Sewing *for the* Home

Contents

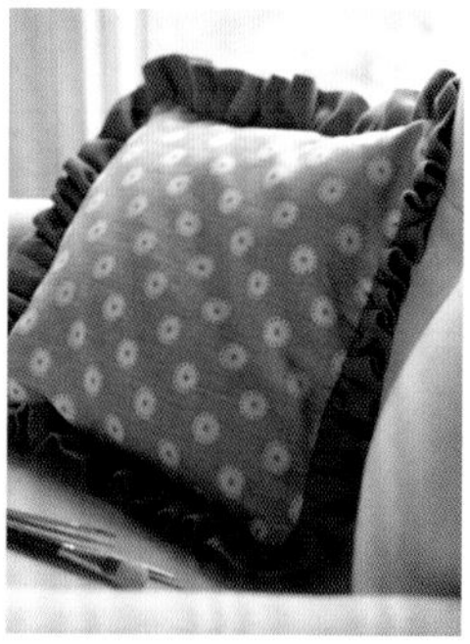

introduction

My passion for fabric printing began 20 years ago on an old ping-pong table in our playroom, whilst my four small children played beneath. To create the fabric needed to make curtains for our house (a converted cowshed), I experimented with potato printing, linocuts, and flour-and-water resist on old linen sheets before moving on to silkscreen printing. Printing on anything I could find, including white t-shirts, pillowslips, and sheets, I developed my first designs inspired by the chickens outside my kitchen door.

Eager friends kindly offered commissions, before **Country Living** magazine published a feature following photo shoots at our house, and this launched the business. These days my business continues to expand; I have now designed ten collections, inspired by the hedgerows, meadows, and woodland surrounding our home, as well as our chickens, designs inspired by our Welsh beach, and the latest block-printed and Swedish collections.

As a child, I was fortunate in going to school on the banks of Lake Windermere in Cumbria. It was an inspirational Arts and Crafts house, whose interior was decorated with stylized flora and fauna, and emphasis was placed upon observing nature, skating on the ice, and gathering reeds for weaving. Ever since then I have continued to marvel at the changing of the seasons and the beauty of the landscape.

Chairs that once belonged to my grandfather and father have been reupholstered more than once, and the search for old furniture took me to junk stores and auctions where I found a huge pleasure reviving discarded chairs and sofas. The wonderful "make do and mend" ethos also supports efforts to reduce our impact upon the planet and preserve the world's resources.

I hope this book will inspire you to discover the fun of making and sewing items. The beautiful step-by-step illustrations will guide you through 50 different sewing projects and you will be amazed at how easy it can be to design and make the interior of your own home.

VANESSA ARBUTHNOTT

Brighten up every corner of your home by mixing and matching stripes and patterns. Easy projects, like tie-top curtains or a simple pillow cover, are a good place to start.

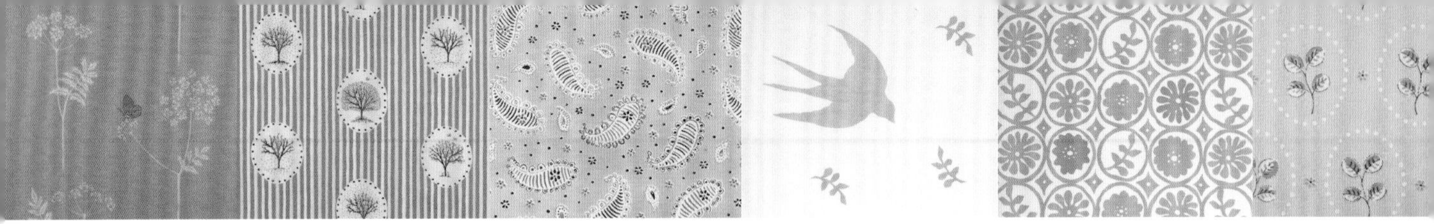

garden inspirations

We were very lucky to find a derelict cowshed, barn, and piggery whilst house-hunting, and this gave us the wonderful opportunity to create a home and garden completely from scratch. The house surrounds the garden on three sides, creating a sheltered lawn, which we have framed with box hedges, roses, and alliums. We also have a scruffy but very productive kitchen garden. Loving the combination of cultivated plants mixed in with wildflowers, cow parsley and buttercups mingle in amongst the flowers and vegetables. I am also a keen birdwatcher, and nothing gives me more pleasure than seeing my lesser spotted woodpecker and the elusive goldfinches at the bird table.

Double doors open out onto our garden, allowing the living room to blend seamlessly with the outside world.

Using leftover scraps of fabrics to make small items like these lavender hearts means nothing is wasted. Filled with lavender from the garden, these little scented hearts can be tucked into drawers and hanging spaces.

Lazy Daisy is based on a traditional sprig pattern.

Daisies

Alliums

Roses

Lavender

Primula

Honeysuckle

nature inspirations

Finding beauty in the delicacy of natural forms occurring in the meadows and woodland is a constant source of peace and tranquility. The pleasures of a country walk are irresistible, and I collect fallen leaves, ferns, cow parsley, and wildflowers to take home to press and draw. For centuries acorns and oak leaves have been shown on fabrics, both woven and printed, and their shapes continue to be very appealing. I have enjoyed giving them a contemporary twist in my designs, and I especially love the serenity of the one-color prints, like Fern and Dragonfly and Woodland Walk.

Fabrics in shades of Buttercup, Clay, and Charcoal from my Meadow collection bring the serenity of nature into the heart of the house.

Ferns

Cow parsley

Butterflies

Songbirds

Hazelnuts

Dragonflies

Photographs of butterflies and flowers taken on a summer walk.

My first drawing for Cow Parsley.

A simple table runner is easy to make and transforms a lunch or supper into a special occasion. The Songbird runner shown here goes beautifully with the French ticking napkins in Raspberry.

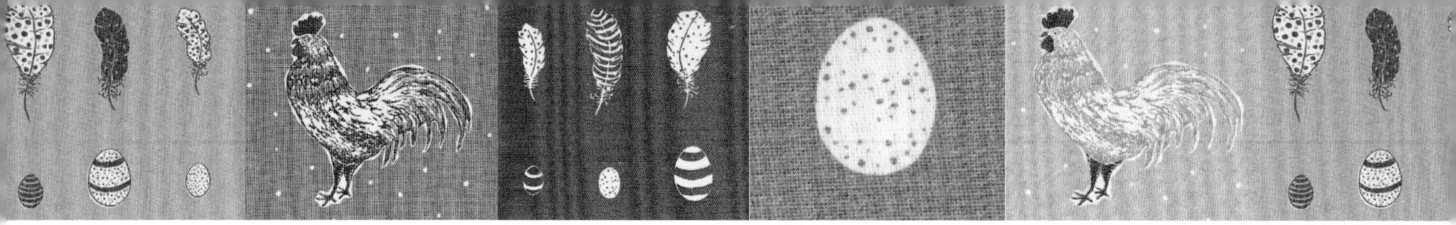

chickens and geese

Living in the country for me wouldn't be the same without keeping chickens, ducks, and geese. They provide background banter, constant companionship, amusement, color, and, of course, delicious eggs. All the wastepaper in the office is shredded and used for their bedding, which in turn makes compost for the vegetable patch. In our garden I collect beautiful feathers discarded by cockerels, hens, ducks, geese, guinea fowl, partridges, and pheasants. The delicate patterns, spots, and stripes of their feathers are irresistible, and I love drawing them. The resulting designs—Feather and Egg and Cockerel and Spot—are still popular after 11 years.

A Feather and Egg tablecloth is set for tea in summer.

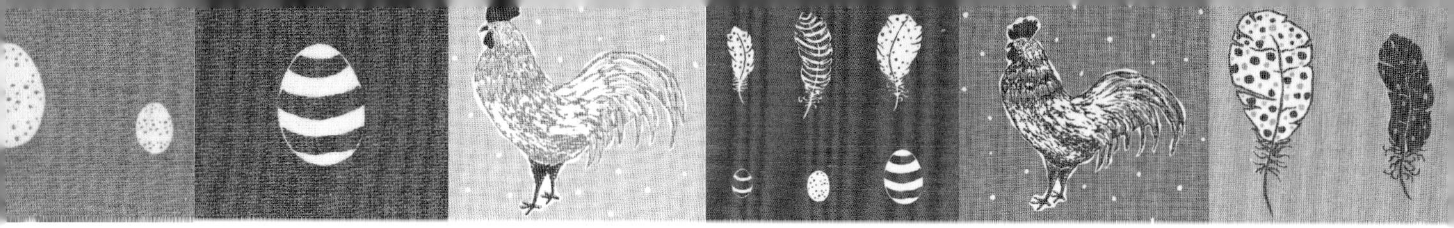

There's something very playful and refreshing about the chicken and cockerel fabrics, but the Feather and Egg design is a touch more sophisticated, so use it when you are designing a scheme for a smart living room. Make a square pillow with a piped edge to give it a tailored look.

Cockerel and Spot was based on our first cockerel.

- Chickens
- Geese
- Ducks
- Spotted feathers
- Eggs
- Cockerels

Every day we collect about six fresh eggs from the coops.

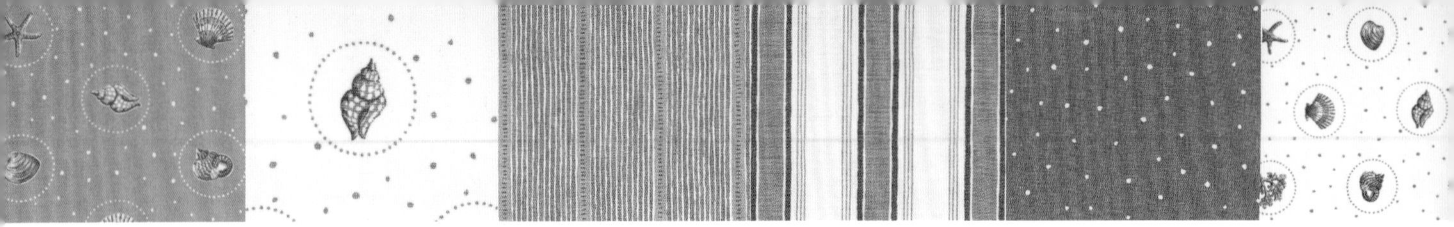

seaside

The Seaside collection was inspired by wonderful childhood memories of summer vacations in Pembrokeshire and Cornwall. I have spent many happy hours beachcombing, at first as a child with my mother and sister, and later with my own children. Rose, Flora, and I still search out beautiful shells, stones, and treasures to fill our buckets and take them home to enjoy. I noticed that the shells often create circular halos in the sand around them, which I have echoed in my shell fabric designs. The best color combinations exist in nature, and here I have used varying tones of watery blues.

The fresh blue and white of the Seaside collection looks summery and pretty, and is particularly suited to a vacation cottage.

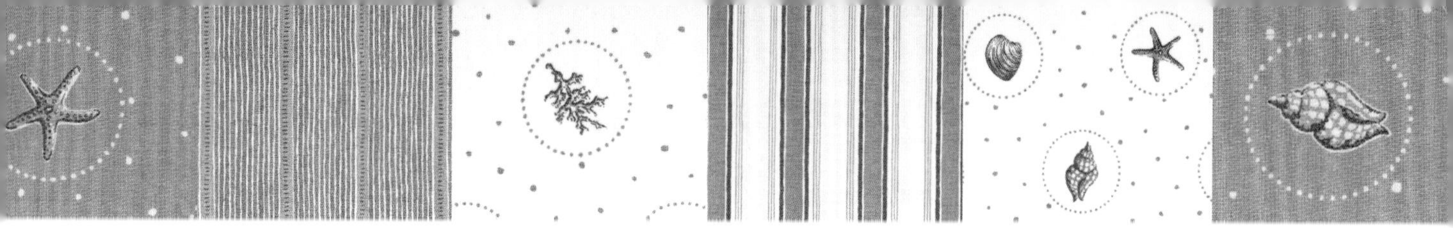

Lots of different shell ideas.

Sea

Sand

Blue sky

Clouds

Shells

Driftwood

The beach in August.

You can't go wrong with the Seaside fabrics, as they look wonderful made up as curtains and chair covers, pillows and shades. The small, allover pattern of the designs means they are economical to cut out, with very little waste. Striped pillows are always useful and can be layered with many of the other patterned fabrics.

hand-printed fabrics

I have a special affinity with hand block printing and screen printing as I used these methods to create my very first fabrics 20 years ago. I found a fresh source of inspiration deep in the bustling markets of Rajasthan in India, where it was exciting to discover the art of traditional block printing still alive and being used for beautiful, simple one-color fabrics. The wooden blocks produce distinctive marks and textures that are so different from the smooth finish of conventional, mechanically printed fabrics, and I was eager to reflect this quality in my designs. I have taken very simple, traditional motifs and printed them as positive and negative images.

Butterfly Dance, in Pigeon and Teal, is partnered with Simple Ticking Ground, in Pigeon, for this armchair, while the pillow cover is Simple Ticking Detail, in Teal.

Printed onto sturdy linen fabric, the Hand Printed fabrics are equally useful made up as a shopping bag, a tablecloth, a pillow, or a pair of long, lined curtains. Try combining the different elements of the range, like the contrast edging on the integral valance at the top of these curtains.

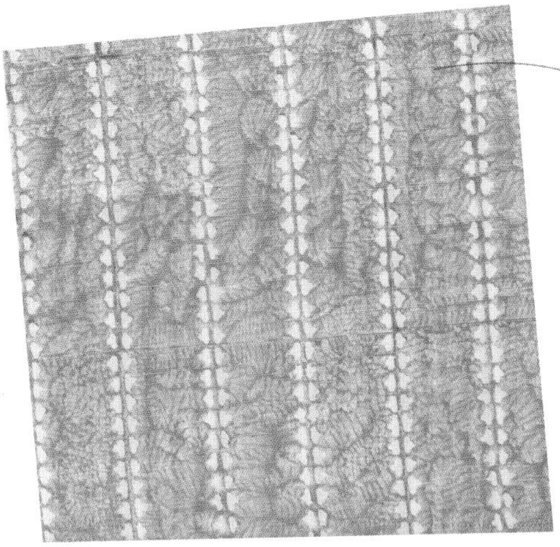

Simple Ticking Ground, in Teal.

Some of the hand-carved wooden butterfly blocks.

Hand-carved wooden blocks

Paisley

India

Tradition

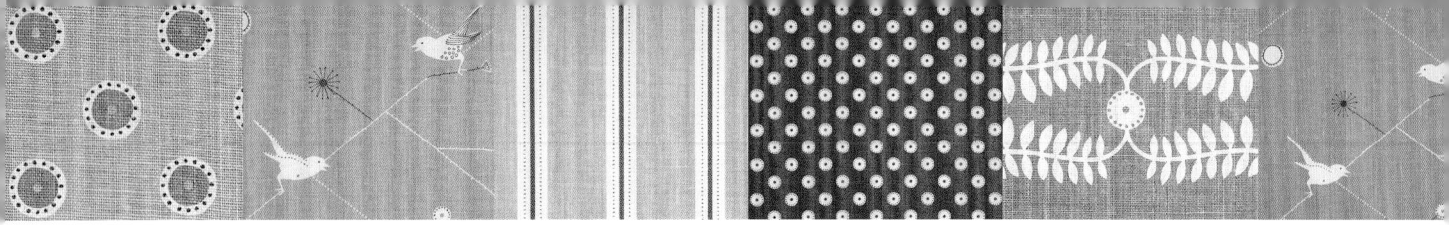

swedish inspirations

For one of my recent collections of printed fabrics, I wanted to bring together some of the striking 1950s patterning I love with the coolness of Scandinavian light. I have always admired the innovative fabric designer Lucienne Day, whose amazing work reflects the tremendous surge of vitality and optimism of those post-war years. The simple stylized birds, trailing leaf forms, and pretty polka-dots are printed in a soft Gustavian palette, in colors like Dove, Dusky Pink, Clay, and Duck Egg, as well as introducing for the first time the bright contemporary colors Lime, Pumpkin, and Sweet Pea.

Soft grays and creams provide the perfect background color for the vibrant pinks and greens.

Polka-dots

Pumpkin

Sweet Pea

Ivy

Trailing leaf

Lime

The bright colors give a striking contemporary feel.

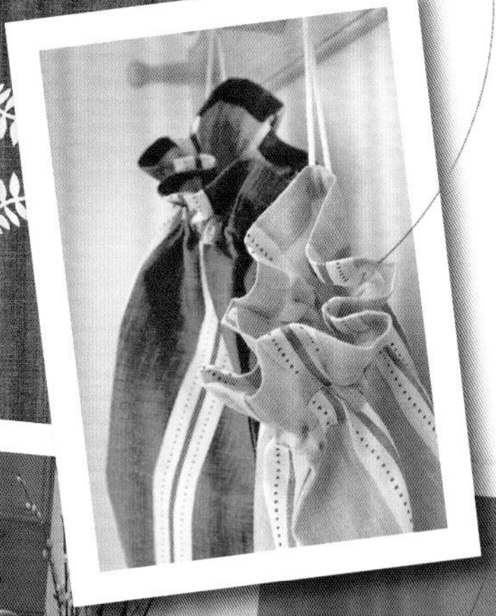

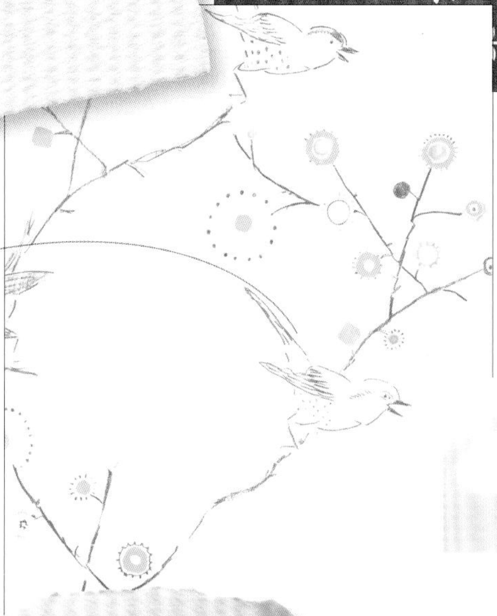

Here's a quick drawing I did for Dawn Chorus.

Take an old wooden chair and give it an instant makeover with some paint and a new seat cover. Sand and wash the wood, and apply a coat of primer and then two topcoats of acrylic eggshell. Make an elegant cover (see page 108) and transform the chair!

chapter 1

curtains

simple unlined curtains

If you haven't made curtains before, this is just the place to start. Unlined, and gathered using a ready-made tape, these short curtains are made in Dawn Chorus, Dusky Pink and Winter, and are perfect for hanging above a sofa placed under a window. For a country look, hang them from a simple wooden pole, or try a curtain track set close to the ceiling (below right).

You will need

- Decorator fabric—see below for yardage
- Narrow two-cord heading tape, the width of each finished curtain panel plus 4in (10cm)
- Matching sewing thread
- Curtain hooks

Estimating yardage

- Measure your window to find the finished length and width of the curtains (see page 204). Add 8in (20cm) to the length for the top and bottom hems, and 2½in (6cm) to the width for the side hems.
- To achieve the proper fullness, this heading needs fabric that measures one-and-a-half to two times the width of the window. For narrow windows, one width of fabric may be enough, but you will need to allow two or more widths of fabric for each curtain panel if your window is wide.

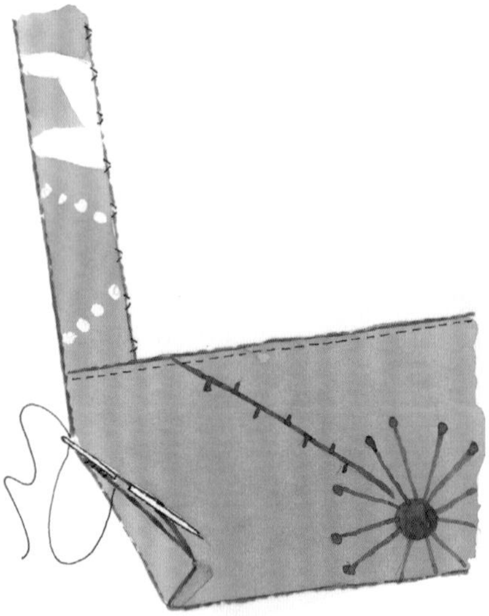

1 Cut out the required number of fabric lengths for each curtain panel. Join the cut fabric lengths to form the panel widths (see page 188). Press a double-fold ⅝in (1.5cm) hem to the wrong side along both side edges of each panel. Pin and hemstitch in place (see page 185). Press a double-fold 2in (5cm) hem to the wrong side along the top and bottom edges of each panel. Pin and machine-stitch in place. Slipstitch (see page 185) the open side edges of the lower hem together and press flat.

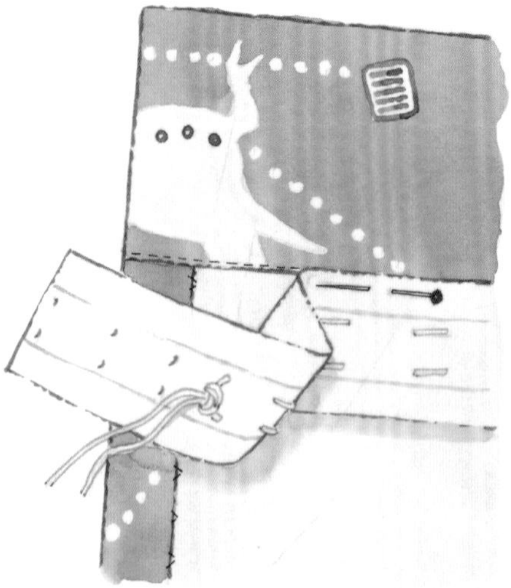

2 On the heading tape, pull the cords out for 2in (5cm) from each end of the tape. Knot the cord ends together at the leading (inner) edge of each curtain panel. Lay the panel wrong side up on a large flat surface. Position the heading tape over the top hem, lining up the top edge of the tape with the stitching line of the hem, and leaving 2in (5cm) of tape extending at each side. Pin in place.

3 Apply the tape as for the Gathered Valance, step 6 (see page 42). Carefully pull up the loose cords, to gather up each panel to half the width of your window. Even out the pleats by hand. Tie the long ends of the cord into a bow, wind into a bundle, and hand-sew to the back of the tape. Never cut the cords, because the panels need to be flattened out for laundering. Insert the curtain hooks about 4in (10cm) apart, placing a hook near each outer edge so the curtains hang straight. Hang from a pole with rings, or from a rod (track).

TIP

If hanging these curtains from a rod in a recess, adjust the position of the tape (and the depth of the top hem) to fit the space between the rod and the top of the recess.

tie-top curtains

Light and breezy at the window of our restored shepherd's hut, these unlined curtains are made in Pretty Maids, Teal and Winter. They are another really easy project to make—simply sew a set of narrow ties and attach them to a pole.

You will need

- Decorator fabric—see below for yardage
- Matching sewing thread

Estimating yardage

- Measure your window to find the finished width and length of the curtains (see page 204). Add 4in (10cm) to the length measurement for the lower hem and ⅝in (1.5cm) for a top seam allowance.
- To achieve the proper fullness, this heading needs fabric that measures one-and-a-half times the width of your window.
- For the facing, allow for a strip of fabric 4in (10cm) deep by the width of each cut curtain panel.
- Calculate how many ties you will need along the top edges of both curtain panels (see page 203). For each tie allow a strip 27½ x 3¾in (70 x 9.5cm).

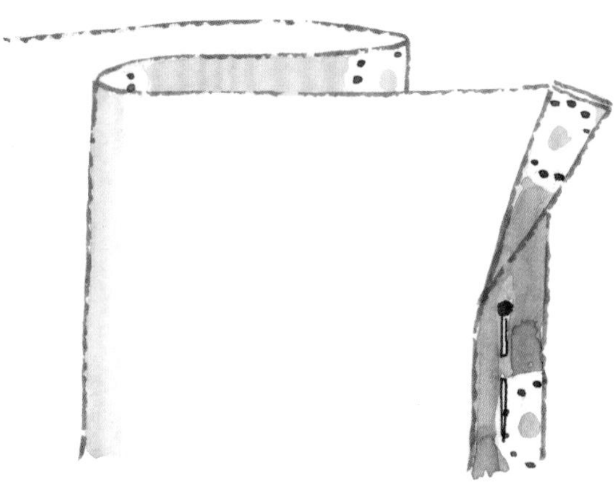

1 Cut out all the required pieces for each curtain panel. Join the fabric lengths, if necessary, to form the finished panel widths (see page 188). Press a double-fold ⅝in (1.5cm) hem to the wrong side along one long edge and both short edges of the facing. Pin and machine-stitch the hems. Press a double-fold ⅝in (1.5cm) hem to the wrong side along both side edges of the curtain panels. Pin and machine-stitch in place.

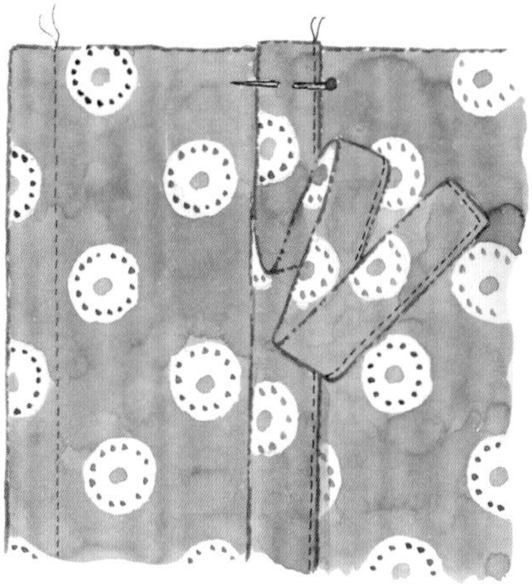

2 Make up the ties using method 1 (see page 202), finishing both ends on each; cut each in half. Decide the positions of the ties, spacing them about 6in (15cm) apart (see page 203), but with the outer ones about 3in (7.5cm) from the edges. Lay out one curtain panel, right side up. Pin two ties at every tie position, one on top of the other, with the raw ends even with the curtain raw edge. Pin and baste in place. Repeat with second panel and remaining ties.

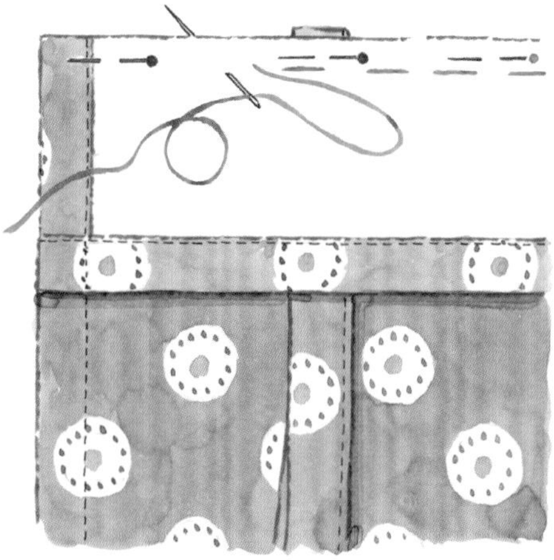

3 With right sides together, and with the raw and hemmed edges even, place a facing on top of each curtain panel, sandwiching the ties in between. Pin and baste the facing in place across the top edge of each curtain panel. Machine-stitch a ⅝in (1.5cm) seam. Remove the basting.

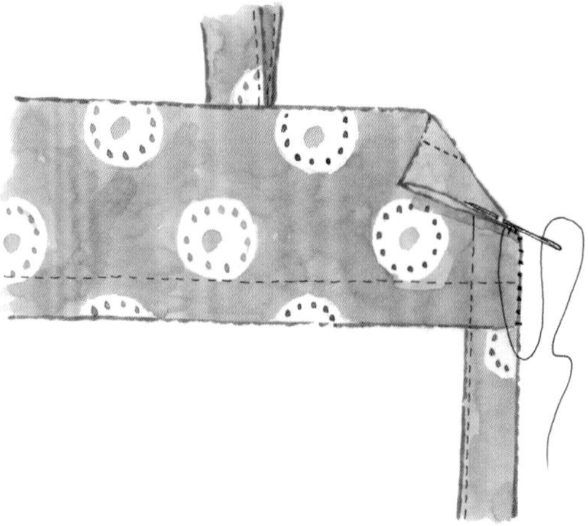

4 Fold the facing over to the wrong side of each curtain panel, exposing the ties, and press the seamed top edge flat. If you wish, machine-stitch close to the top edge. Pin and baste the lower edge of the facing to the curtain, and machine-stitch in place. Slipstitch (see page 185) the open side edges together. Press a double-fold 2in (5cm) hem along the lower edge of each curtain; pin, baste, and either hemstitch (see page 185) or machine-stitch in place. Slipstitch each lower hem's open side edges. Remove all the basting. Use the ties to hang the curtains from the pole.

contrast-lined curtains

The magnificent cockerel in our garden was the inspiration for Cockerel and Spot, and this fresh color combination of Straw, Duck Egg, and Raspberry makes it the perfect choice for a kitchen or dining room. Rather than use a plain lining fabric, designed to be hidden, I used a traditional French mattress ticking in red and white, that accentuates the country style of the room.

You will need

- Main decorator fabric for the outer panel—see below for yardage
- Contrast decorator fabric for the lining—same yardage as the main fabric
- Matching sewing thread
- Pencil-pleat heading tape—the width of each finished curtain panel, plus 4in (10cm)
- Weights for hems (see page 193)
- Small piece of muslin for covering the weights
- Curtain hooks

Estimating yardage

- Measure your window to find the finished width and length of the curtains (see page 204).
- The main fabric should measure the finished length plus 6in (15cm) for the lower hem and ¾in (2cm) for the top hem, by the finished width plus 1¼in (3cm) for seam allowances.
- The lining should measure the same length and width as the main fabric.
- For wide windows like these, you will need to allow two or more widths of fabric for each panel. For narrow windows, one width may be enough.

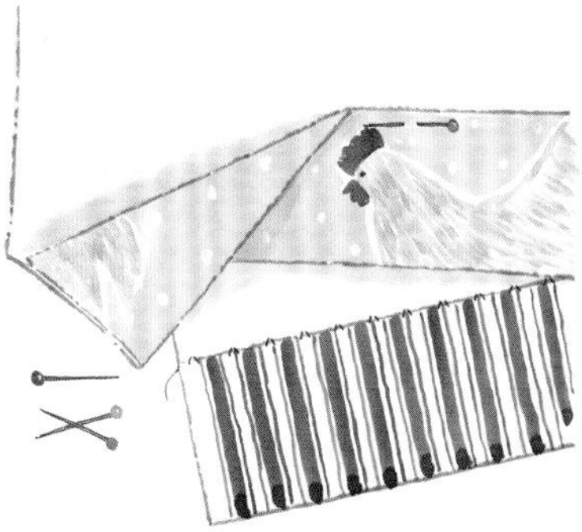

1 From the main and lining fabrics, cut out the pieces for the curtains. Join the main-fabric lengths and join the lining lengths to form the finished panel widths (see page 188). Press a double-fold 3in (7.5cm) hem to the wrong side along the lower edge of each main-fabric panel and each lining panel. Pin the hems in place, then slipstitch (see page 185).

2 With right sides together and raw edges of the main and lining fabrics even, pin each outer panel to a lining panel down the side edges. Stitch ⅝in (1.5cm) seams.

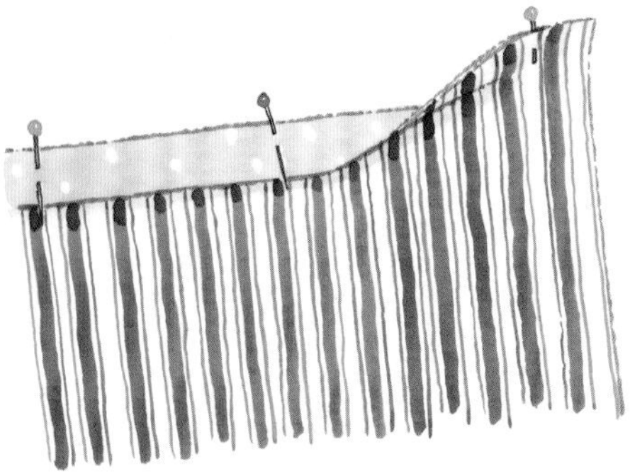

3 Press the seams open, turn right side out, and press the seams so they run along the side edges. On each panel, pin the main fabric and lining together along the top raw edges, then press a ¾in (2cm) hem to the lining side of the panel. Pin in place.

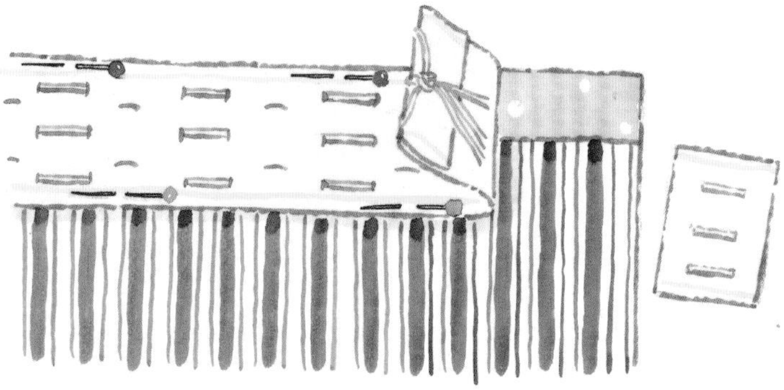

4 For each panel, cut a length of heading tape to the width of the panel plus 4in (10cm). With the lining side of the panel facing up, pin the heading tape along the hemmed top edge, leaving 2in (5cm) of tape extending at each side edge. Remove the pins holding the top hem in place as you go. At the leading edge (the left-hand edge of the right-hand panel, or the right-hand edge of the left-hand panel), pull the cords free of the excess tape and knot the cord ends together. Trim away 1¼in (3cm) of the excess tape and turn under the remaining ¾in (2cm), in line with the side edge of the panel. Tuck the knotted cord ends under the tape, and pin the tape in place.

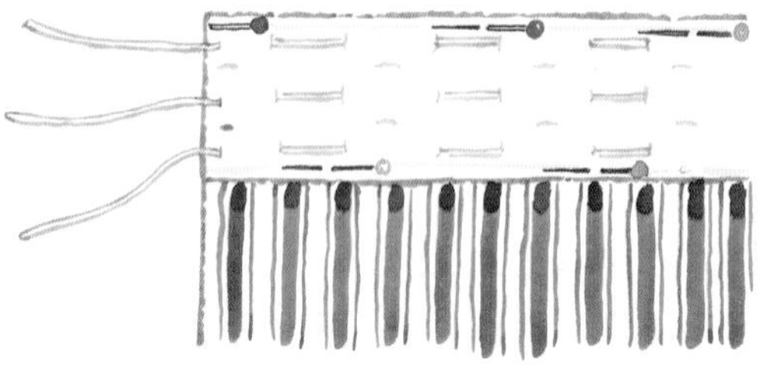

5 For each panel, remove the pins at the other end of the tape, and pull the cords free of the excess tape. Trim and fold the end of the tape under, as in step 4, but leave the cord ends free. (Do not trim them.) Pin the tape in place.

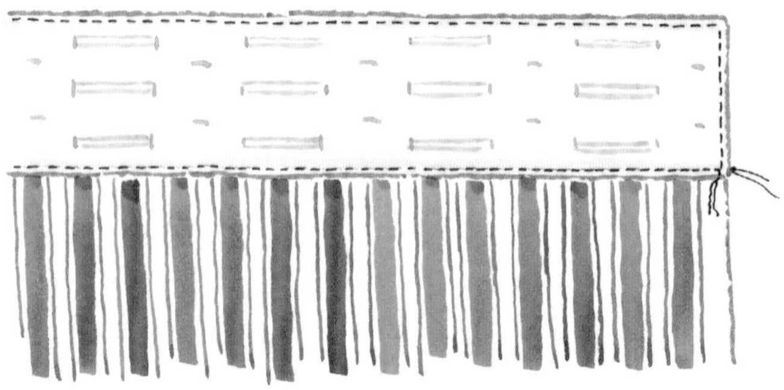

6 Machine-stitch the tape in place on each panel, stitching along the top edge and then along the end, stopping when you get to the bottom of the tape. Go back to where you started stitching and machine-stitch along the edge of the end of the tape (leaving the loose cord ends free) and then the lower edge of the tape, so that you are stitching in the same direction as for the previous stitching line. Stop when you get to the end of the tape. Remove all the pins.

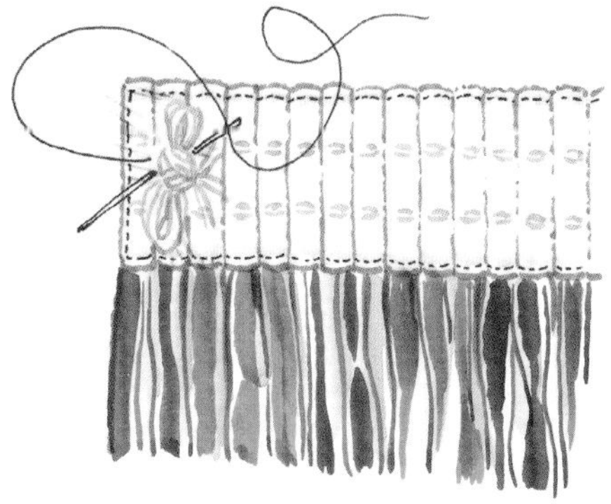

TIP

Use a simple narrow, two-cord heading tape for pretty country-style curtains, or pinch-pleat tape to create a more tailored finish.

7 Pull up the tape cords evenly, gathering each panel to fit half the width of the window. Tie the long ends of the cord into a bow and wind into a bundle. Hand-sew to the back of the tape. (Never cut the cords, as the panels will need to be flattened out for laundering.)

8 Cover the required number of weights with muslin (see page 193). Pin and hand-sew them to the lining at the lower corners and at the base of any seams. Slipstitch the hem edges of the main fabric and lining together for 2in (5cm) to conceal the weights. Insert drapery hooks into the heading tape, about 4in (10cm) apart, placing a hook near the outer side edge so the panel hangs straight. Use the hooks to hang the panels from a pole with rings.

ruffle-top curtains with contrast border

Walking my lively whippet, Ruby, down our narrow lane and into the quiet woods, where she instantly rushes off following the scents of rabbits and hares, I have time to look around and collect beautiful leaves, ferns, and flowers to take home, press, and draw. I often sit down quietly to watch the birds, butterflies, and insects passing All the natural organic forms offer me endless inspiration for designs. These long curtains, in a beautiful shade of green I call Lichen, hang in our hallway. I have lined them in Plain Check, also in Lichen, to make the view into the house from the garden more interesting. The checked ruffle-tops flop over to the front from the wooden poles for a relaxed effect, and the lining is repeated down the leading edge of the curtains. This is an easy project if you have some experience of sewing, but if you are more of a novice, take it slowly using the step-by-step illustrations, and you will find they are not quite as complicated as they look.

Coordinating fabrics with a large pattern, like Fern and Dragonfly, with the smaller, geometric pattern of Plain Check, is an interesting way to layer two designs together. Another option (left) is to use a striped pattern for the lining.

You will need

- Main decorator fabric—see below for yardage
- Lining fabric—see below for yardage
- Contrast decorator fabric—see below for yardage
- Matching sewing thread
- Narrow two-cord heading tape—the width of each finished curtain panel, plus 4in (10cm)
- Weights for hems (see page 193)
- Small piece of muslin for covering the weights
- Curtain hooks

Estimating yardage

- Measure your window to find the finished width and length of the curtains (see page 204). To the length, add 6in (15cm) for the lower hem and 3½in (9cm) for the top ruffle.
- To achieve the right fullness, this heading needs a fabric fullness of one-and-a-half to two times the width of your window.
- The lining should measure the width of the main fabric minus 2in (5cm), by the length of the main fabric minus 5in (12.5cm).
- For each edging strip, allow one strip of contrast fabric 7in (17.5cm) wide, by the finished length of your curtains plus 4⅛in (10.5cm) for the top ruffle and seams. There is one edging strip for each curtain panel.
- For each top facing, allow one strip of contrast fabric 4in (10cm) wide, by the width of your finished curtain plus 4in (10cm).

TIP

When you are making a large pair of curtains like this, it's important to keep the layers of fabric flat, so smooth out a blanket on the floor and lay out the fabrics on top. This way you will be able to press hems in place, and pin and stitch fabrics into position without disturbing them. This is especially important when you are making lined curtains, as you will find they don't hang straight from the pole if they slip out of line at this stage.

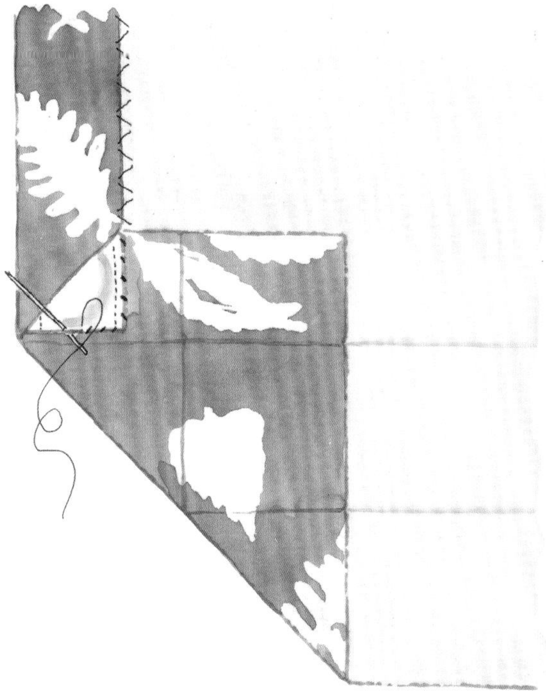

1 From the main, contrast, and lining fabrics, cut out all the pieces. Join the main fabric lengths to form the finished panel widths (see page 188). Repeat for the lining fabric and the top facings. Lay the main-fabric panel, wrong side up, on a flat surface. Press a double-fold 3in (7.5cm) hem along the lower edge, and a single 2in (5cm) hem down the leading edge (the left-hand edge of the right-hand panel, or the right-hand edge of the left-hand panel). Catchstitch (see page 187) the raw side hem edges in place, starting and finishing 8in (20cm) from the top and lower edges. Make a mitered corner where the hemmed edges meet (see page 192). Hand-sew a covered weight into the lower hem (see page 193). Slipstitch the mitered edges together and hemstitch the lower hem (see page 185).

2 Lay the lining, wrong side up, on a flat surface. Press a double-fold 2in (5cm) hem along the lower edge, and a single 1in (2.5cm) hem down the right-hand side of the right panel, or the left-hand side of the left panel (in other words, the mirror image of the main fabric). Hemstitch the lower hem in place. With wrong sides together, lay the lining on top of the curtain panel, leaving a 1in (2.5cm) border of main fabric showing along the pressed lower and side edges. Pin in place. If necessary, trim away the lining down the other side edge so that it is even with the main fabric panel. Also trim away the top edge of the lining, so that it is 3in (7.5cm) below the top edge of the main fabric panel. Baste the layers of fabric together along the top and side raw edges. Hemstitch the lining to the curtain panel along the pressed side edge.

3 With right sides together, pin a contrast-edging strip to the raw side edge of the curtain panel, with the lower edge of the strip extending ⅝in (1.5cm) beyond the lower hemmed edge of the main fabric. Machine-stitch a ⅝in (1.5cm) seam and press the seam toward the contrast strip.

4 Press a single ⅝in (1.5cm) hem along the lower edge and along the other long edge of the contrast strip. Fold the contrast strip to the wrong side so that it is folded in half lengthwise, wrong sides together, and the pressed side edge is even with the seam line. Pin in place and hemstitch along the long side edge, and slipstitch along the open lower edge of the contrast strip.

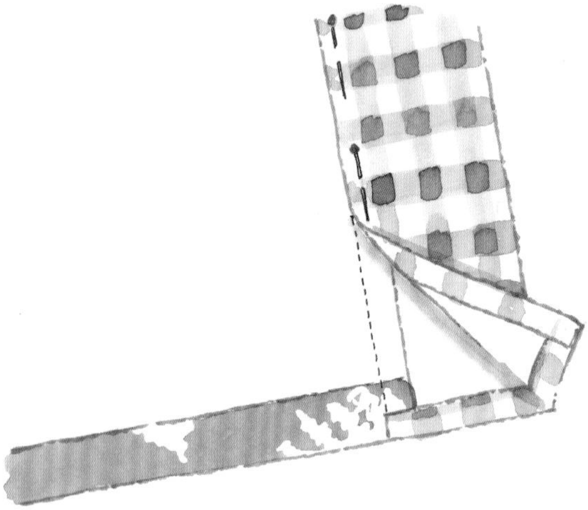

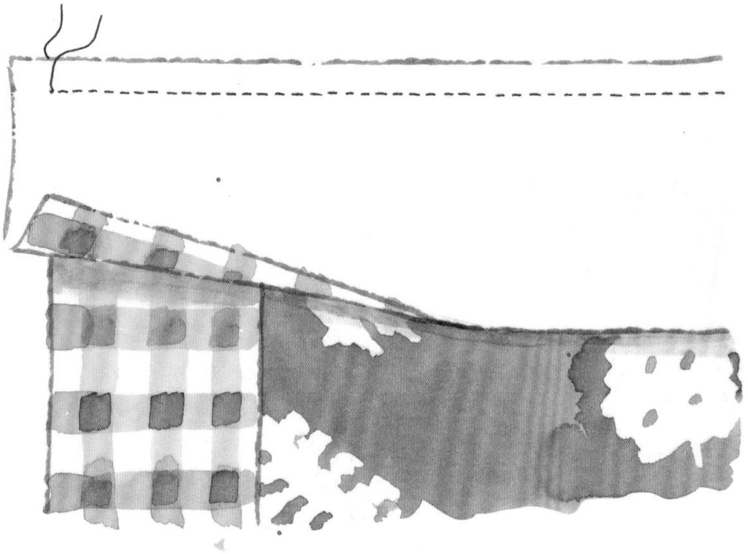

5 With right sides together, pin one long edge of the contrast top facing to the top raw edge of the curtain panel, with the facing extending ⅝in (1.5cm) beyond each side edge. Machine-stitch a ⅝in (1.5cm) seam and press the seam toward the facing.

6 Press a single ⅝in (1.5cm) hem to the wrong side along each side edge of the facing strip, then bring the facing over to the lining side of the panel with the seam line running along the top; press. Baste the raw edge of the facing in place through all layers of fabric, then slipstitch down the open side edges.

7 Lay the panel, wrong side up, on a large surface. Position the heading tape centrally over the raw edge of the top facing, with 2in (5cm) extending at each side edge; pin in place. At the leading edge, pull the cords free of the excess tape and knot the ends together. Trim away 1¼in (3cm) of the excess tape and turn under the remaining ¾in (2cm), in line with the edge, tucking the knotted cord ends under the tape. At the other end of the tape, pull the cords free of the excess tape; trim and turn under the end of the tape, but leave the cord ends free. Machine-stitch up one end of the tape, along the top edge, and down the other end. Machine-stitch the lower edge of the tape and remove the basting.

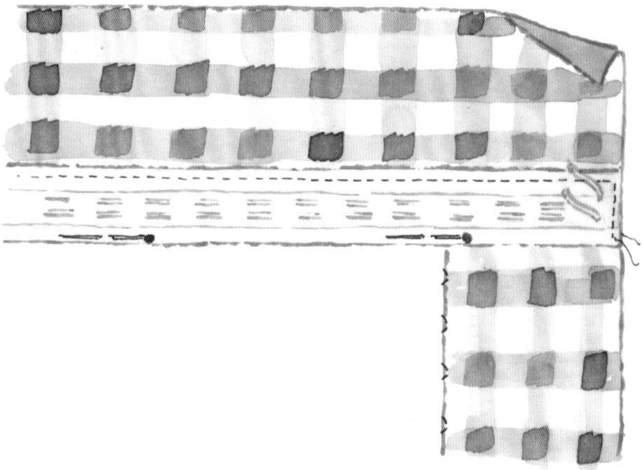

8 Pull up the tape cords evenly, to gather up the panel to half the width of your window. Even out the gathers by hand. Tie the long loose ends of the cord into a bow and wind into a bundle; hand-sew to the back of the tape. (Never cut cords, because the panels need to be flattened out for laundering.) Insert curtain hooks about 4in (10cm) apart, placing a hook near each outer edge. Repeat steps 1–8 for the second curtain, and hang the curtains using the hooks. Arrange each top facing so that it folds over to the front, forming a ruffle.

appliquéd-stripe curtains

In May and June, on my way home from an evening walk, I often pick a bunch of cow parsley to put in a pitcher on the windowsill. I love this pretty pair of short curtains, made from Seaweed and Shells, with a soft, gathered valance trimmed with Deckchair Stripe in Denim. This creates a sea-like, wavy line and adds a nautical air.

1 From the main and lining fabrics, cut out the pieces for the curtain panels. Press a 2in (5cm) hem to the wrong side along both side edges of each main-fabric panel. Catchstitch (see page 187) the side hems, starting at the upper edge and ending 8in (20cm) from the lower edge of each panel.

2 On each main-fabric panel, press a double-fold 3in (7.5cm) hem to the wrong side along the lower edge. Make a neat mitered corner at both bottom corners (see page 192). Catchstitch the side and lower hems in place. Slipstitch the mitered edges together (see page 185).

TIP

Link the curtains with the rest of the room by making the appliqué stripe in fabrics used in other soft furnishings, like pillows and slipcovers.

You will need

- Main decorator fabric—see below for yardage
- Lining fabric—see below for yardage
- Contrast vertically striped decorator fabric—see below for yardage
- Matching sewing thread
- Narrow two-cord heading tape—the width of each finished curtain panel, plus 4in (10cm)
- Curtain hooks

Estimating yardage

- Measure your window to find the finished width and length of the curtains (see page 204). To the length, add 6in (15cm) for the lower hem and 2in (5cm) for the top hem.
- For narrow windows like these, you will need to allow one width of fabric for each panel. For wider windows, you may have to allow two widths of fabric. Also allow for a 2in (5cm) hem down each side of each panel.
- The length of the lining needs to be the cutting length calculated for your main fabric, less 3in (7.5cm), and its width needs to be the finished width of your curtain panels, with no extra allowances.
- For the appliquéd stripes on the curtains, you will need a length of vertically striped fabric the same length as the finished curtain panels, plus 2⅝in (6.5cm) for the top and lower hems.

3 Decide on the desired width of the appliquéd stripe, and add 1¼in (3cm) for hem allowances. For each panel, cut a strip to this width from the contrast fabric, centering the stripe(s). Press a ⅝in (1.5cm) hem to the wrong side along each long edge and one end. Clip away part of the hem allowance at the corners, as shown.

4 On the right side of each main-fabric panel, measure 1in (2.5cm) from the inner side edge (the so-called leading edge, which will meet the other curtain), and mark a line from top to bottom with pins. Lightly draw the line using a ruler and dressmakers' chalk, and remove the pins. Lay the strip of contrast fabric, right side up, on the right side of the curtain panel, lining up one long edge of the strip with the chalked line, and the pressed short end with the hemmed lower edge. Pin and baste. Starting at the upper edge of the panel, machine-stitch the strip in place close to one long folded edge and then across the folded end. Go back to the upper edge of the panel and stitch in the same direction down the other long edge of the strip. Remove the basting stitches.

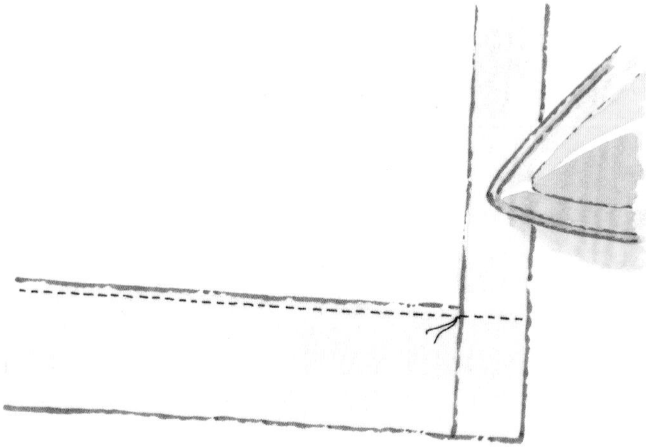

5 For each lining-fabric panel, press a double-fold 2in (5cm) hem to the wrong side along the lower edge. Machine-stitch the lower hem in place. Press a 1in (2.5cm) hem to the wrong side down each side edge.

6 With wrong sides together, lay one lining panel on top of one curtain panel with the top raw edges even and 1in (2.5cm) of main fabric showing around the side and lower edges. Pin the lining in place along the side and upper edges. Slipstitch the lining to the main fabric down both side edges. Repeat for the other panel.

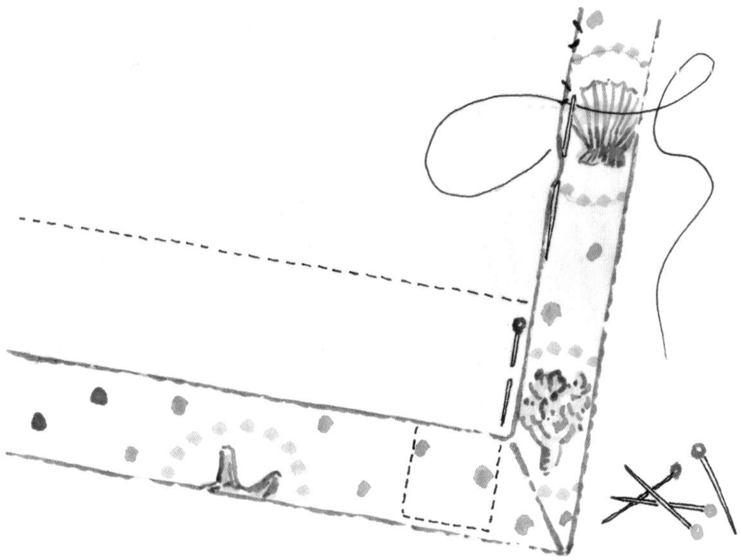

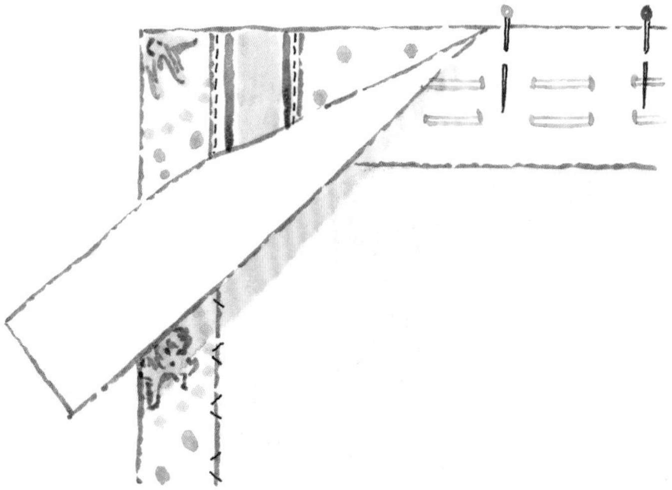

7 For each panel, baste the top raw edges together, then press a 2in (5cm) hem to the lining side and pin in place. Cut a length of heading tape the width of the curtain plus 4in (10cm). Attach the heading tape as shown for Contrast-Lined Panels, steps 4–7 (see pages 28–29), and then remove the basting.

8 Make a gathered valance to top the curtains (see pages 40–43). Before pulling up the cords, make another contrast strip as in step 3 and appliqué it 1in (2.5cm) up from the lower edge using the same method as in step 4. (Both ends of the stripe are turned under at the side edges, as at the bottom edge of the curtain in step 4.)

gathered valance

A gathered valance, hung over a pair of lined curtains, is a traditional way of keeping out drafts and hiding the workings of a rod, but I love the way it softens the tops of the curtains. I made this valance in Cow Parsley, Sand and Cornflower and hung it over a matching pair of curtains at the French windows.

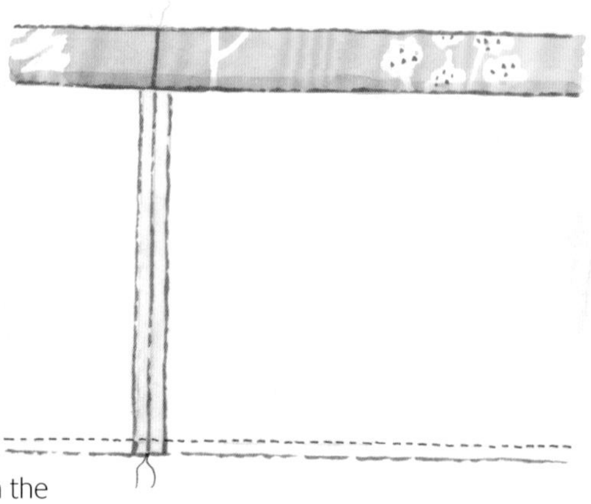

1 From the main fabric and lining, cut out the pieces for the valance. Join fabric and lining widths to obtain the correct valance panel width (see page 188). With right sides together, lay the lining panel on top of the main-fabric panel, with the lower edges even and the seams matching. Pin and machine-stitch the pieces together along the bottom edge with a ⅝in (1.5cm) seam. Press the seam open.

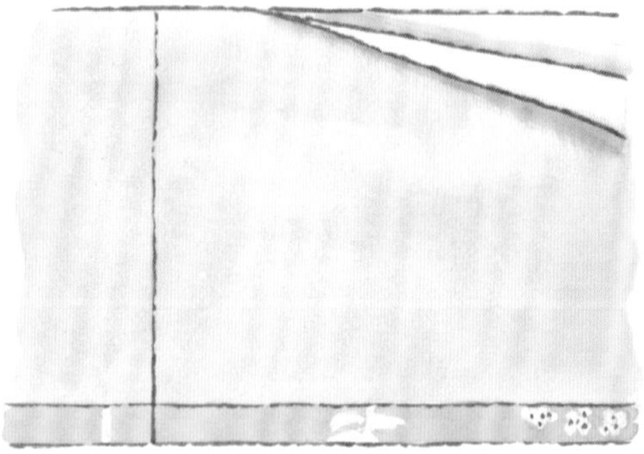

2 Fold the lining over to the wrong side of the main-fabric panel, so they are now wrong sides together. Match the raw edges at the top and sides so that a 1⅜in (3.5cm) strip of main fabric shows along the lower edge of the lining. Very lightly press the fold along the lower edge.

TIP

A valance can also be hung from a valance rod, a drapery rod, or a pole. There is no need to allow for returns on a rod or pole, so the valance will use a little less fabric.

You will need

- Main decorator fabric—see below for yardage
- Lining fabric—see below for yardage
- Matching sewing thread
- Narrow two-cord heading tape, the width of the finished valance panel plus 4in (10cm)
- Hook-and-loop tape, the width of the gathered-up valance panel plus 4in (10cm)
- Valance shelf (see page 211)
- Angle irons and screws
- Drill, screwdriver, staple gun

Estimating yardage

- Prepare a wooden valance shelf as shown on page 211, attaching it to the wall with the angle irons.
- To find the finished gathered width of the valance, measure along the front and the two side edges (the returns) of the valance shelf. The size of the valance panel prior to gathering needs to be twice this measurement, plus 1¼in (3cm) extra for the seams. You may need to join fabric lengths to obtain the correct width.
- Decide on the finished depth of the valance (the depth is usually about one-sixth of the length of your shade or curtains) and add 3½in (9cm) for the top and bottom hems.
- The lining should be the same width as the main fabric, and the length of the main fabric minus 2¾in (7cm).

3 Refold the valance so the right sides of the main fabric and lining are together again. Making sure the top edges are even, pin and machine-stitch a $\frac{3}{8}$in (1cm) seam down each side edge of the valance.

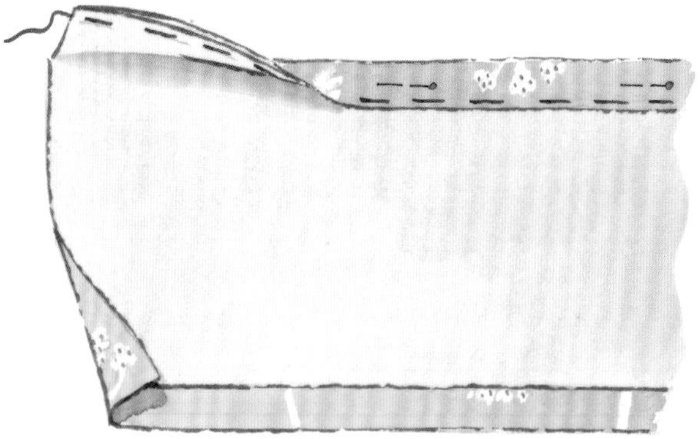

4 Turn the valance panel right side out. Baste the top raw edges together, then press the seamed side edges and the lower folded edge flat. Press 1$\frac{1}{2}$in (4cm) to the wrong side along the basted top edge of the valance panel, and pin in place. Slipstitch the open side edges of the hem together (see page 185).

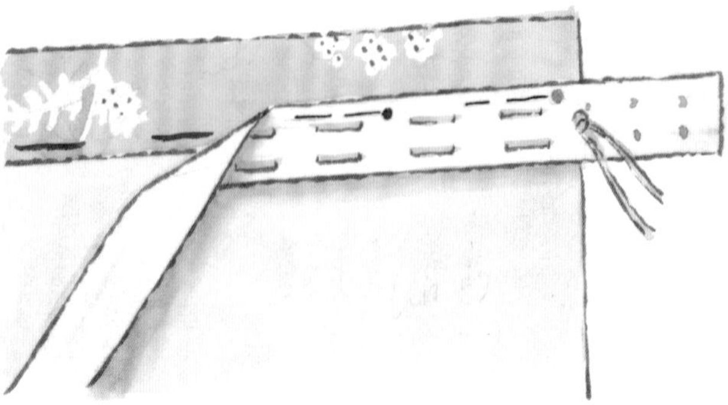

5 Pull the cords of the heading tape out for 2in (5cm) from each end of the tape, and knot the cords at one end. Lay the panel on a flat surface, wrong side up. With 2in (5cm) of tape extending beyond each side edge, pin the tape to the valance 1in (2.5cm) down from the pressed top edge.

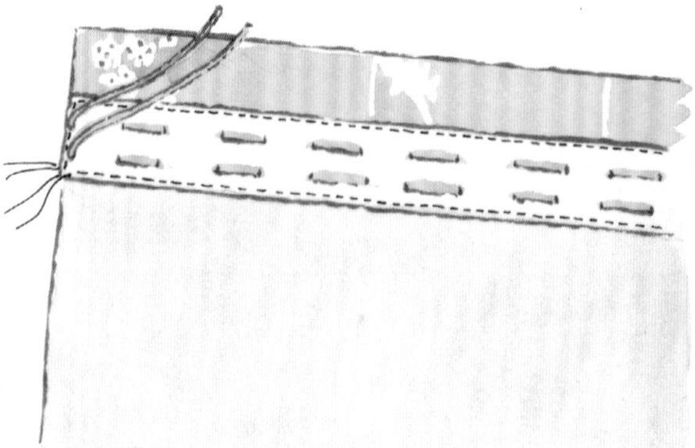

6 Trim away some of the excess tape at both ends, leaving $\frac{3}{4}$in (2cm) to fold under in line with the edges of the panel; pin. Machine-stitch up one short end of the tape, along the top edge, and along the other short end, making sure you leave the loose cord ends free. Machine-stitch the lower edge of the tape, stitching in the same direction as before.

The valance is softly gathered with a ready-made tape, which allows you to adjust the folds by hand for an even fit. If you wish, you could add a contrast trim to the valance to match the curtain.

Hook-and-loop tape makes it easy to remove the valance for cleaning—just press the edge of the valance onto the valance shelf and peel off when you need to.

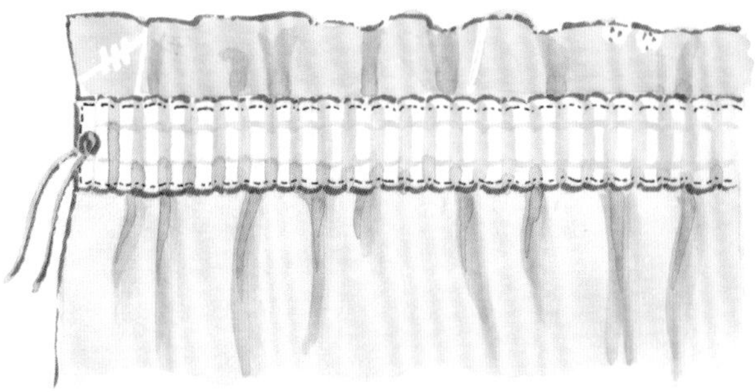

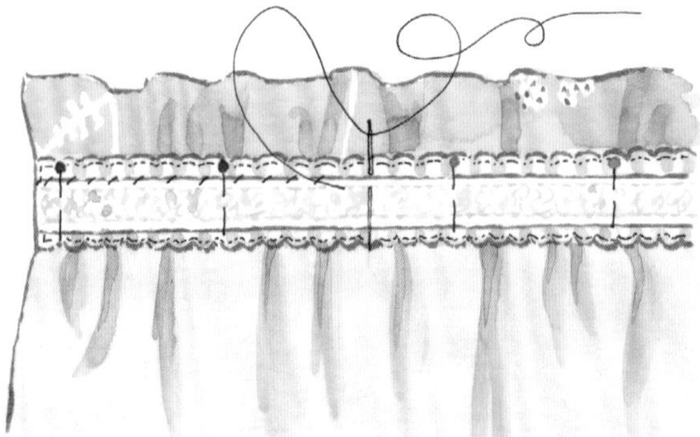

7 Pull up the loose cords to gather the valance to fit the valance shelf. Knot the free cord ends together, but do not trim them. Space the gathers evenly along the length of the valance. Tie the long ends of the cords into a bow and wind into a bundle. Hand-sew to the back of the tape.

8 Pin the loop side of the hook-and-loop tape to the gathered-up heading tape, and sew along all edges using overhand stitch (see page 186). Staple the hook side of the hook-and-loop tape to the front and returns of the valance shelf. Attach the valance panel to the valance shelf by pressing the two sides of the hook-and-loop tape together.

pinch pleat curtains with contrast leading edge

For a really classic curtain heading you can't beat pinch pleats as the folds fall into clean, fluted lines every time. We gave these curtains, made in Pretty Maids, in Mushroom, Teal, and Winter, a touch of something a bit more special with a leading edge of Plain Linen in Teal, to coordinate with the polka-dots in the main fabrics.

1 From the main, contrast, and lining fabrics, cut out the pieces. Join the main-fabric lengths to form the finished panels (see page 188). Repeat for the lining. Lay out each main-fabric panel, wrong side up. Press a double 3in (7.5cm) hem to the wrong side along the lower edge, and a single 2in (5cm) hem to the wrong side down the outer side edge. To miter the corner, leave the lower double hem folded but unfold the side hem and mark where the lower-edge fold comes to on it. Now unfold just one of the lower-edge folds, refold the side hem, and mark where the side fold comes to on the lower-edge fold.

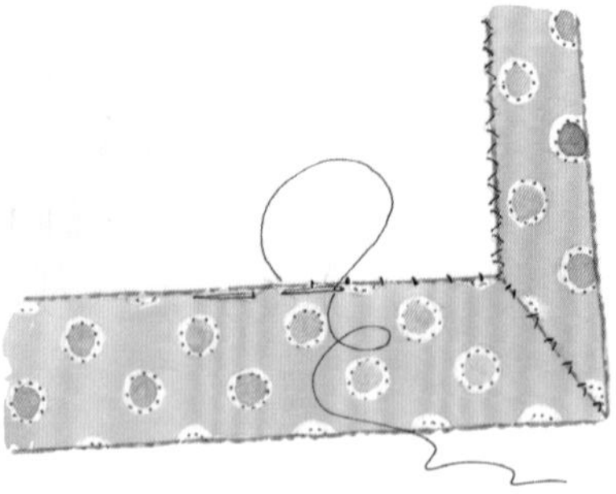

2 Unfold the side hem again and fold in the corner along a line between the two marks. Refold the hems, forming the miter. Hand-sew covered weights into the lower hem (see page 193), with one weight ¾in (2cm) from the inner (unhemmed) side edge. On each panel, catchstitch (see page 187) the raw edge of the side hem in place, finishing 8in (20cm) from the top edge. Slipstitch the miter and hemstitch the lower hem (see page 185).

You will need

- Main decorator fabric—see below for yardage
- Contrast decorator fabric, for edging —see below for yardage
- Lining fabric—see below for yardage
- Matching sewing thread
- 4in- (10cm-) wide buckram or stiffener the finished width of each curtain panel
- Weights for hem (see page 193)
- Small piece of muslin for covering the weights
- Pin hooks

Estimating yardage

- Measure your window to determine the finished width and length of the curtains (see page 204). To the length, add 6in (15cm) for the lower hem and 2in (5cm) for the top hem.
- To achieve proper fullness, this heading needs fabric that is two-and-a-half to three times the width of your window.
- The lining should measure the width of the main fabric, minus 2in (5cm), and the length should be 5in (12.5cm) shorter than that of the main fabric.
- For the edging strips, allow one strip for each panel, measuring 7in (17.5cm) wide, by the finished length of your curtains plus 1¼in (3cm) for the top and lower hems.

3 Press a 2in (5cm) hem to the wrong side along the top edge of each main-fabric panel, mitering the corner where this hem meets the side hem. Slipstitch the miter. Slip the buckram or stiffener underneath the side and top hems. On the unfinished edge of the curtain, trim the buckram so it finishes ⅝in (1.5cm) from the raw edge. Pin in place.

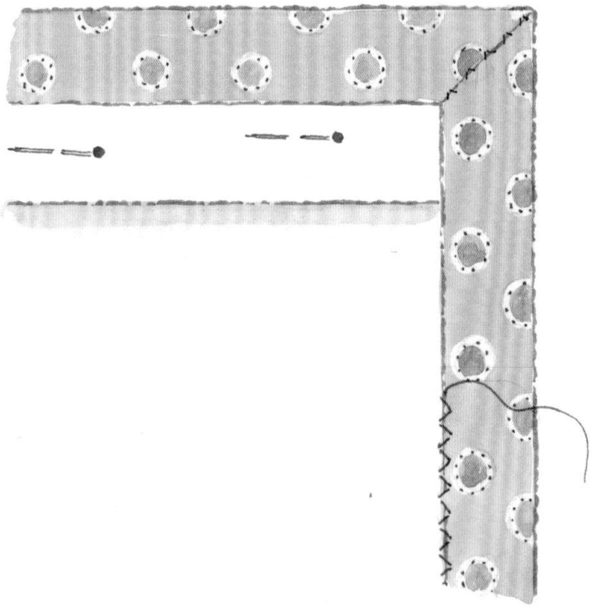

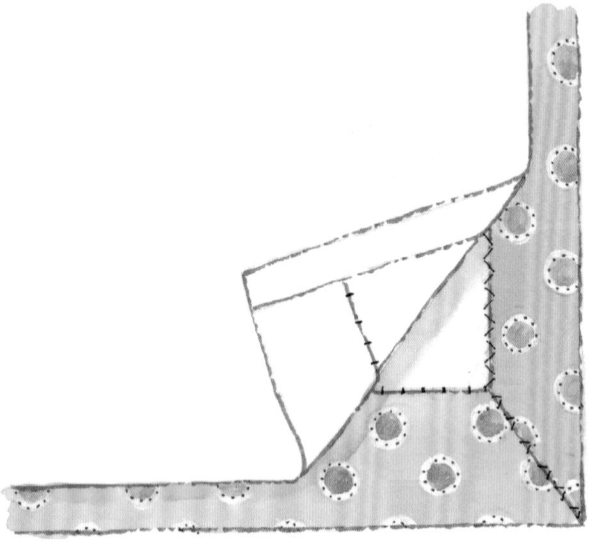

4 Lay each lining panel, wrong side up, on a flat surface. Press a double-fold 2in (5cm) hem to the wrong side along the lower edge, and a single 1in (2.5cm) hem along the top edge and down the outer side edge (on the lining this is the right edge of the left panel, and the left edge of the right panel). Hemstitch the lower hem in place. With wrong sides together and the raw side edges even, lay the lining on top of the curtain panel, leaving a 1in (2.5cm) border of main fabric showing around the three hemmed edges. Pin and hemstitch the lining to the curtain panel along the finished top edge and side edge.

5 Baste across each curtain panel just beneath the lower edge of the buckram to hold it in place. With right sides together and raw edges even, pin one long edge of a contrast-fabric strip to the unfinished edge of each lined curtain panel, with the strip extending ⅝in (1.5cm) beyond the top and lower edges. Machine-stitch through all thicknesses.

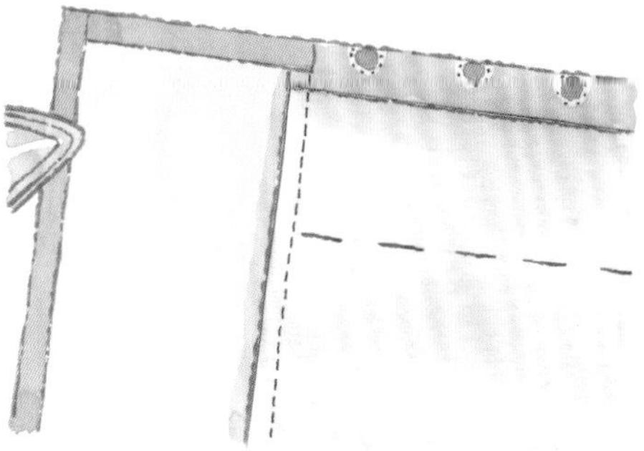

6 On each panel, press the seam toward the contrast strip. Press a single ⅝in (1.5cm) hem to the wrong side along the top, lower, and long side edges of the contrast strip.

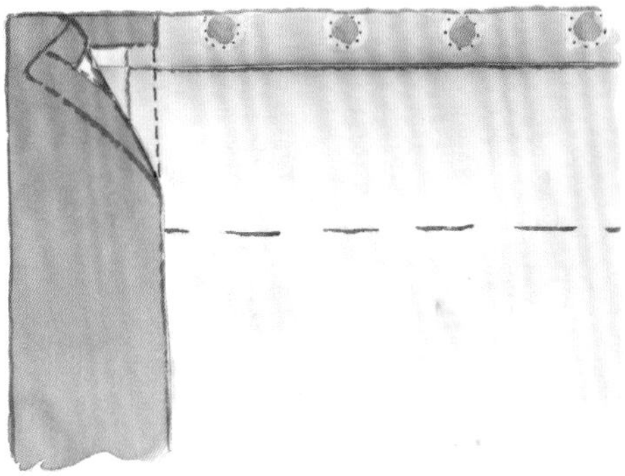

7 On each panel, fold the contrast strip to the wrong side down its length, and pin the long pressed edge to the seam line stitched in the previous step. Hemstitch the strip in place along the side edge, and across the open top and lower edges.

Pinch pleats are a classic curtain-making technique and do exactly what they say; they are pinched together by hand and stitched at the backs and fronts to hold them in place. Pin hooks are pushed into the back of each set of pleats so you can make them slightly longer or shorter if you need to.

8 Calculate the spaces between the heading pleats (see page 206) and complete the curtains as for the Valance-Topped Curtain, steps 10–12 (see pages 52–53). However, instead of pinching the large pleats in step 11 into two small pleats, pinch them into three equal-sized small pleats. Remove the basting.

valance-topped curtain

Printed by hand from carved wooden blocks, Life and Eternity Detail uses the ancient Eastern motif we now know as paisley. The design has been used in woven fabrics for centuries, and I adapted it for my Hand Printed range to connect with its Indian heritage. These curtains, in Teal, are topped with an integral pinch-pleat valance, edged in Simple Ticking Ground, also in Teal, from the same collection.

You will need

- Main decorator fabric—see below for yardage
- Contrast decorator fabric—see below for yardage
- Lining fabric—see below for yardage
- Matching sewing thread
- 4in- (10cm-) wide buckram or stiffener—see below for yardage
- Weights for hems (see page 193)
- Small piece of muslin for covering the weights
- Pin hooks

Estimating yardage

- Measure your window to determine the finished width and length of the curtains (see page 204). To the length, add 1⅝in (4cm) for seams. To the width, add 4in (10cm) for side hems.
- To achieve proper fullness, this heading needs a fabric fullness two-and-a-half to three times the width of your window.
- For the valance, determine the finished depth—as a rough guide it should be about one-fifth or one-sixth of the finished curtain drop. Allow for a ⅜in (1cm) hem at the base and a 2in (5cm) hem at the top. The width should be the same as your finished curtain width, plus ¾in (2cm) for each side hem.
- The lining should measure the width of the main fabric minus 2in (5cm), by the length of the main fabric minus 5in (12.5cm).
- For the curtain hem border, allow a contrast strip 7⅝in (19cm) deep, by the width of the finished curtain plus 4in (10cm) for side hems.
- For the valance side edging strips, allow for two contrast-fabric strips that are each 1¾in (4.5cm) wide, by the finished depth of your valance plus 2⅜in (6cm) for hem and seams. For the valance bottom edging strip, allow for one contrast-fabric strip that is 1¾in (4.5cm) deep, by the finished width of the valance plus ¾in (2cm) for seams.

1 From the main, contrast, and lining fabrics, cut out all the pieces. Join the main-fabric lengths to form the finished panel widths (see page 188). Repeat for the valance, lining, and contrast strips. With right sides together and raw edges even, pin and machine-stitch one long edge of a curtain hem border to the lower edge of the main-fabric panel with a ⅝in (1.5cm) seam. Press the seam open. Lay the panel wrong side up on a flat surface and press a 3in (7.5cm) double-fold hem to the wrong side of the hem border, so that a 1in (2.5cm) strip remains visible on the right side of the panel.

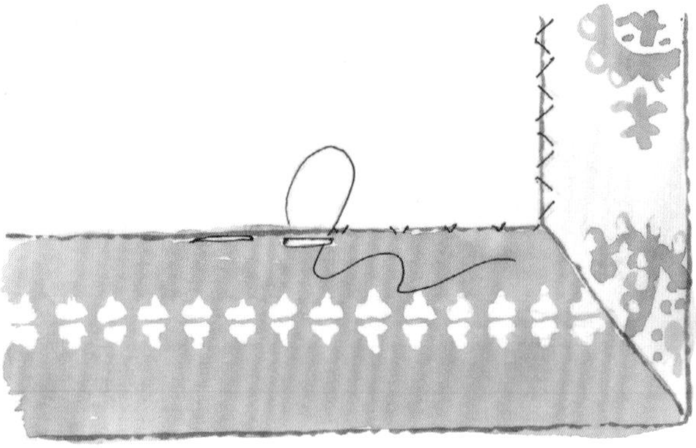

2 Press a single 3in (5cm) hem to the wrong side down each side of the curtain panel. Miter the corners where the side and lower hems meet (see page 44, steps 1 and 2). Hand-sew covered weights into the lower hem at the side edges (see page 193). Catchstitch (see page 187) the raw edges of the side hems in place, finishing 8in (20cm) from the top edges. Slipstitch the miter and hemstitch the lower hem (see page 185).

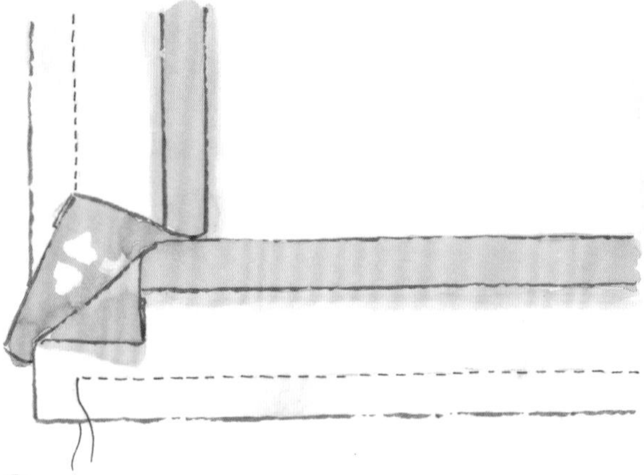

The edges of the fold-over valance and the bottom of the curtains are trimmed with a coordinating Simple Ticking Ground, cut into strips and mitered at the corners to define the edges.

3 Press ⅜in (1cm) to the wrong side along one long edge of each remaining contrast strip. With the right side of one of the short strips to the wrong side of the valance, pin and machine-stitch the raw long edge of this strip to the side edge of the valance with a ⅜in (1cm) seam, starting and finishing ⅜in (1cm) in from each end. Repeat to attach the remaining short strip to the other side edge of the valance. Attach the long strip to the lower edge of the valance in the same way. Press the seams toward the valance.

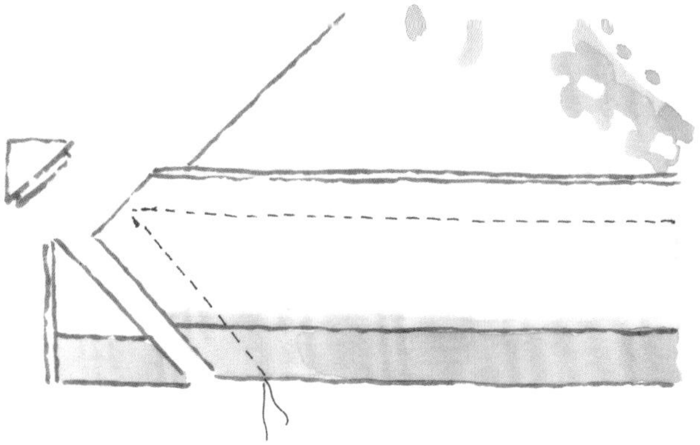

4 Fold the valance diagonally at one corner so that the contrast strips lie on top of each other, with right sides together and pressed edges even. Pin the strips together. Now fold over the strips diagonally at the corner, bringing the raw edges even. Press the diagonal fold in place.

5 Unfold the valance corner and, using the press line as a guide, machine-stitch diagonally across the strips, finishing at the end of the first rows of stitching. Trim away the fabric at the corner, leaving a ¼in (5mm) seam allowance, and finally trim away the bottom edge of the strips close to the stitching. Repeat with the remaining corner.

6 Turn the strips right side out, carefully pushing out the corners. Pin and then hemstitch the pressed edge in place on the right side of the valance. Lay the valance on top of the main panel, centering it between the side edges and with the top raw edges even and right sides up. Pin and baste the layers together along the top, side, and bottom edges. Machine-stitch the valance to the main panel along the top edge only, with a 2in (5cm) seam. Remove the basting.

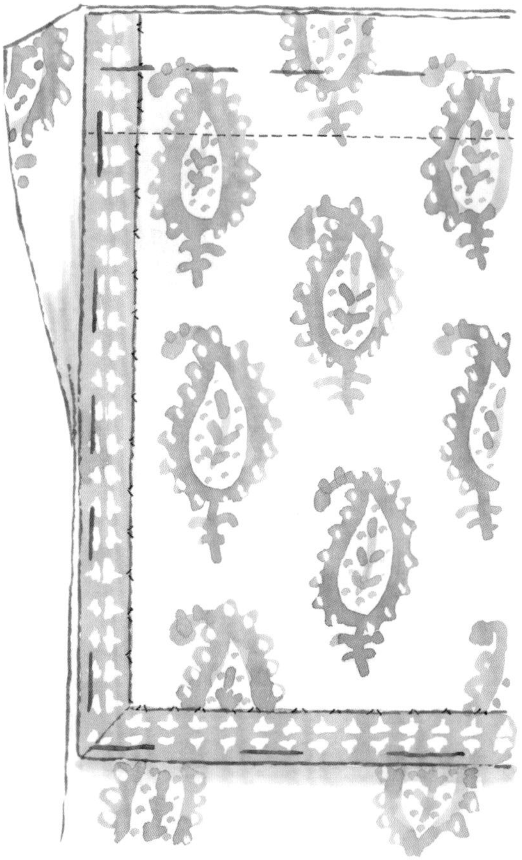

TIP

Using two different fabrics from the same range makes a pretty, coordinated look, and I like to layer pillows on chairs and sofas that go with the curtains. In the main picture (page 49), I added a pillow made in Life and Eternity Ground, also in Teal, that picks up the denser blue of the edgings.

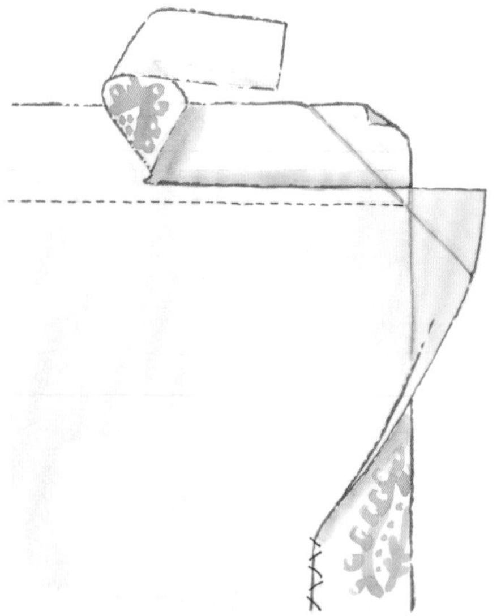

7 Press a 2in (5cm) hem to the wrong side along the top of the curtain panel, so that the stitching line sits right on the top fold. Miter the corners where this hem meets the side hems (see page 192), but before slipstitching the mitered edges together, open out the top fold and trim away the top edge of the main panel only, leaving a ½in (1.2cm) seam allowance. Refold the corners and slipstitch the mitered edges together.

8 Cut a strip of buckram or stiffener to fit the width of the top edge and slip it underneath the side and top hems. Pin in place. Lay the lining out, wrong side up, on a flat surface. Press a double-fold 2in (5cm) hem along the lower edge, and a single 1in (2.5cm) hem along the top of the panel and down each side edge. Hemstitch the lower hems in place.

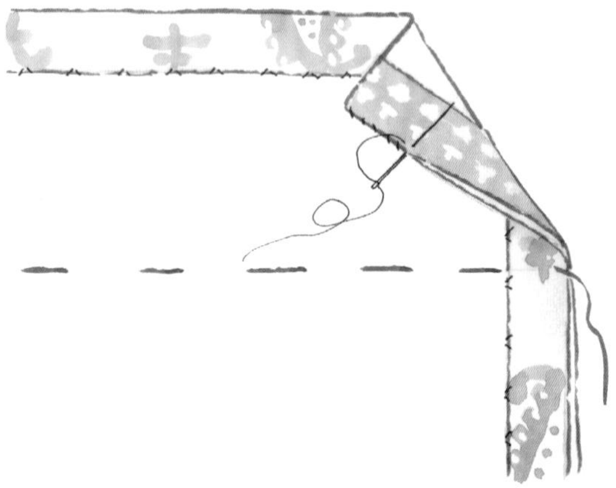

9 With wrong sides together, lay the lining on top of the curtain panel, leaving a 1in (2.5cm) border of main fabric showing around all edges. Pin and hemstitch the lining to the curtain panel along the finished top and side edges. Baste across the curtain panel just beneath the lower edge of the buckram to hold it in place, through all layers. Slipstitch the side edges of the valance to the main curtain panel from the top edge to the buckram basting line.

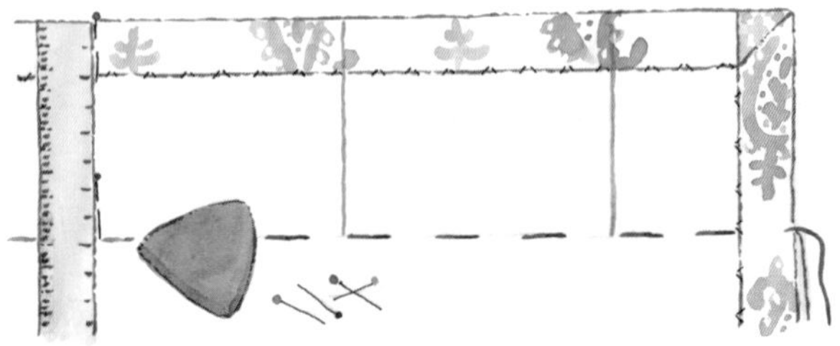

10 Calculate the spaces between the heading pleats (see page 206). With pins, mark the position of each pleat along the top edge of the panel. Using dressmakers' chalk and a ruler, draw vertical lines (at a right angle to the top edge) on the wrong side of the curtain panel, working from the pins down to the basted line beneath the buckram heading.

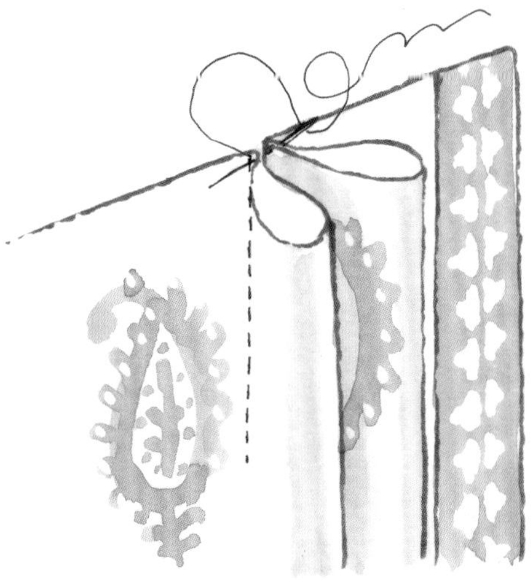

11 With wrong sides together, bring each pleat together and pin along the chalk lines. Machine-stitch each pleat along the pinned line, ending at the lower edge of the buckram. Make sure the machined line is at a right angle to the top edge. At the top edge of each pleat, pinch the fabric into two equal-sized half-pleats. Hand-sew the top of each pleat together firmly with overhand stitches (see page 186). Also hand-sew the two half-pleats together at the base of each pleat. Remove all basting stitches.

12 From the wrong side, insert a pin hook into the seam of each pleat so that the curtain panels can be hooked onto a track or pole.

The bottom border of Simple Ticking Ground gives a deeper tone to the edges of the curtains that brush the floor, which is particularly useful if the main fabric is white, like this one.

upholstered cornice

This project takes a few do-it-yourself skills, and needs a basic toolbox if you want to have a go. But it's worth the effort if you want more of a challenge and it will give you a beautiful old French-style window treatment over a set of long, lined curtains, just right for tall windows. As an alternative, try teaming the cornice with a classic Roman shade. The cornice is made using traditional upholstery techniques, with a staple gun and a curved needle. I have made mine in Cow Parsley, in Stone and Cornflower and lined it in Plain Check, Stone, which is used for the piping that enhances the lower edge.

You will need

- Main decorator fabric for the cornice (pelmet) front—see right for yardage
- Contrast decorator fabric for the lining and the piping—see right for yardage
- Matching sewing thread
- Medium-size cable cord or piping cord—see right for yardage
- Sheet of ⅜in- (1cm-) thick MDF (medium-density fiberboard) or plywood
- Lightweight batting (wadding)—see right for yardage
- Flathead screws
- Tape
- Fabric adhesive
- Two angle irons (or three if the window is wide) and screws
- Paper for making a pattern
- Jigsaw, drill, staple gun
- Curved upholstery needle

Estimating yardage

- Measure your window to determine the length of your cornice (pelmet) and decide on the finished depth. As a general rule, the depth is usually about one-sixth of the length of your shade or curtains.
- MDF or plywood cut into four pieces for the cornice box (pelmet box): one front piece to the finished length, by the depth at the deepest point; one top piece to the finished length, by 5⅝in (14cm) wide; and two side panels to the finished depth minus ⅜in (1cm), by 5⅝in (14cm) wide.
- For the main fabric, allow for a piece of fabric the finished length plus 12in (30cm), by the finished depth, adding ⅝in (1.5cm) all around. If necessary, allow for it to be made from a central piece and two side pieces, adding ⅝in (1.5cm) seam allowances all around each piece.
- For the contrast lining, allow for a piece of fabric the finished length plus 12in (30cm), by the finished depth, adding ¾in (2cm) all around. If necessary, allow for it to be made from a central piece and two side pieces, adding ⅝in (1.5cm) seam allowances all around each piece.
- For the cable cord or piping cord, allow enough to fit around the lower edge of the cornice box (front and sides).
- For covering the cord, gauge the width of your fabric strip. To do this, measure around the cord and allow an extra 1¼in (3cm) for seam allowances. Allow for enough bias strips of contrast fabric, of this width, to fit the length of your cord (see page194).
- You will need enough batting to fit the outside of the front and sides of the cornice box.

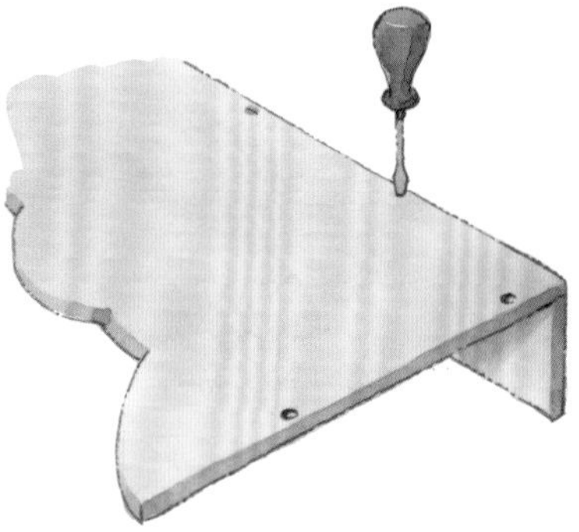

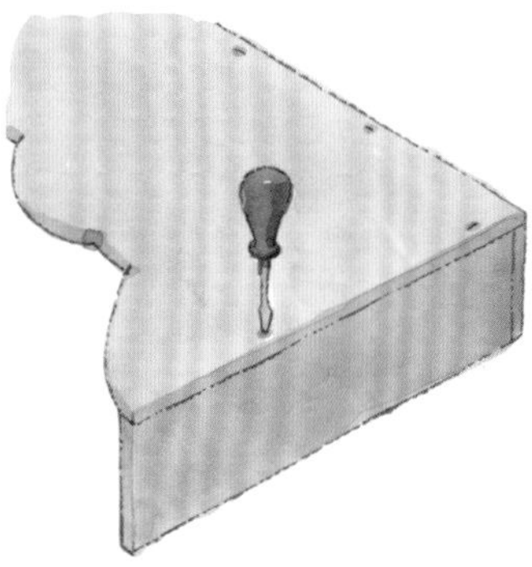

1 On paper, draw around the rectangular front piece of the cornice box, and then draw the desired shape along the lower edge of the paper. Cut out to create a pattern for the front. (Folding the pattern in half crosswise and then cutting through both halves at once will ensure the shaped edge is symmetrical.) Draw around the wooden side pieces on paper and cut out a pattern for each side. Place the shaped pattern on the MDF or plywood front piece, draw around the lower shaped edge, and then cut it out with a jigsaw. Drill two holes ⅛in (3mm) from each side edge and six equidistant holes ⅛in (3mm) from the top edge. On the top piece, drill two holes ⅛in (3mm) from each end. Screw the front piece to the top piece through the six holes along the top edge of the front, as shown.

2 To complete the cornice box, screw the front piece to the front edge of each side piece through the two holes along each side edge of the front. Screw the top piece to the top edge of each side piece through the two holes at each end of the top piece, as shown.

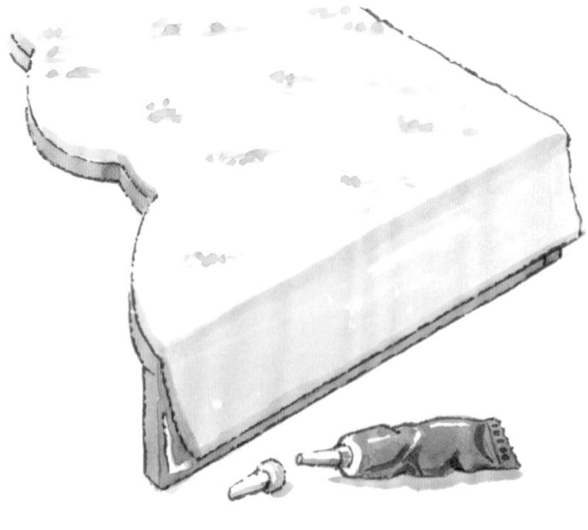

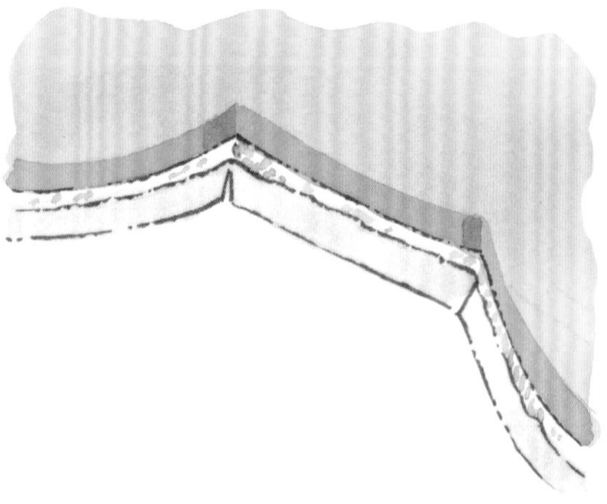

3 Lay the front pattern flat and place a side pattern at each side, keeping them ⅜in (1cm) apart (the thickness of the wood). Temporarily tape the sides to the front, maintaining the gaps between them. Use the taped patterns to cut out the front and sides as one piece from the batting (wadding). Attach the batting to the front and sides of the cornice box with fabric adhesive.

4 Using the taped patterns, cut out the front and sides as one piece from the main fabric, adding a ⅝in (1.5cm) hem allowance all around. If your cornice is too long for the fabric, cut a central piece and two side pieces and join them, right sides together, with ⅝in (1.5cm) seams, positioning the seams symmetrically. Lay the main fabric piece on a flat surface, wrong side up. Center the padded front of the cornice box on top, with ⅝in (1.5cm) of the fabric showing all around. Snip into the hem allowance of the fabric on any curves or inner corners along the bottom edge.

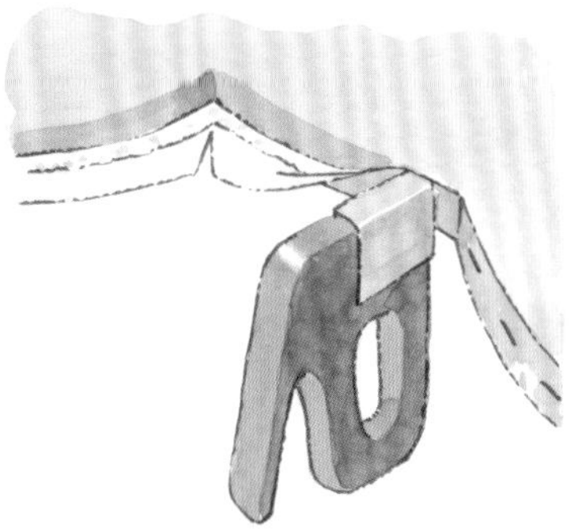

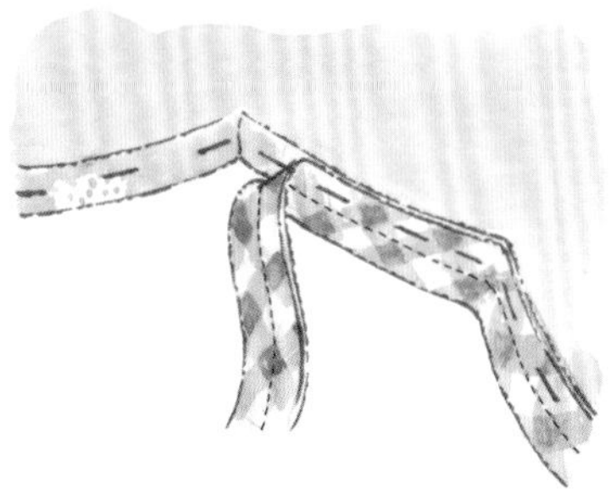

5 Using the staple gun, carefully fasten the fabric to the cornice box, placing the staples along the edges of the board and slightly stretching the fabric as you work, as shown here. Fold the fabric at the corners to get it around the side edges.

6 Cut out and join bias strips of contrast fabric and cover the cord with the strips (see page 196). Staple this piping to the lower edges of the cornice front and sides, making sure that the cord faces outward and the flanged edges lie along the lower edges of the cornice, as shown.

TIP

Slipstitching makes an invisible edge, but for a quicker version, neatly staple the lining to the edges, then disguise the staples by gluing braid trim on top.

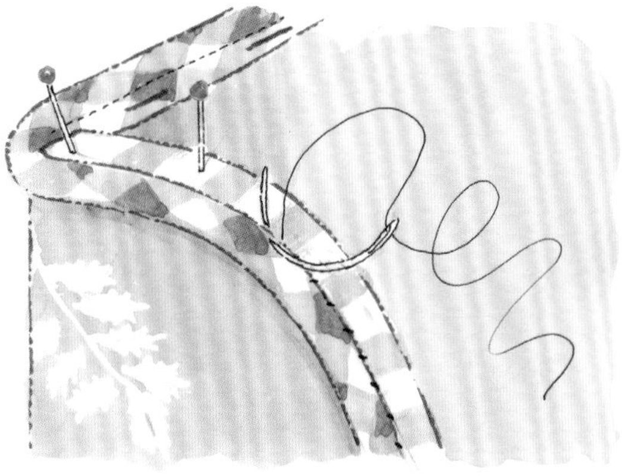

7 Remove the tape from the patterns and use the front pattern to cut out the front from the contrast lining fabric, adding a ¾in (2cm) hem allowance all around. Fold under a ⅜in (1cm) hem along the lower edge of the lining, and pin the lining to the front cornice lower edge, butting the folded edge up to the piping. Snip into the corners as you work. Smooth out the lining fabric along the inside of the cornice box front, pushing it well into the corners. Staple it in place at the sides and top. Using the curved upholstery needle, slipstitch (see page 185) the pinned lower edge of the lining to the cornice.

8 Using the patterns for the sides, cut out two side pieces from the contrast fabric, adding a ¾in (2cm) hem allowance all around. Turn under a ⅜in (1cm) hem along the lower edge of each. Pin and slipstitch the lining sides to the lower piped edge, as for the front piece. Now turn under the other edges and staple the fabric along the side back edges and the front and top inside edges. Install the cornice above your shade or curtains using the angle irons (see page 211).

chapter 2

shades

roller shade

A roller shade must be the easiest type of shade to make, so rather than buying one ready-made, using a patterned fabric like Wild Rose, in Buttercup and Charcoal, means you can color-coordinate a window covering with pillows and throws. The fabric needs to be stiffened and is simply taped to the roller at the top.

You will need

- Closely woven, lightweight, colorfast fabric—see below for yardage
- Matching sewing thread
- Roller shade kit with side pulley mechanism
- Liquid or spray fabric stiffener
- Double-sided tape
- Drill, screwdriver, saw, carpenter's square (set square)

Estimating yardage

- Measure your window to determine the finished width and length of the shade (see page 208). Add 12in (30cm) to the length for the bottom casing and to allow the roller to be covered with fabric, and add 2in (5cm) to the width to allow for shrinkage during the stiffening process. There is no need to add side hem allowances, as the stiffened fabric will not fray.

TIP

A roller shade works well if it is fitted under an upholstered cornice (see page 54), which hides the top of the shade. This is useful if you need to use the conventional roll, which allows the shade to sit close to the window, meaning the reverse side of the fabric is visible at the top.

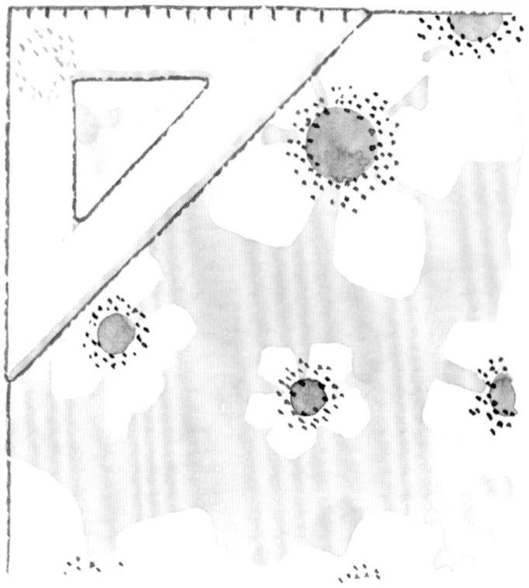

1 Decide on how your shade will roll up. (If you don't want to see the roller—and the wrong side of the fabric—at the top, choose "reverse roll," as in the photo. Or, if you want the shade to sit close to the window frame with the roller in front, choose "conventional roll.") Following the instructions in the kit, mount the brackets from the kit at the top of the window and, if necessary, cut down the top metal roller to the correct width.

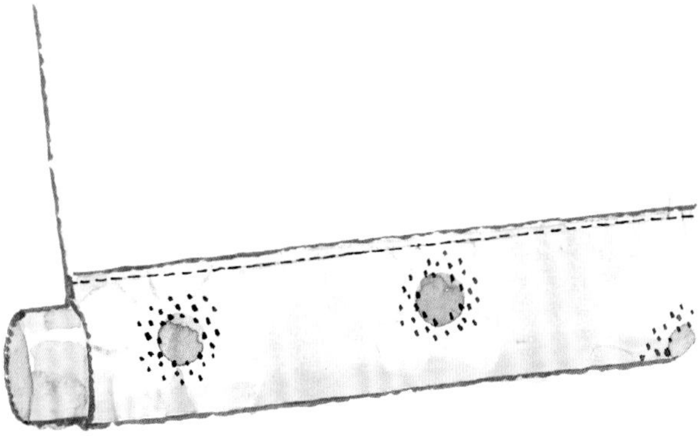

2 Stiffen the fabric following the manufacturer's instructions. Allow it to dry and then press flat. Cut the fabric to the required width, using a carpenter's square (set square) to make sure that all corners are absolutely square. Lay the fabric panel, wrong side up, on a flat surface. Fold up 1½in (4cm) at the bottom edge and machine-stitch it in place close to the raw edge. Cut the bottom weight bar ¾in (2cm) shorter than the width of the shade and slide it into the casing.

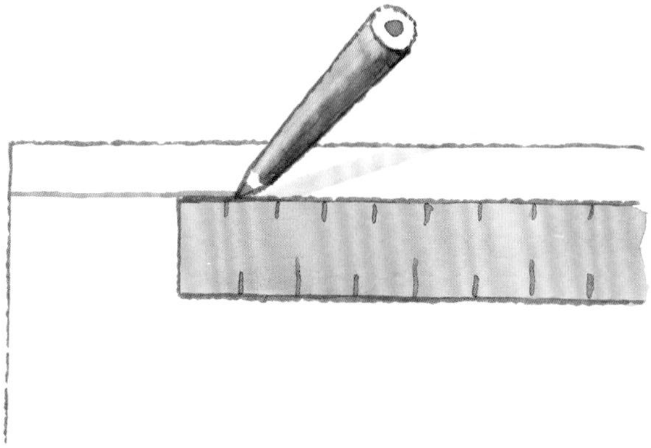

3 Lay the shade on a flat surface, and draw a chalk line the width of the tape from the top edge and parallel to the edge—for a reverse-roll shade mark this line on the wrong side of the fabric, and for a conventional-roll shade mark the line on the right side of the fabric. Stick a length of double-sided tape along the top edge of the shade, on the same side of the fabric as the chalk line.

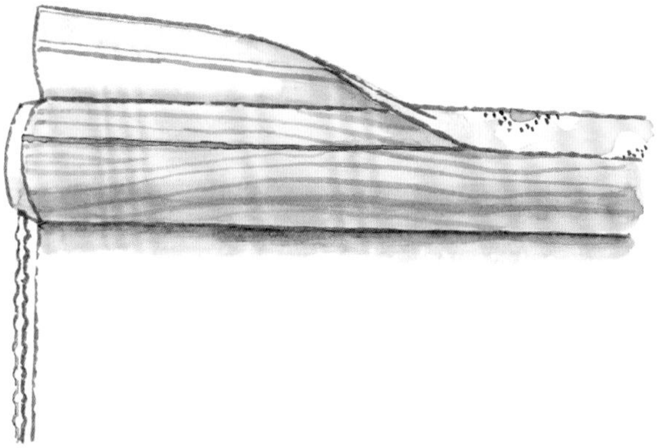

4 Remove the backing from the tape and press the top edge of the fabric onto the roller, so the top edge is aligned exactly along the guideline on the roller. Roll up the shade by hand, and slot it into the brackets. Adjust the side pulley mechanism following the manufacturer's instructions.

unlined roman shade with bottom border

Roman shades are wonderfully easy to make, especially if they are unlined, but a trim of coordinating fabric makes them a bit more interesting. Inspired by the first swallows of summer, Swallow Dive, in Duck Egg and Speedwell, trimmed with Little Leaf, in Forget-me-not and Denim, evokes optimistic days of warmth and light.

You will need

- Main decorator fabric—see right for yardage
- Contrast decorator fabric—see right for yardage
- Matching sewing thread
- Hook-and-loop tape the width of the finished shade
- Dowel rods ⅜in (1cm) in diameter, as long as the width of the finished shade minus 1½in (4cm)
- One thin 1in- (2.5cm-) wide wooden slat as long as the width of the finished shade minus 1½in (4cm)
- Small Roman shade rings
- Fine Roman shade cord
- 1 x 2in (2.5 x 5cm) wooden lath the width of the finished shade
- Brass screw eyes
- Wooden acorn and brass cleat
- Angle irons (optional)
- Screws
- Breakaway cord connector
- Adjustable breakaway orbs
- Staple gun, saw, drill, awl (bradawl)

Estimating yardage

- Measure your window to find the finished width and length of the shade (see page 208).
- The main-fabric panel should measure the finished length of the shade plus 1⅝in (4cm) for seams and hems plus 2in (5cm) per dowel rod pocket (see page 209 to work out how many dowel rod pockets you will need), by the finished width plus 5in (12cm) for hems. You may need to join lengths to achieve the required finished width, using flat fell seams (see page 189). Also allow main fabric for covering the lath (see page 210).
- The contrast-fabric border on the lower edge should measure the finished width of the shade plus 5in (12cm), by 7¼in (18cm).

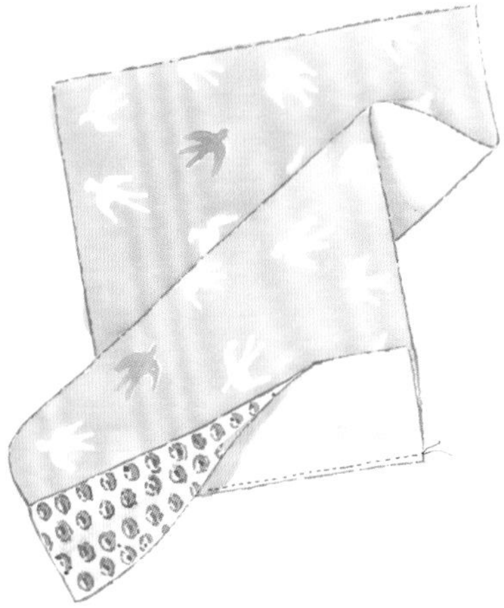

1 Cut out the required number of main-fabric lengths, joining the widths, if necessary, with flat fell seams (see page 189), to form the finished panel. From contrast fabric, cut out one border piece. With right sides together and raw edges even, pin one long edge of the border to the lower edge of the shade. Machine-stitch a ⅝in (1.5cm) seam. Press the seam allowance toward the border.

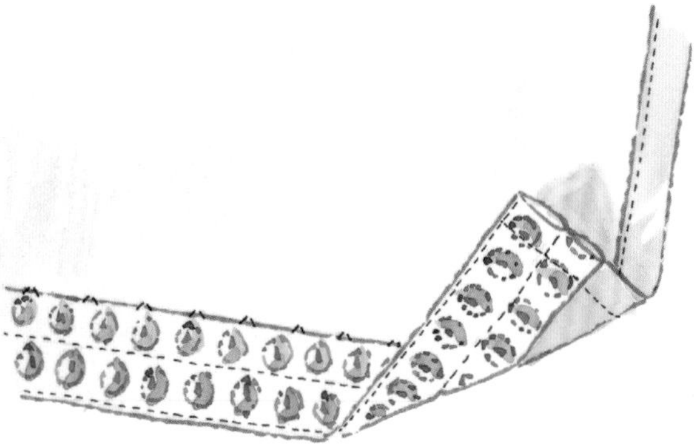

2 Along each side edge of the fabric panel, press a double-fold 1¼in (3cm) hem to the wrong side; pin and machine-stitch each in place along the first pressed edge. Along the lower edge of the border, press ⅝in (1.5cm) to the wrong side, then press a further 3in (7.5cm) to the wrong side so that the first pressed edge lies along the border stitching line. Pin and hemstitch (see page 185) in place. Machine-stitch close to the lower pressed edge of the border and then machine-stitch parallel to this but 1½in (4cm) above it to form a casing.

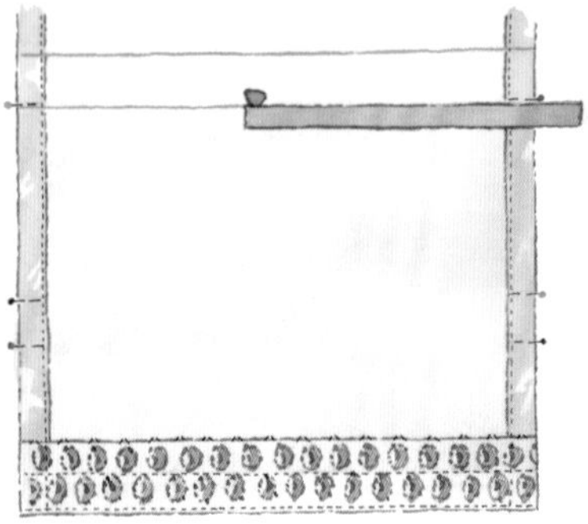

3 Lay the shade, wrong side up, on a flat surface, and use pins to mark the positions for the dowel rod pockets along the side hems, working up from the top edge of the border. The two marks for each rod pocket should be 2in (5cm) apart, and the spacing of the rod pockets should be as explained on page 209. Using dressmakers' chalk and a long ruler, lightly draw lines across the shade, joining the pins.

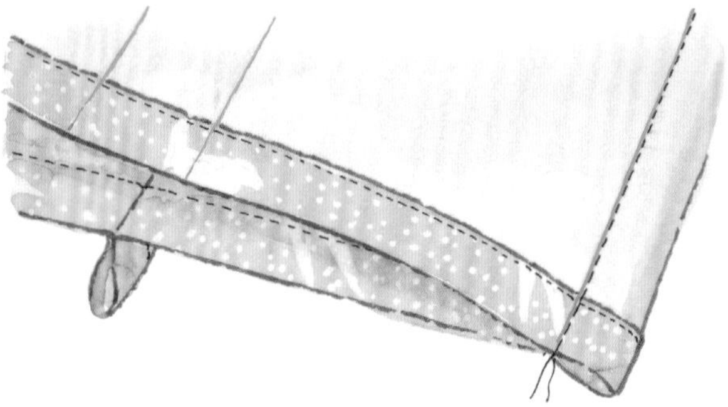

4 Fold the shade crosswise, with right sides together, so that the two chalk lines indicating a rod pocket are on top of each other. Pin in place and press. Machine-stitch along the chalk line to form a 1in- (2.5cm-) wide rod pocket. Repeat for the other rod pockets.

5 Measure the length of the finished shade from the border seam line and mark the position of the shade's top edge with pins. Press the top hem to the wrong side along the pin line. Trim the hem allowance to ⅝in (1.5cm) and pin in place. Attach the fluffy (loop) side of the hook-and-loop tape to the wrong side of the shade at the top, as for the Lined Swedish Shade, step 3 (see page 72). Insert the dowel rods through the dowel rod pockets, and insert the wooden slat into the lower casing in the border. Slipstitch (see page 185) the open ends of the border and the edges of the dowel rod pockets to enclose the wooden slat and dowels.

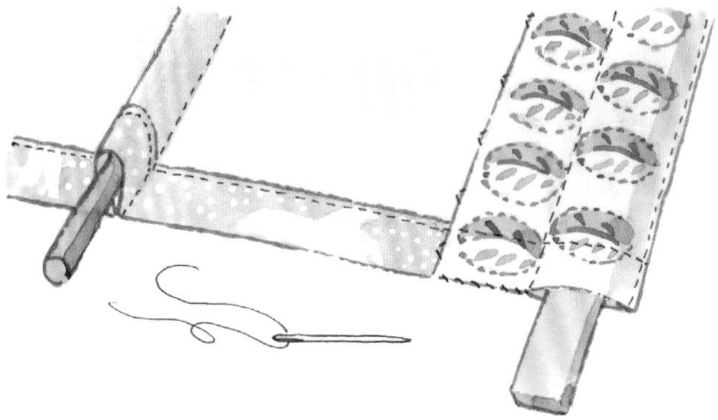

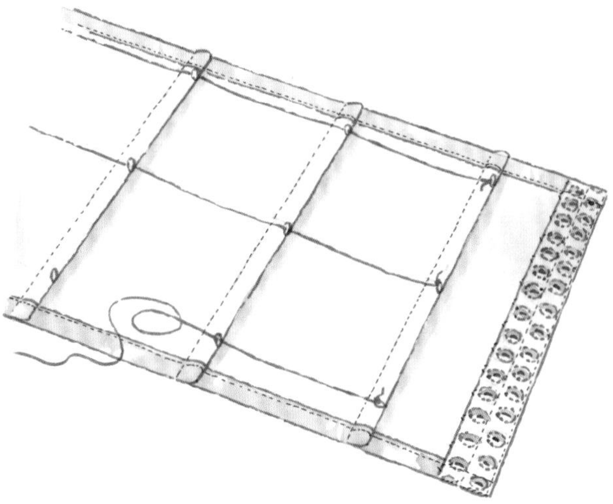

6 Lay the shade wrong side up on a flat surface. Position the cording rings 2in (5cm) in from each side of the shade and at equal intervals across it, about 12in (30.5cm) apart. Hand-sew the rings securely to the folded edge of each pocket. Tie a length of the Roman shade cord to the bottom ring of each column and thread it up through the line of rings above it.

7 Cover the wooden lath with the main fabric and attach the hook side of the hook-and-loop tape (see Wooden Laths for Shades, page 210, steps 1–3). Attach the shade using the hook-and-loop tape, then attach the screw eyes (see page 210, step 4). Thread the cords through the corresponding screw eyes and thread them across and through the remaining screw eyes to the operating side. Make sure that the shade is lying flat and that the cords are all pulled through smoothly. Thread the cords through one end of the breakaway cord connector, then knot the cord ends together about 4in (10 cm) from the last screw eye. Thread a single length of cord through the other remaining part of the breakaway cord connector and knot the end securely. Now fasten the connector together and attach the acorn to the end to your chosen length. Fit the shade above the window, and install a cleat on the wall or window frame, as for the Lined Swedish Shade, step 7 (see page 73). Important: You must ensure that your shade and its cords comply with the latest legislation on child safety.

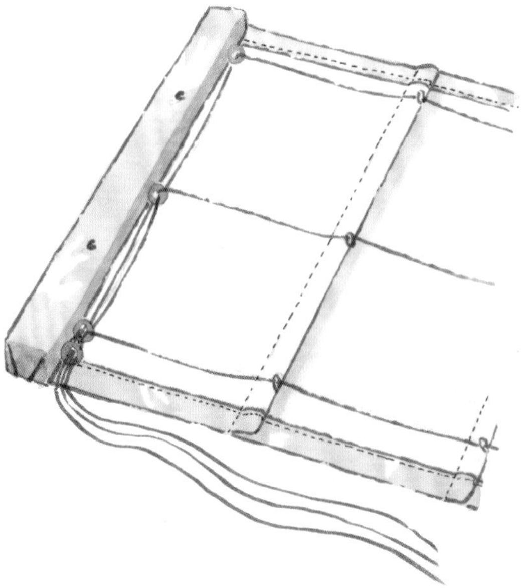

COULEUR & HABITAT
KÜNKEL AFRICAN ELEPHANTS
YOSHITOMO NARA DRAWING FILE
BIRDS & PEOPLE
SURVIVAL

lined roman shade with border

Borders add definition to a Roman shade, helping to bring out the colors in a scheme. They are added to the main fabric before it is made up. Made in Origami Linen in Turquoise and Saffron, this shade is bordered with Plain Linen in Turquoise.

You will need

- Main decorator fabric—see below for yardage
- Contrast decorator fabric for borders—see below for yardage
- Lining fabric—see below for yardage
- Matching sewing thread
- Hook-and-loop tape the width of the finished shade
- Roman shade tape (a special tape that has a casing woven along its center, with fabric loops attached)—see below for yardage
- Dowel rods ⅜in (1cm) in diameter, 1½in (4cm) shorter than the width of your finished shade
- One thin 1in (2.5cm-) wide wooden slat, 1½in (4cm) shorter than the width of your finished shade
- Fine Roman shade cord
- 1 x 2in (2.5 x 5cm) wooden lath as long as the width of your finished shade
- Brass screw eyes
- Wooden acorn and brass cleat
- Angle irons (optional)
- Screws
- Breakaway cord connector
- Adjustable breakaway orbs
- Bodkin or large tapestry needle, staple gun, saw, drill, awl (bradawl)

Estimating yardage

- Measure your window to determine the finished width and length of the shade (see page 208).
- Decide on the finished width of side borders and the depth of the bottom border; they are usually the same width/depth—between about 1in (2.5cm) and 4in (10cm). The border in the photo is 3¼in (8cm).
- The main-fabric panel should measure the finished shade length minus the finished border depth plus 2in (5cm), by the finished shade width minus twice the finished border width plus 1¼in (3cm). Also allow main fabric for covering the lath (see page 210).
- Each of the two contrast-fabric side borders should measure the same as the main-fabric panel cut length plus the finished bottom border depth plus 2⅝in (6.5cm), by the finished border width plus 2⅝in (6.5cm). The bottom border should measure the same as the main-fabric panel cut width plus twice the finished border width plus 4in (10cm), by the finished border depth plus 2⅝in (6.5cm).
- The lining should measure the finished length of the shade, by the finished width of the shade.
- For the Roman shade tape, calculate the dowel rod spacing for your shade length (see page 209) and then allow for a length of tape the width of your shade multiplied times the number of rods calculated, plus 20in (51cm).

1 From the main fabric and lining, cut out the required number of lengths, joining the lengths, if necessary, with flat fell seams (see page 189) to form the finished main-fabric and lining panels. From contrast fabric, cut out the two side borders and the bottom border. On the main-fabric panel, measure ⅝in (1.5cm) up from the bottom edge and ⅝in (1.5cm) in from one side edge; mark with a pin. Repeat at the other side.

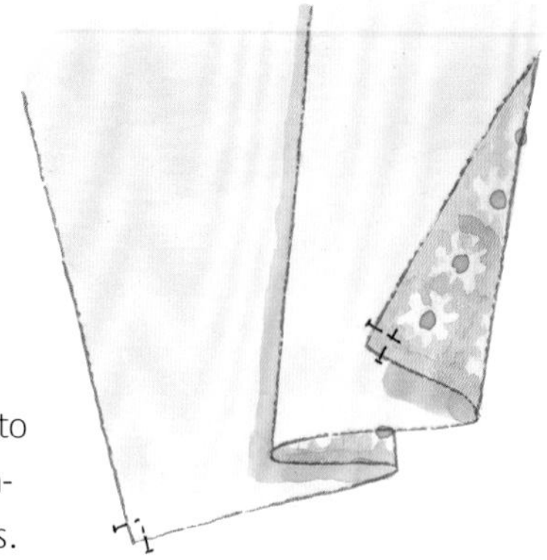

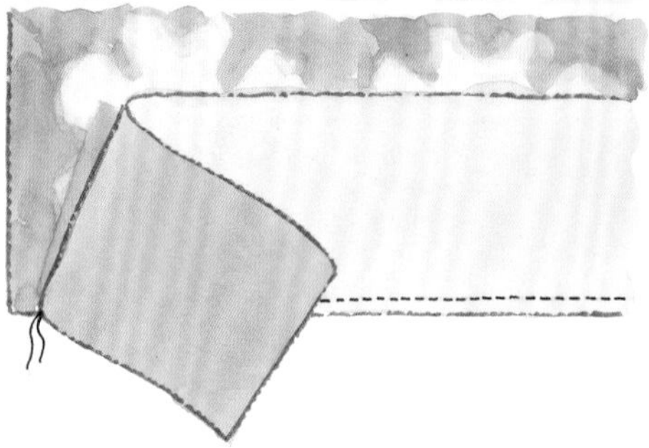

2 With right sides together, pin the bottom border to the main fabric along the lower edge, with the border extending beyond the main fabric by the same amount at each side edge. Machine-stitch a ⅝in (1.5cm) seam between the marked corners.

3 With right sides together, pin one side border to one side edge of the main fabric, with the edges even at the top; machine-stitch a ⅝in (1.5cm) seam from the top edge to the point you marked at the bottom edge. Repeat to attach the remaining side border to the other side edge. Press the seam allowances toward the borders.

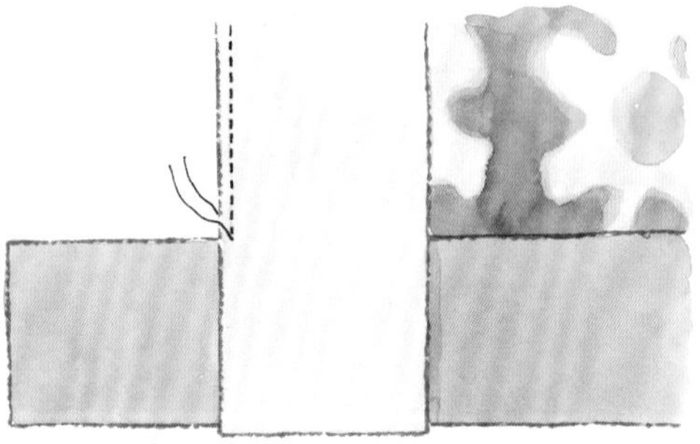

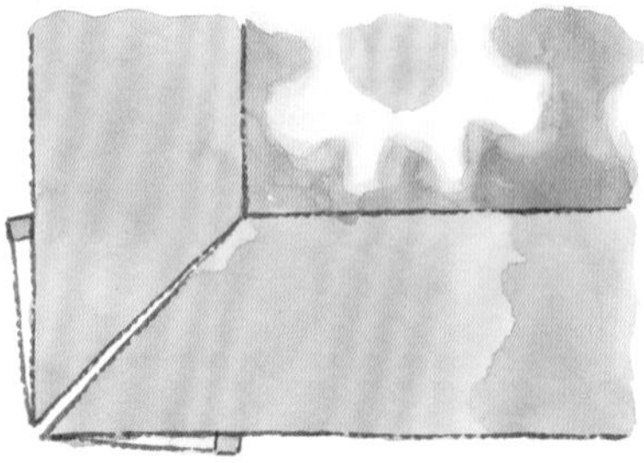

4 Turn under the bottom end of one side border and the adjacent end of the bottom border diagonally from the outer corner to the point at which the stitching lines meet, so that the folded edges meet; press. With right sides together, and stitching into the corner, pin and stitch along the press lines to form a miter. Trim the seam allowances to ¼in (5mm) and press open. Repeat for the other bottom corner.

5 On the long raw edge of each side border, press 2in (5cm) to the wrong side of the shade, and then, after doing the side borders, do the same for the bottom border. Do not miter the corners this time. Catchstitch the raw edges in place (see page 187). On the lining panel, press a single 1in (2.5cm) hem to the wrong side along the side and bottom edges. Place the lining on the panel with wrong sides together and with the top raw edges even; 1in (2.5cm) of the border will be showing at the side and bottom edges. Pin and baste the lining to the panel around all edges. Hemstitch (see page 185) the lining to the borders along the side and bottom edges, leaving 1in (2.5cm) unsewn at the bottom of each side edge; remove the basting. To form a channel for the wooden slat, topstitch 1½in (4cm) from the lower edge.

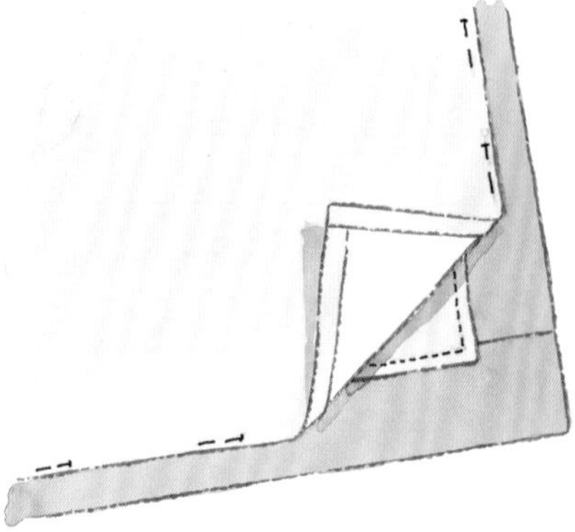

6 Measure the length of the finished shade and mark the position of the top edge with pins. Press the top hem to the wrong side along the pin line. Trim the hem allowance to ⅝in (1.5cm) and pin in place. Attach the fluffy (loop) side of the hook-and-loop tape to the wrong side of the shade at the top, covering the raw edges of the main fabric and lining. Machine-stitch the hook-and-loop tape in place around all edges.

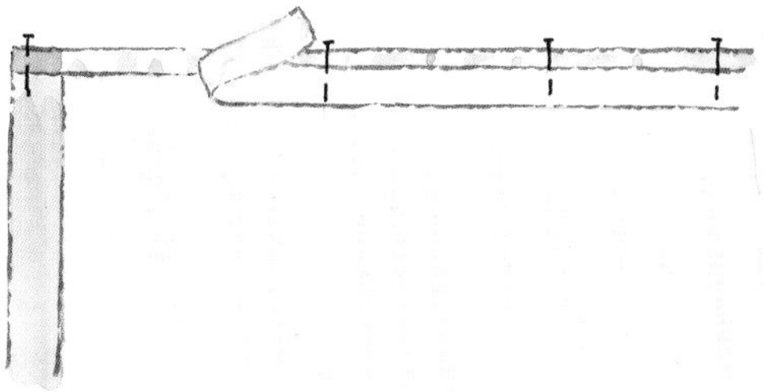

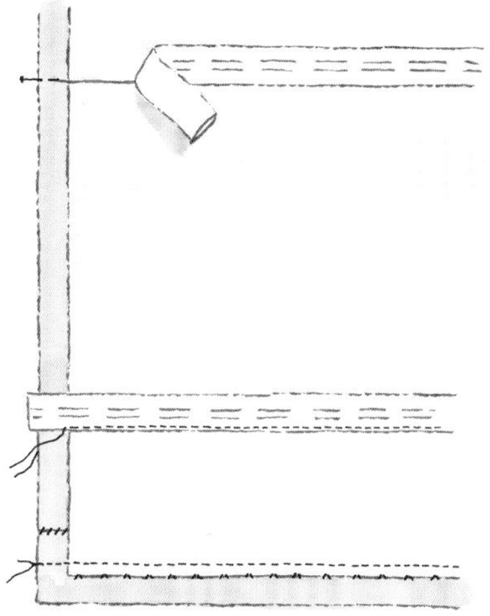

7 Calculate the spacing positions for the Roman shade tape, measuring up from the base of the shade (see page 209). Lay the shade, wrong side up, on a flat surface, and mark the positions with pins along each side hem. Lightly draw lines across the shade, joining the pins, using dressmakers' chalk and a long ruler. Cut lengths of tape ½in (1cm) longer than the width of the shade, making sure that the loops on each are aligned. Place on the shade, with the bottom of each tape along the chalked line, and ¼in (5mm) overhanging at each end. Pin and machine-stitch along the lower edge of each tape, starting and finishing ¾in (2cm) in from the ends of the tape.

8 Insert the dowel rods through the casings in the tapes, and the wooden slat into the casing on the lower edge. Slipstitch (see page 185) the open ends of the casing to enclose the slat, and hemstitch in place the remaining 1in (2.5cm) of the lining side edges. To neaten the raw ends of the Roman shade tape, turn in a double ⅜in (1cm) hem at each end, and hand-sew in place.

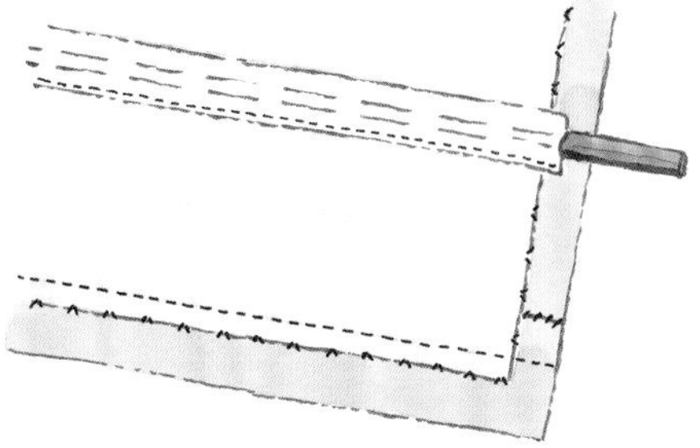

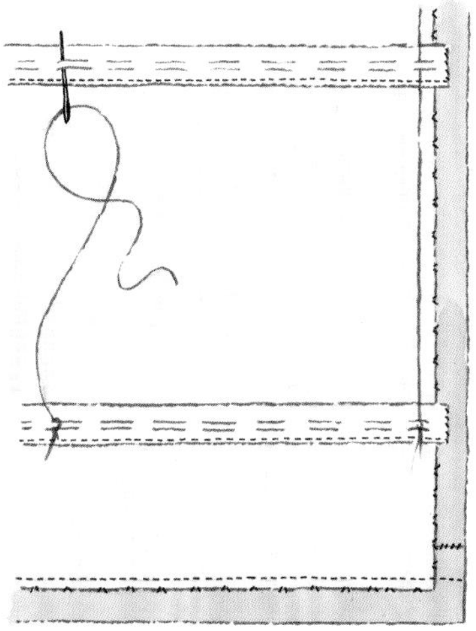

9 Lay the shade, wrong side up, on a flat surface. On the Roman shade tapes, measure and mark the cord positions for the head rail. Mark vertical rows with pins, placing the first and last rows 2in (5cm) in from the side edges. The remaining vertical rows should be spaced evenly across the center of the shade, about 12in (30.5cm) apart. Thread a length of the Roman shade cord through each of the loops at your pin positions in the bottom strip of Roman shade tape. Using a bodkin or tapestry needle, thread each length of cord vertically through the corresponding loops in each length of tape, at your pin positions, securing in place with an adjustable breakaway orb (sewn onto the tape). Complete the shade as for the Unlined Roman Shade with Bottom Border, step 7 (see page 65). Important: You must ensure that your shade and its cords comply with the latest legislation on child safety.

lined swedish shade

These beautifully simple shades are traditional in Sweden, where the winter days are short and sunlight is treasured. Rather than heavy drapes, windows in cottages and palaces alike are often dressed with simple unlined woven checks, made into curtains or traditional roll-up shades. This shade is a useful way of introducing two fabrics into a room—the photo on the right uses For the Love of Rose, in Duck Egg, as the main fabric and Stripe & Dash, in Duck Egg and Cornflower, as the contrast fabric. When the shade is down, only the front fabric shows, but during the day, when the shade is rolled up, you can see both fabrics.

You will need

- Main decorator fabric—see right for yardage
- Contrast decorator fabric—see right for yardage
- Matching sewing thread
- Hook-and-loop tape the width of the finished shade
- One dowel rod, ⅜in (1cm) in diameter, the width of the finished shade minus ¾in (2cm)
- ¾ x 1½in (2 x 4cm) wooden lath the width of the finished shade
- Two 1¼in (3cm) clear plastic D-rings or round rings
- Fine Roman shade cord
- Angle irons (optional)
- Screws
- Breakaway cord connector
- Wooden acorn and brass cleat
- Saw, drill, staple gun

Estimating yardage

- Measure your window to determine the finished width and length of the shade (see page 208).
- The main-fabric panel should measure the finished width plus 1¼in (3cm) for seams, by the finished length plus 2¼in (6cm) for hems. You may need to join lengths to achieve the required finished width. Also allow main fabric for covering the lath (see page 210).
- The contrast-fabric backing panel should measure the same length and width as the main-fabric panel. Also allow contrast fabric for two tab loops, each 12 x 3¼in (30 x 8.5cm).

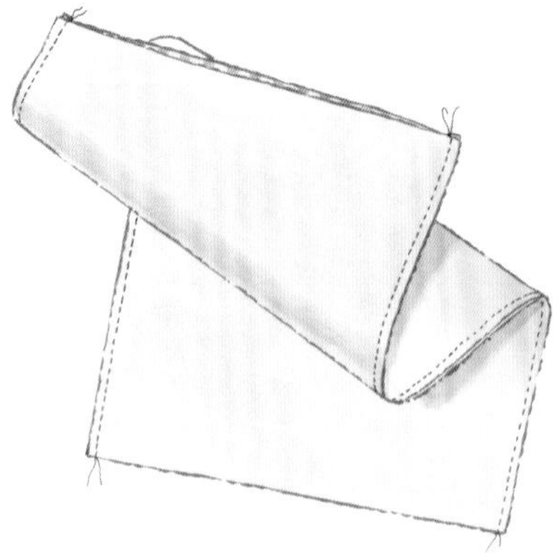

1 Cut out the required number of main-fabric lengths, joining the widths, if necessary, with flat fell seams (see page 189), to form the finished panel. Do the same for the contrast backing fabric. With right sides together, pin and machine-stitch the backing to the main panel down the side edges, with ⅝in (1.5cm) seams. Turn right side out and press flat, with the seams exactly along the edges of the shade.

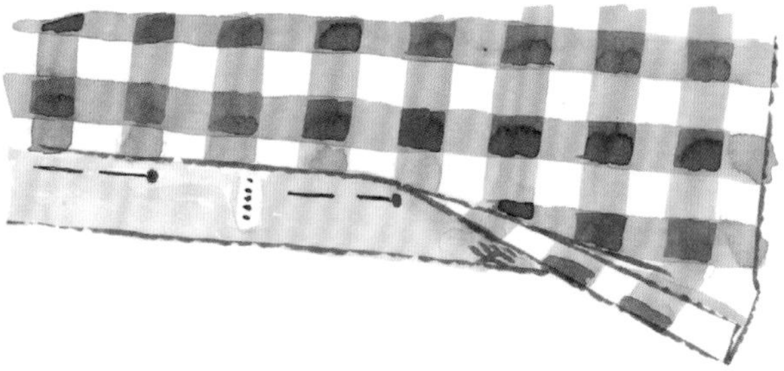

2 On the lower edge, fold over and press a ⅝in (1.5cm) hem to the contrast-fabric side of the panel, then fold and press over a further 1in (2.5cm) hem. Pin and machine-stitch in place close to the first pressed edge, to form a casing.

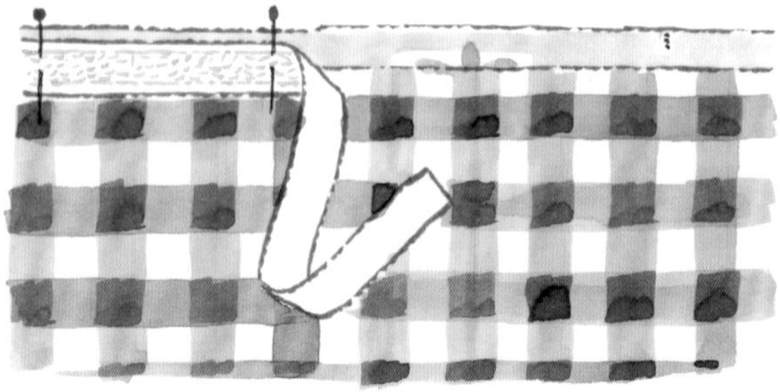

3 On the top edge, fold over and press a ⅝in (1.5cm) hem to the contrast-fabric side of the panel, and baste. Pin the fluffy (loop) side of the hook-and-loop tape to the contrast-fabric side of the shade at the top, covering the raw edge. Machine-stitch the tape in place along both long edges (stitching in the same direction each time) and across both ends of the tape.

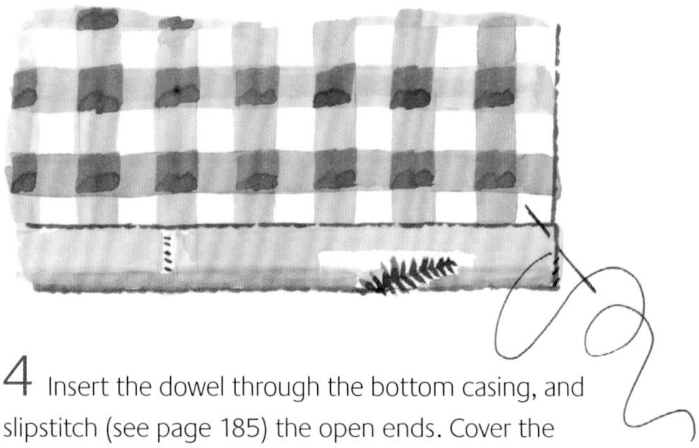

4 Insert the dowel through the bottom casing, and slipstitch (see page 185) the open ends. Cover the wooden lath with main fabric and attach the hook side of the hook-and-loop tape (see Wooden Laths for Shades, page 210, steps 1–3).

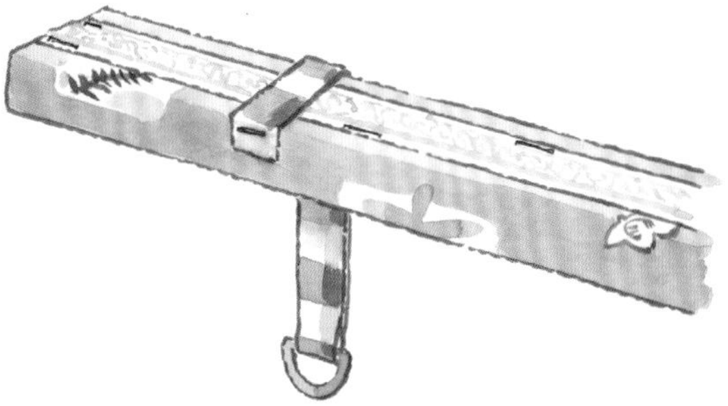

5 Cut out and make up the two tab loops as for Ties, method 2 (see page 203) without finishing the ends. Thread a ring onto each tab loop, then fold each loop in half with the seams together and raw edges even. Staple the raw ends of the tabs to the back of the wooden lath, about 4in (10cm) in from each end, so that the loops come over the top of the lath and hang down in front, on top of the hook-and-loop tape.

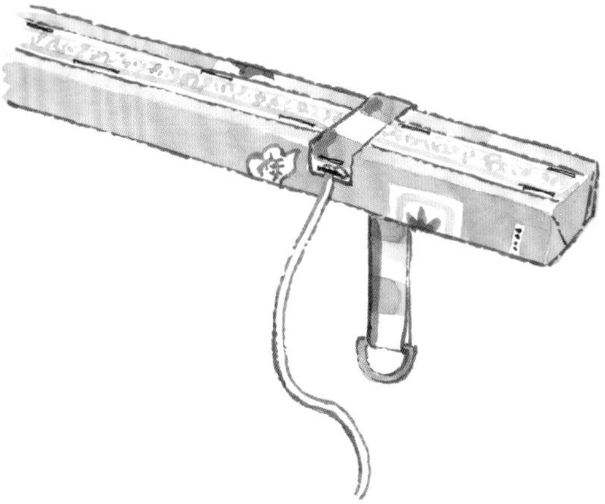

6 Cut two lengths of cord, each as long as four times the drop of the shade. Tie a knot at one end and staple each knot to the back of the wooden lath over the end of each tab loop, so that the cords hang down from the lath.

7 Attach the shade to the lath with the hook-and-loop tape. To mount the shade above the window, open the hook-and-loop tape as far as the pilot holes. (There is no need to remove the shade totally from the lath.) Screw the lath to the wall or window frame through the pilot holes, then reattach the sides of the shade along the lath. Install a cleat on the wall or window frame, positioning it on the same side as the draw cords, to secure the cords when the shade is raised.

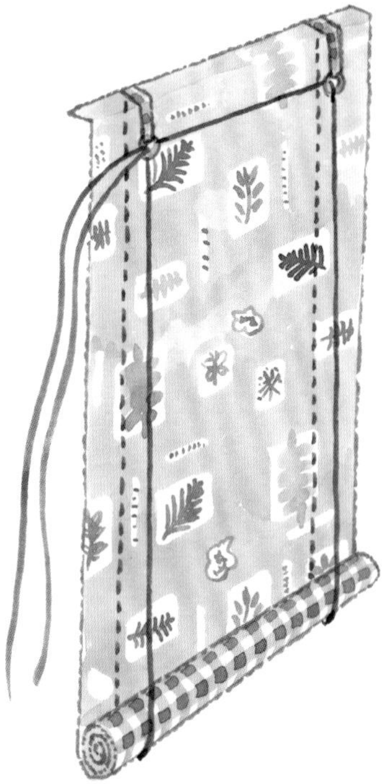

8 To create the operating mechanism, thread the shade by bringing the cords (which are hanging down the back of the shade) under the bottom edge, and bring them up the front to pass through their corresponding rings, as shown. Pass one of the cords across the top of the shade and through the second ring to bring both cords over to the operating side. Thread the cords through one end of the breakaway cord connector, then knot the cord ends together about 4in (10cm) from the last screw eye. Thread a single length of cord through the other remaining part of the breakaway cord connector and knot the end securely. Now fasten the connector together and attach the acorn to the end to your chosen length. Roll up the base of the shade, by hand, and secure it at your selected position by winding the cord around the cleat. Important: You must ensure that your shade and its cords comply with the latest legislation on child safety.

chapter 3

pillows

the easiest pillow

Here's a wonderfully simple way to make a pillow. With no zipper, ties, or buttons, it's basically just a front and two back pieces that overlap at the back to make an envelope. With only four straight seams, a pillow cover can be made in under an hour. If you are a complete beginner, this project is ideal for you, so try making a few in different fabrics to perfect the technique.

You will need

- Decorator fabric—see below for yardage
- Matching sewing thread
- Pillow form
- Snaps (optional)

Estimating yardage

- Measure the pillow form. For the front piece, allow ⅝in (1.5cm) all around for seams. For the two back pieces, allow for each to be the same depth as the front piece, and a width equal to half the width of the pillow form plus 5in (13cm).

TIP

If you like your pillows to be very plump, with very taut covers, simply cut the pieces slightly smaller.

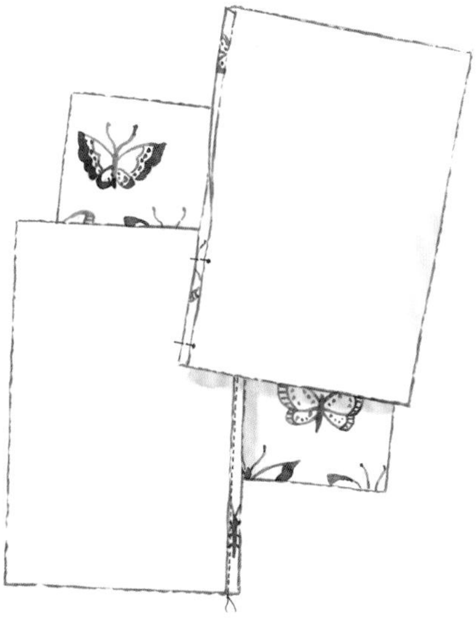

1 Cut one front piece and two back pieces from the fabric. Press a double 1in (2.5cm) hem to the wrong side along one long edge of each back piece. Pin and machine-stitch both hems in place, stitching close to the first pressed edge on each.

2 Lay the front piece right side up on a flat surface, then place the back covers on top, right sides down, with raw edges even and the hemmed edges overlapping at the center. Pin, then baste the pieces together around all four sides. Machine-stitch a ⅝in (1.5cm) seam around all four sides.

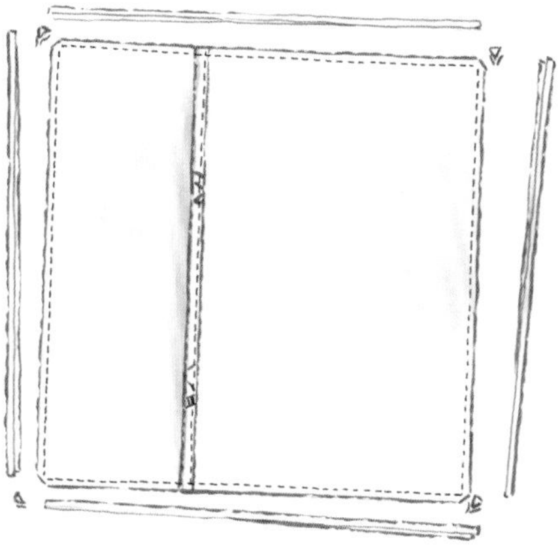

3 Remove the basting. Trim the seam allowances to ⅜in (1cm), and snip off the corners of the seam allowances. Turn the pillow cover right side out. Carefully push out the corners using a sharp pair of scissors, and press the seamed edges flat. Insert the pillow form through the back opening, and smooth the back overlaps flat.

4 If your pillow form is large, you may wish to sew snaps to the underside of the overlap and the right side of the underlap. This will stop the opening from gaping and keep the front nice and taut.

ruffled cushion

This is a good example of how changing the color can give a completely different look to the same fabric. Also in Stripe and Dash fabric, like the Curvy Cushion (see page 82), but in the richer colorway of Cranberry, this cushion has a wide ruffle around three sides and narrow ties which loop neatly around the chair back.

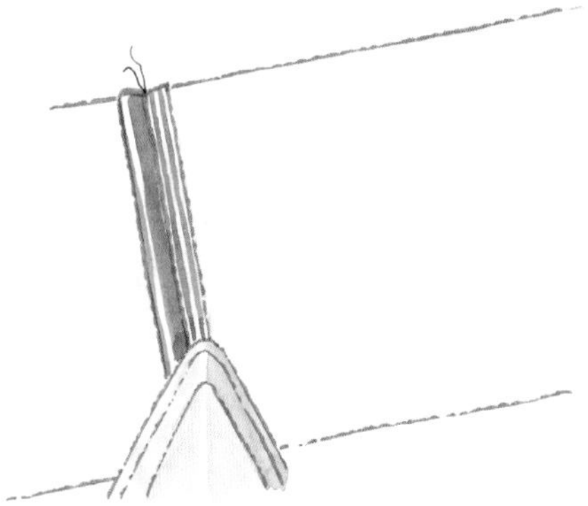

1 From the fabric, cut out one top piece, two base pieces, and the ruffle pieces. With right sides together, join the ruffle pieces into a long strip, using ⅝in (1.5cm) seams. Press the seams open.

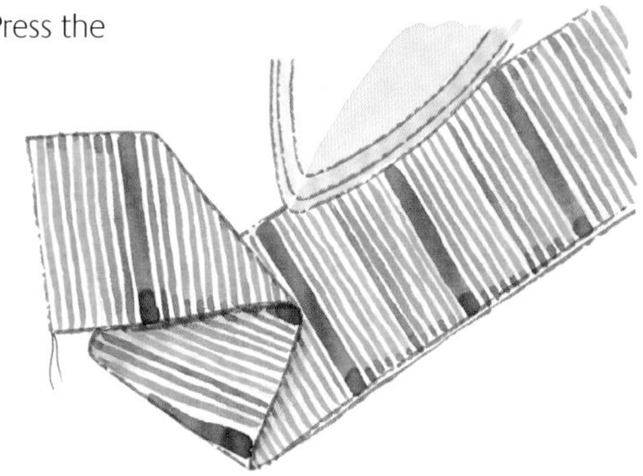

2 With right sides together, fold the ruffle strip in half lengthwise. Pin and machine-stitch across both ends, with ⅝in (1.5cm) seam allowances. Trim the seam allowances to ¼in (5mm) and snip off the corners of the seam allowances. Turn the seamed ends right side out, and carefully push out the corners with a pointed object, such as a pair of scissors. Press the seamed edges flat, and then press the ruffle in half all along its length, wrong sides together.

You will need

- Decorator fabric—see below for yardage
- Matching sewing thread
- Ready-made square or rectangular pillow form to fit your chair seat
- Zipper 3in (7.5cm) shorter than the width of the pillow form

Estimating yardage

- Measure the length and width of the pillow form.
- For the top, allow one piece of fabric that is the size of the pillow form, plus a ⅝in (1.5cm) seam allowance all around.
- For the base, divide the form size into two halves. Allow for two pieces of fabric, each the size of one of these halves plus a ⅝in (1.5cm) seam allowance all around each.
- Allow 7½in (19cm) for the width of the ruffle strip. For the length, add the width of the pillow form to twice its length, then double this total, and add 1¼in (3cm) for seam allowances. You will need to join fabric pieces to obtain the correct length for your ruffle, so allow an extra 1¼in (3cm) to the length of each fabric piece for seam allowances.
- Allow for four ties, each 2¼ x 10in (6 x 25.5cm).

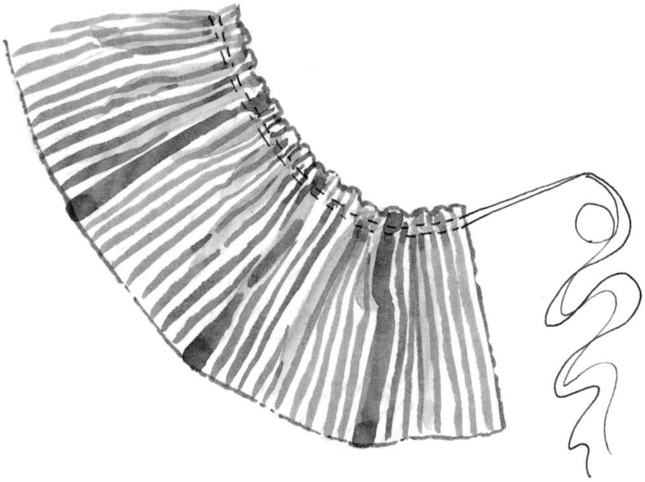

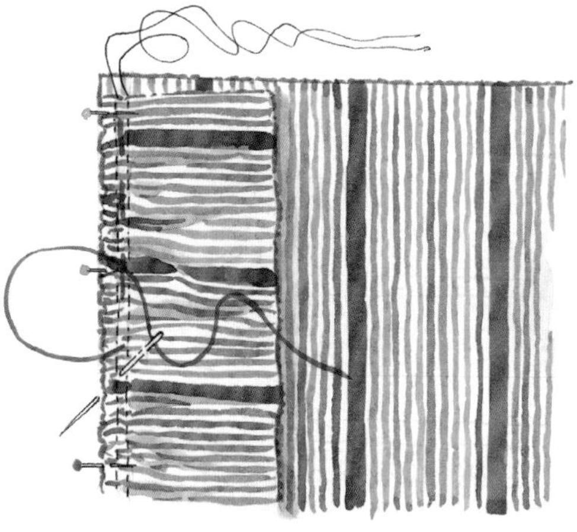

3 With the raw edges of the ruffle even, sew two parallel rows of gathering stitches (see page 198) along the raw edges of the ruffle, spacing the rows roughly ¼in (5mm) apart. Carefully pull the threads to gather the ruffle evenly until it fits around the front and sides of the top piece.

4 Place the ruffle on the right side of the top piece, with raw edges even. Pin in place along the front and side edges, starting and finishing ⅝in (1.5cm) from the back edge. Baste the ruffle in place, and then machine-stitch a ⅝in (1.5cm) seam around the front and side edges. Remove the basting stitches.

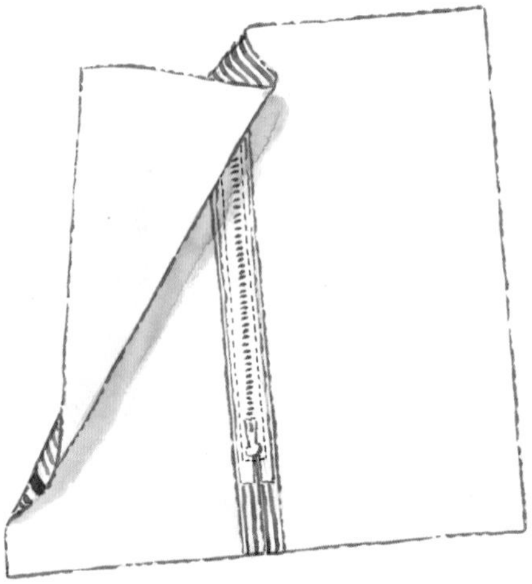

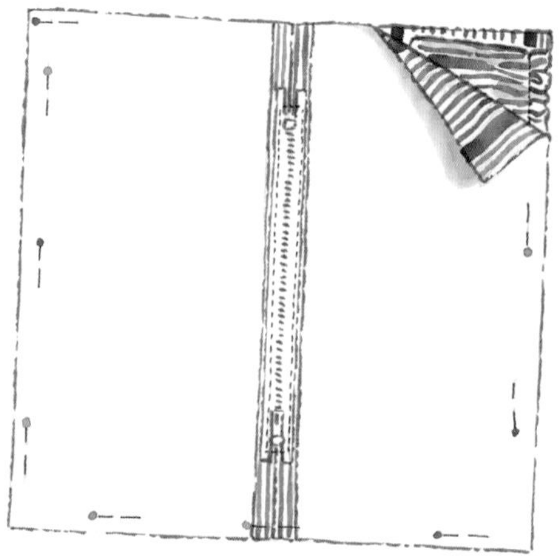

5 With right sides together, pin and baste the two base pieces together along one long edge, using a ⅝in (1.5cm) seam. Machine-stitch along the basting for 1½in (4cm) at each end of the seam, leaving the basting stitches in the center intact. Press open the seam, and insert the zipper (see page 201). Remove the basting.

6 Pin the base to the top piece, with right sides together and the ruffle sandwiched between the two layers. Machine-stitch a ⅝in (1.5cm) seam around the front and sides, starting and finishing ⅝in (1.5cm) from the back edge. Snip off the corners of the seam allowances at the front. Press under ⅝in (1.5cm) on the raw back edges of the top and base. Turn right side out.

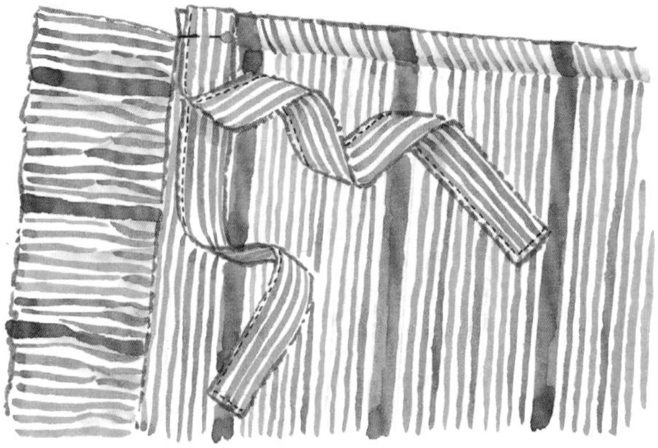

7 Make four ties following method 2 (see page 203), finishing one end of each. Open out the pressed back edge of the base. With raw edges even, place two ties, one on top of the other, at each side of the opened-out back edge, as shown. Pin and baste the ties in place. Machine-stitch the ties along the pressed line, stitching over the same place several times to reinforce. Remove the basting stitches.

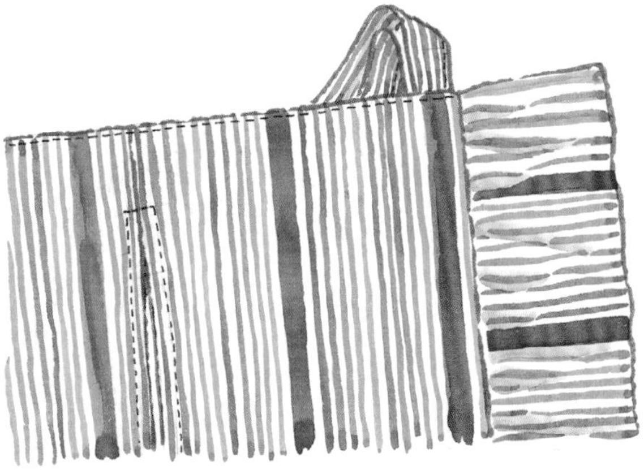

8 Fold the pressed seam allowances back to the wrong side, so that the ties are projecting from the cover. Open the zipper. Pin and baste the pressed-under edges together, with the ends of the ties sandwiched between them. Machine-stitch the edges together, close to the pressed edge. Insert the pillow form through the opening in the base, and close the zipper.

TIP

When joining the top piece to the base in step 6, be careful not to accidentally catch the folded edge of the ruffle in the seam.

curvy cushion

Finding a vintage or neglected garden chair and upgrading it with a coat of paint and a new cushion is a wonderful way to furnish a home on a budget. Old metal chairs like this one can be found in junk stores, although there are plenty of reproductions available in chain stores too. A relaxed seat cushion, in Stripe and Dash, Apple Green and Raspberry, has soft ties to hold the cushion in place for use as a bedroom chair.

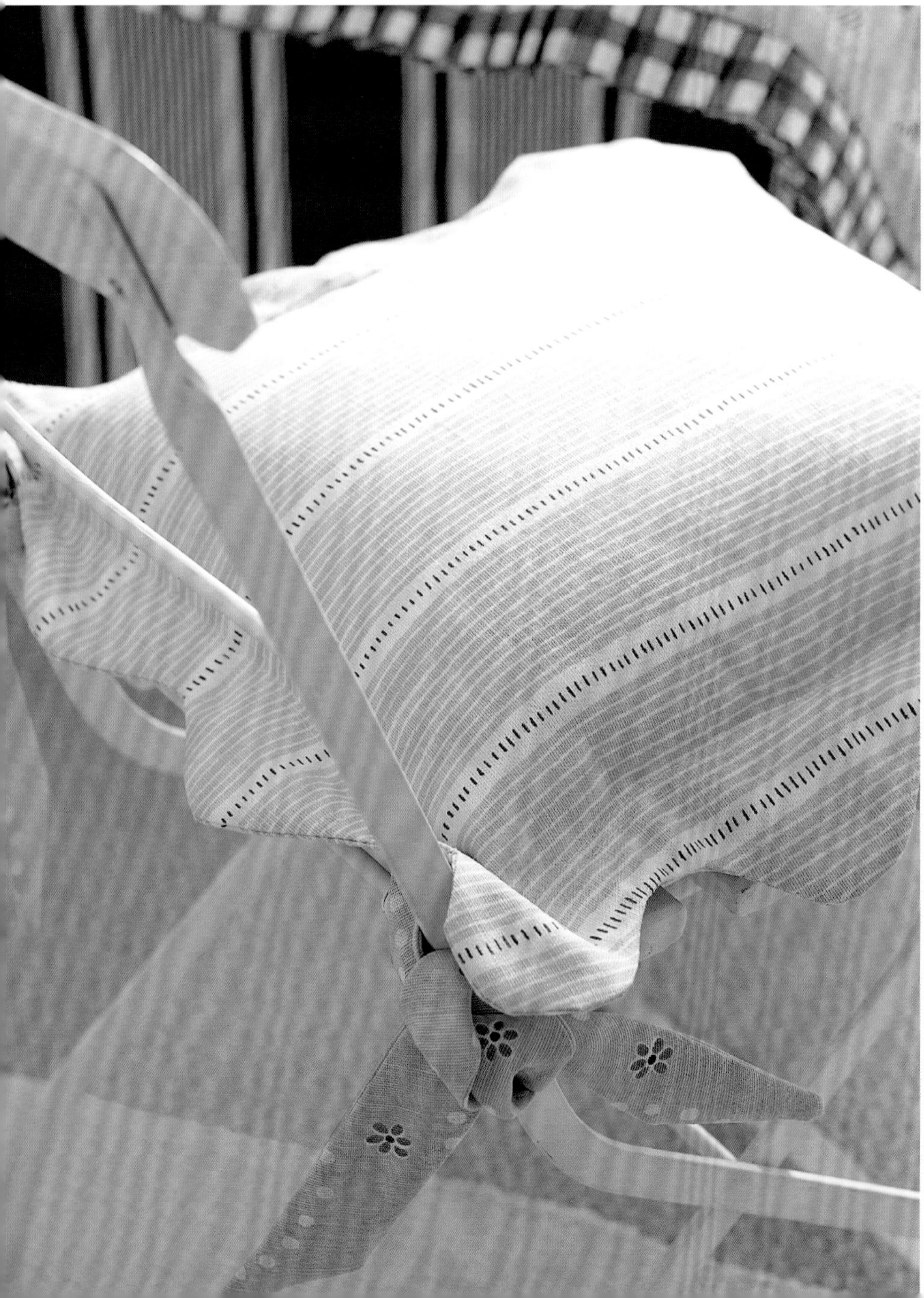

You will need

- Main decorator fabric—see below for yardage
- Contrast decorator fabric—see below for yardage
- Matching sewing thread
- 14in (36cm) square pillow form
- 10in (25cm) zipper
- Paper for making patterns

Estimating yardage

- For the main fabric, make a paper pattern following steps 1 and 2. Allow for one top and two base pieces, plus a ⅝in (1.5cm) seam allowance all around.
- For the contrast fabric, allow for two ties 3¾in (9.5cm) wide by 30in (76cm) long.

TIP

This is a lovely cushion to make for a garden chair like this, but is such a pretty shape that it would look just as good used as a scatter cushion on a sofa or easy chair. Simply omit the ties and add it to a clutch of pillows made from different patterns and colors.

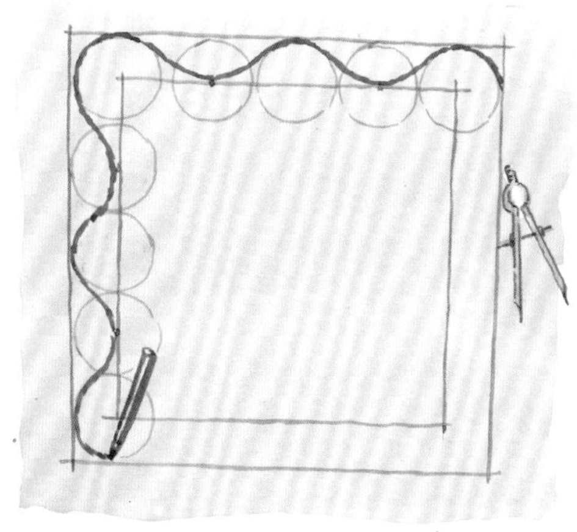

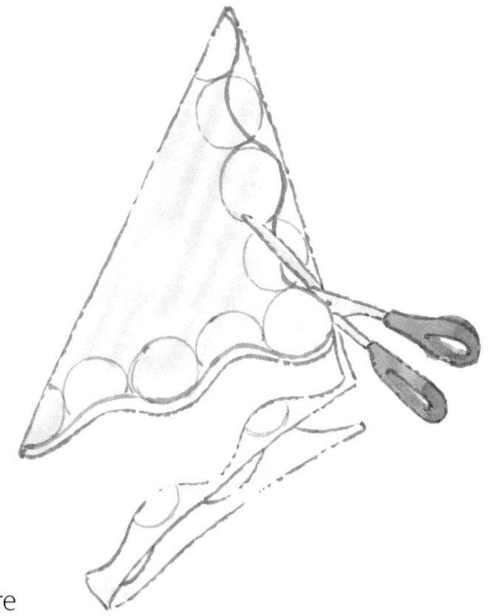

1 Draw a 20in (51cm) square on paper and then draw another square 2in (5cm) inside the edges of the first. Starting at one corner of the inner square, draw a 4in (10cm) circle using a compass, with the spike of the compass on the corner of the inner square and the outer edge of the circle touching the sides of the outer square. Continue drawing circles along to the next corner, and then down the adjacent side to that corner, marking the center of each circle where you placed the compass spike. Now draw a wavy line to join all the circles passing through each alternate center mark, as shown.

2 Cut out the larger square and fold the pattern diagonally in half. Cut along the wavy line through both layers of paper as shown, and then open it out to create the pattern for the top. For the base pattern, fold the top pattern in half parallel to two edges, draw around it onto paper, and cut out the new pattern.

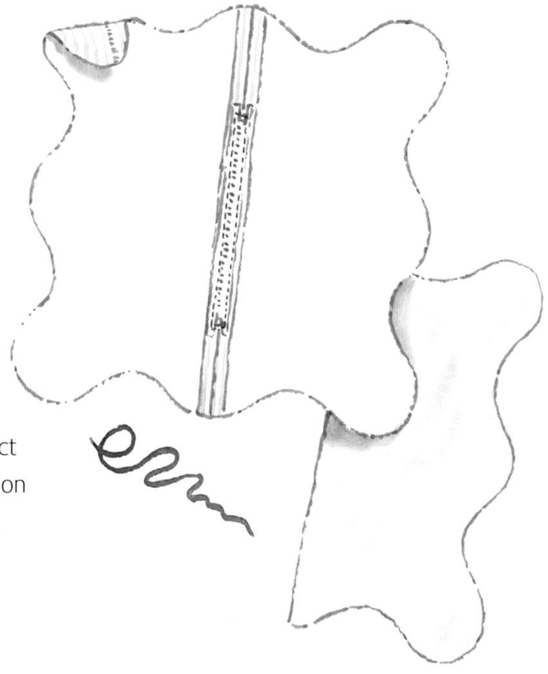

3 From the main fabric, cut out one top and two base pieces, adding a ⅝in (1.5cm) seam allowance all around each piece. With right sides together, pin the two base pieces together along the straight edges; baste a ⅝in (1.5cm) seam. Machine-stitch along the basting for 5⅝in (14.5cm) at each end of the seam, leaving the basting stitches intact in the center. Insert a zipper into the basted portion of the seam (see page 201). Remove the basting.

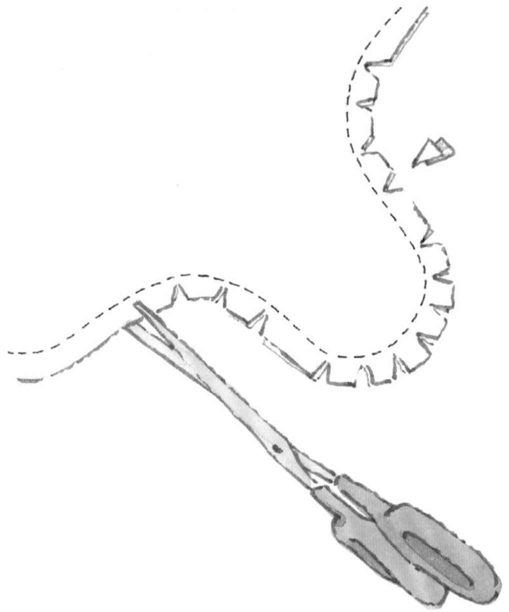

4 Open the zipper. With right sides together and all edges even, pin and baste the top and base pieces together around the shaped outer edge. Machine-stitch a ⅝in (1.5cm) seam all around the shaped edge. Remove the basting stitches and clip into the seam allowances on the curves(see page 190). Turn the cover right side out and press the seamed edges flat.

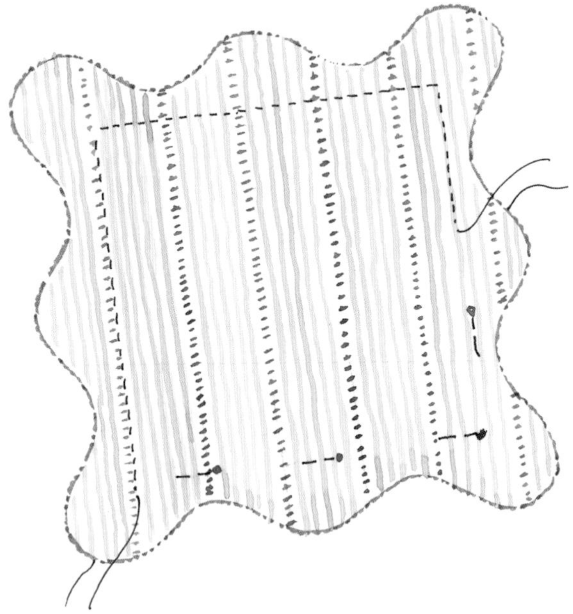

5 On each edge, measure 3in (7.5cm) in from the outermost curves of the cover, and mark with lines of pins, to mark out a 14in (36cm) square in the center of the cover. Baste around the pinned square through both layers to mark the position, then machine-stitch around the basted square. Remove the basting.

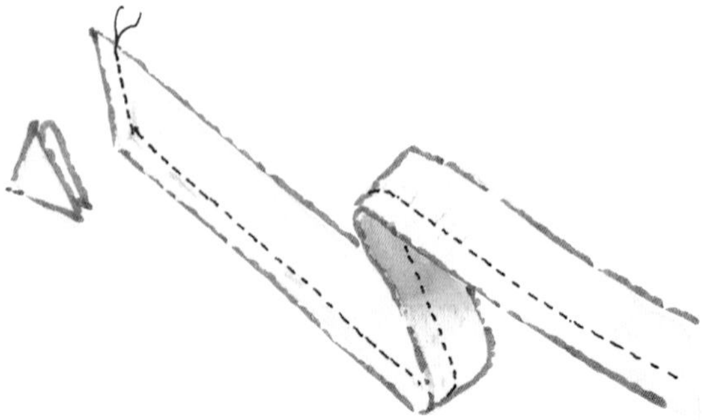

6 From contrast fabric, cut out two ties, each 3¾ x 30in (9.5 x 76cm). With right sides together, fold the ties in half, bringing the long edges together. Trim each end diagonally down from the folded edge to form a slanted end. Make up the ties following method 2 (see page 203).

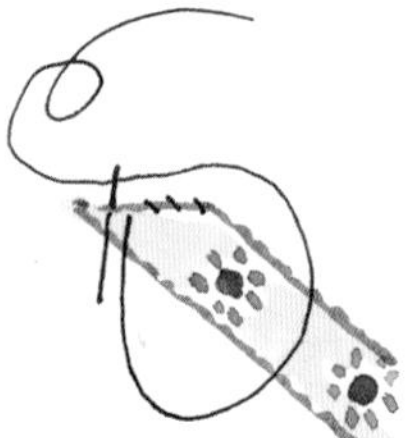

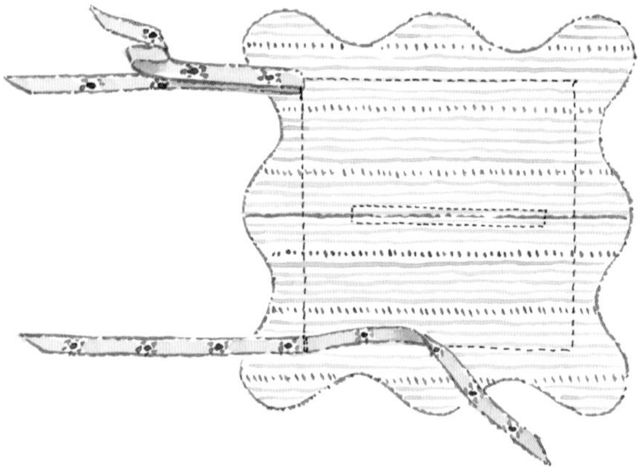

7 Place the cover on the chair seat, with the base on top. Using pins, mark the tie positions on the back edge of the stitched inner square. Fold each tie in half crosswise and mark its center with a pin. Open out each tie, pin in the center to the marked position, and machine-stitch across the center of each tie through all layers, reverse stitching at the ends. Insert the pillow form through the zipped opening.

tailored bolster pillow

Made in For the Love of Rose, in Duck Egg, and Stripe & Dash, in Duck Egg and Cornflower, this pillow is a classic round bolster shape. I use mine to soften the edges of a wooden bench, partnering it with a box-edge seat cushion to make it a more comfortable place to relax.

You will need

- Decorator fabric—see right for yardage
- Medium-sized cable cord or piping cord—see right for yardage
- Matching sewing thread
- Bolster form
- Zipper 4in (10cm) shorter than the length of the bolster form
- Paper for making patterns

Estimating yardage

- Measure the length, circumference, and diameter of the bolster form.
- For the fabric, make a paper pattern following step 1. Allow for one main piece and two end pieces. Also allow for enough bias strips (see page 194) of this fabric to cover the cord.
- For the cord, allow twice the circumference plus 4in (10cm).

TIP

For an alternative to making your own piping, hand-sew decorative drapery cord around the ends of the bolster after the cover has been completed.

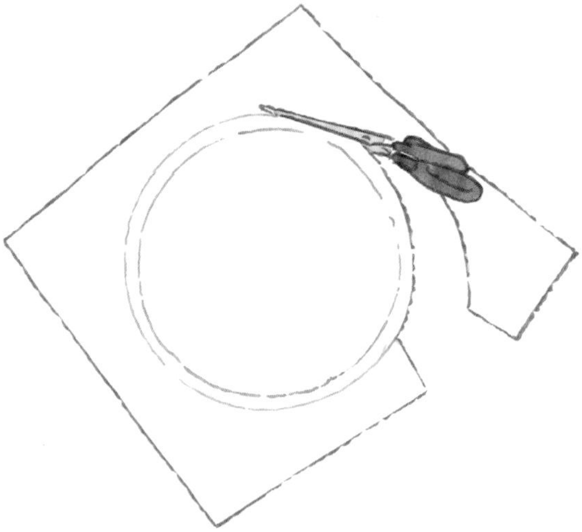

1 On paper, draw the main rectangular pattern piece to the length of the pillow form by the circumference, and add a ⅝in (1.5cm) seam allowance all around. Cut out the pattern piece. For the end pieces, draw a circle to the diameter of the pillow form and add a ⅝in (1.5cm) seam allowance all around. Cut out the pattern piece. From the fabric, cut out one main piece, two ends, and the bias strips.

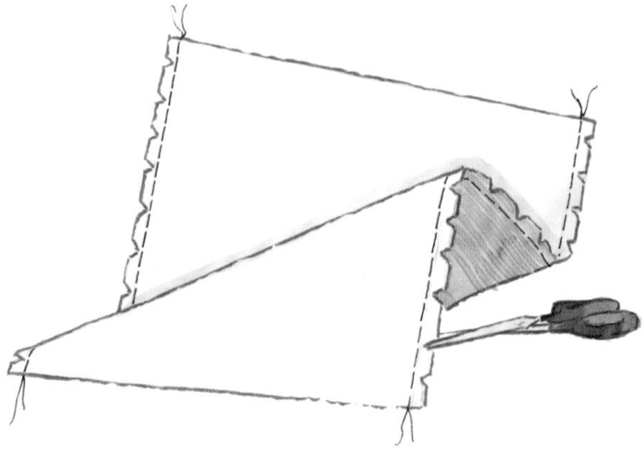

2 Staystitch (see page 183) ⅜in (1cm) from the circumference edges of the main piece and then clip into the seam allowances at regular intervals, no closer than ⅛in (3mm) from the stitching line.

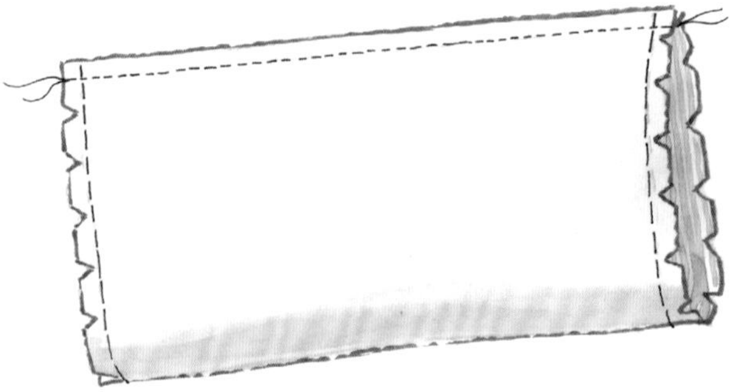

3 Fold the main piece in half, with right sides together, bringing the unclipped edges together to make a cylinder. Pin and baste the edges together with a ⅝in (1.5cm) seam.

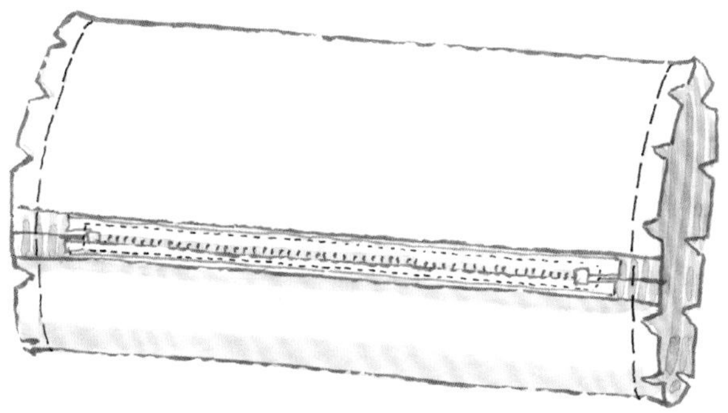

4 Machine-stitch a 2in- (5cm-) long seam at each end, leaving the center seam basted in place. Press open the seam and insert the zipper (see page 201). If you have difficulty machine-stitching the zipper into the fabric cylinder, stitch as far as the center from one end, then remove from the machine, turn the cylinder around, and stitch toward the center from the other end. Remove all basting stitches.

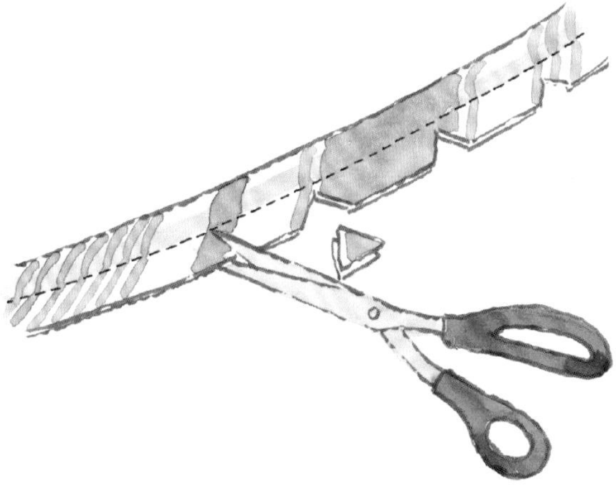

5 Make up the piping (see page 196). Clip into the seam allowances at regular intervals, getting no closer than ⅛in (3mm) to the stitching line, to help the piping fit around the curves of the bolster ends.

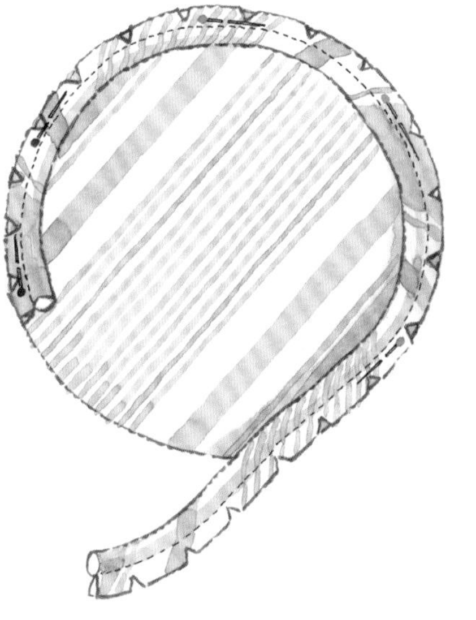

6 Cut the piping into two equal lengths. Pin and baste a length onto the right side of each circular end piece. Join the ends of the piping and stitch in place (see page 197).

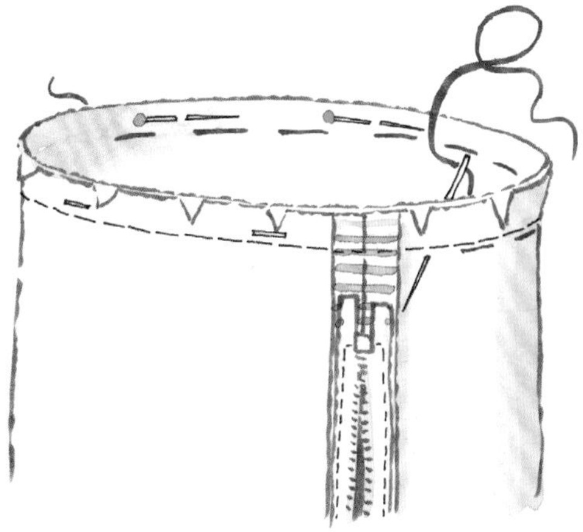

7 Open the zipper in the main piece, and with right sides together, pin the piped end pieces to the clipped ends of the main piece. Pin and baste them in place. Using a zipper foot on your machine, and working with the end pieces on top, stitch the pieces together, stitching on top of the piping stitching as close to the piping as possible. Remove the basting stitches and turn the cover right side out. Insert the bolster form through the opening and close the zipper.

piped pillow

This is a classic pillow to add to your repertoire. Edged with self-colored piping and with a zipper to close, it can be made in any fabric, for any room in the house. This is one of my particular favorites, made up in Feather and Egg, Duck Egg and Denim.

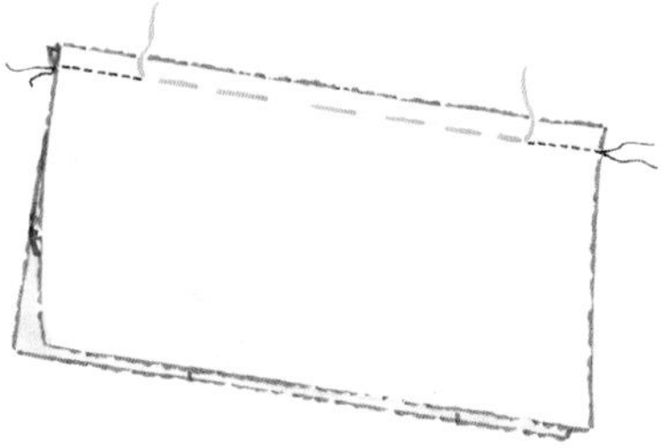

1 From the fabric, cut out the front, two back pieces, and bias strips. With right sides together, pin and baste the two back pieces together along one long edge, using a ⅝in (1.5cm) seam. Machine-stitch along the basting for 2in (5cm) at each end of the seam, leaving the basting stitches in the center intact. Press open the seam and insert the zipper (see page 201). Remove the basting.

2 Join the bias strips to the required length and cover the cord with them (see page 196). Pin and baste this piping to the right side of the front around all four edges, with raw edges even. At each corner, snip into the seam allowance of the piping so it will bend around the corner. Join the ends of the piping and machine-stitch it in place (see page 197).

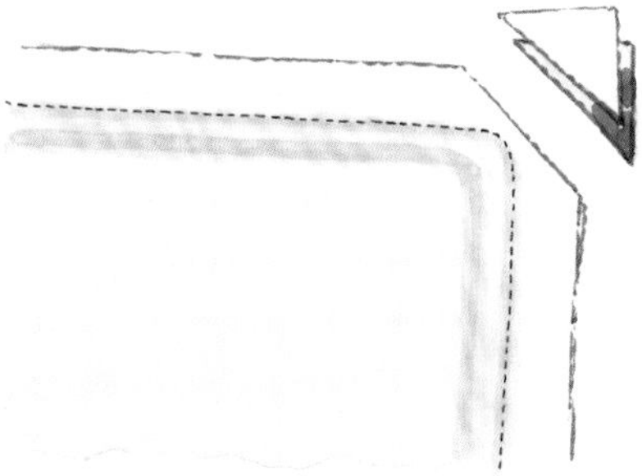

3 Pin the front to the back, with right sides together and the piping sandwiched between the two layers. Undo the zipper and baste a ⅝in (1.5cm) seam around the edges of the front and back pieces. Using a zipper foot, and working with the front piece on top, machine-stitch the front and back together. Remove the basting, snip off the corners of the seam allowances, and turn right side out. Insert the pillow form through the opening in the back, and close the zipper.

You will need

- Decorator fabric—see below for yardage
- Medium-thick cable cord or piping cord—see below for yardage
- Matching sewing thread
- Square or rectangular pillow form
- Zipper 4in (10cm) shorter than the width of the pillow form

Estimating yardage

- Measure the length and width of the pillow form.
- For the front, allow one piece of fabric that is the size of the pillow form, plus a ⅝in (1.5cm) seam allowance all around.
- For the back, divide the form size into two halves. Allow for two pieces of fabric, each the size of one of these halves plus a ⅝in (1.5cm) seam allowance all around each.
- For the cable cord or piping cord, you will need enough cord to go around the edges of the pillow form, plus 4in (10cm).
- For covering the cord, gauge the width of your fabric strip. To do this, measure around the cord and allow an extra 1¼in (3cm) for seam allowances. Allow for enough bias strips of fabric, of this width, to fit the length of your cord.

three-paneled pillow

Never throw away any scraps of fabric, as you can combine them to make a pillow like this one. It's fun piecing all the fabrics you have used elsewhere in the room to make a pillow for a bed, chair, or sofa. Here, the fresh colors of Four Seasons, in Speedwell, Denim, and Straw, together with Wild Rose, in Buttercup, Clay, and Charcoal, have been combined with the summer swallow of Up In The Air, in Duck Egg, Speedwell, and Cornflower. Piping made from Little Leaf in Forget-me-not and Denim is a lovely finishing touch.

You will need

- Decorator fabric in four coordinating patterns—see below for yardage
- Matching sewing thread
- 20 x 12in (51 x 30cm) rectangular pillow form
- 8in (20cm) zipper
- 2yd (1.8m) of medium-thick cable cord or piping cord

Estimating yardage

- For the first fabric, allow for one center-front panel measuring 13¼in (33cm) deep by 9¼in (23cm) wide.
- For the second and third fabrics, allow for one side-front panel each, measuring 13¼in (33cm) deep x 7¼in (18.5cm) wide.
- For the fourth fabric, allow for two back panels, each measuring 13¼in (33cm) deep x 11¼in (28.5cm) wide; two bias strips, each measuring 13¼in (33cm) deep x 1¾in (4.5cm) wide; and enough bias strips to fit the length of your cord (see page 194).

TIP

The front panels are separated by narrow strips, which are folded and stitched into the seams. If you want to make a slightly easier project, simply omit these strips and make straight seams instead. You can do the same with the piping too.

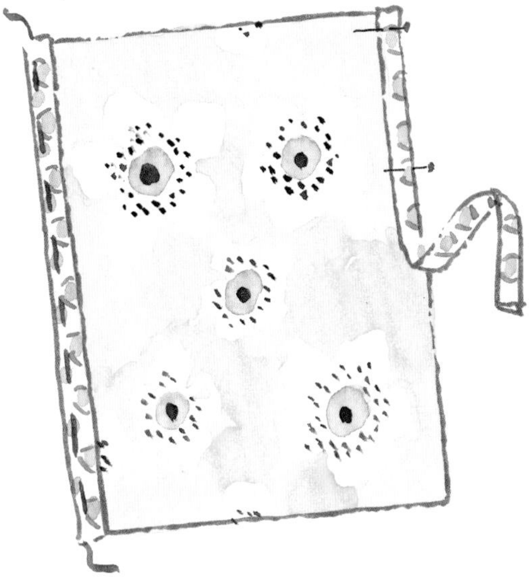

1 Cut out one center-front panel from the first fabric, one side-front panel each from the second and third fabrics, and two back panels from the fourth fabric. Also cut out from the fourth fabric the two short bias strips and the bias strips for covering the cord. With wrong sides together and raw edges even, fold each short bias strip in half lengthwise; press. Pin and baste a folded strip to the right side of the center-front panel along each long edge of the panel, with raw edges even.

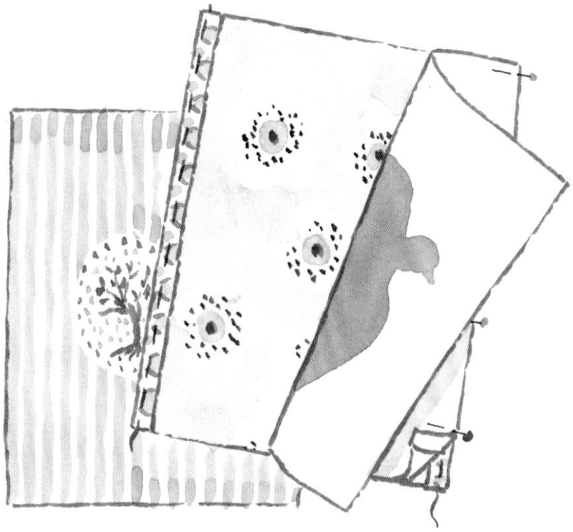

2 With right sides together and raw edges even, pin and baste one long edge of the side-front panel to a long edge of the center-front panel, sandwiching the folded bias strip in between. Machine-stitch a ⅝in (1.5cm) seam. Repeat for the other bias strip, the other side-front panel, and the other side edge of the center-front panel. Press the seams toward the center front and remove the basting.

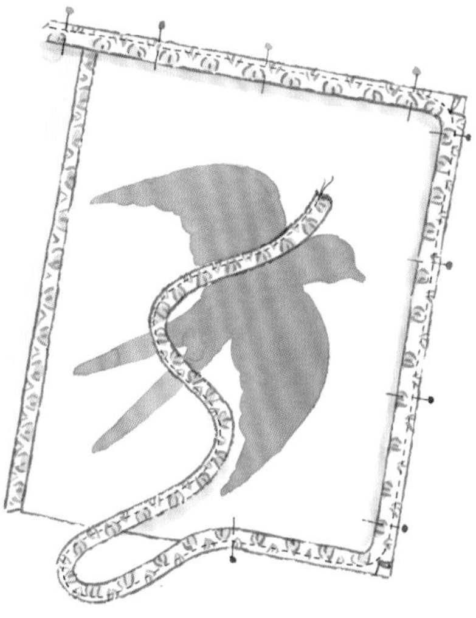

3 Cover the cord with the bias strips and apply to the outer edges of the front panel (see pages 196–197).

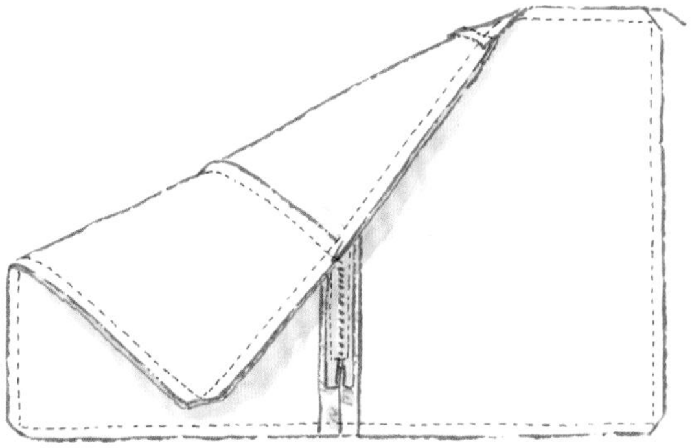

4 With right sides together, pin and baste the two back pieces together along one long edge, using a ⅝in (1.5cm) seam. Machine-stitch along the basting for 2in (5cm) at each end of the seam, leaving the basting stitches in the center intact. Press open the seam and insert the zipper (see page 201). Remove the basting. Complete the pillow cover as for the Piped Pillow, step 3 (see page 89).

pillow with knife pleats

This is a smart little tailored pillow that looks more complicated than it is. The basic pillow, made from Life and Eternity Detail, in Teal, is a simple rectangle with a zipper inserted in the back to close. What makes it special is the decorative edging made from a pair of pleated strips, one at either end, in Simple Ticking Ground, Teal. This is a pillow that looks perfect with a contemporary-style armchair, like my button-backed tub chair.

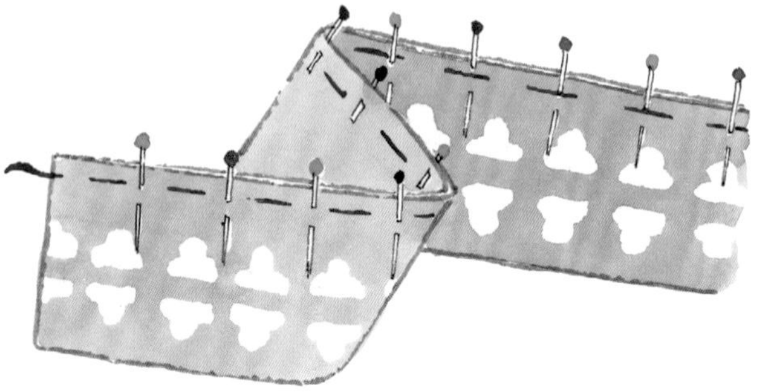

1 Cut out the pleating strips and fold each in half lengthwise, with right sides together and raw edges even. Pin and machine-stitch a ⅝in (1.5cm) seam at each short end. Turn right side out, pushing out the corners, and press in half lengthwise, with raw edges even. Baste the raw edges together. Taking one strip at a time, and using pins for markers, divide the long, raw, basted edges into 1in (2.5cm) sections.

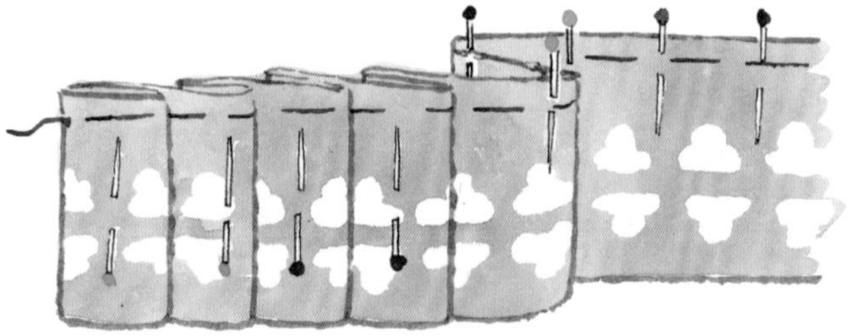

2 Start to pleat the pinned edge by bringing the first pin into line with the third pin (and the second pin on the fold between them); pin in place. Now take the fourth pin into line with the sixth pin (and the fifth pin on the fold between them); pin in place. Continue in this way until you reach the end of the strip and have made 12 pleats. The finished pleated strip should measure 12in (30cm). Baste and press the pleats.

You will need

- Main decorator fabric—see below for yardage
- Contrast decorator fabric—see below for yardage
- Matching sewing thread
- 20 x 12in (51 x 30cm) rectangular pillow form
- 8in (20cm) zipper

Estimating yardage

- For the main fabric, allow for one front panel, measuring 21¼ x 13¼in (54 x 33cm), and two back panels, measuring 13¼ x 11¼in (33 x 28.5cm).
- From contrast fabric, allow for two pleating strips each measuring 37¼ x 4¼in (93 x 11cm).

TIP

Make your own individual look by adapting this pillow to make a variety of different styles; gather the strips instead of pleating them and you will have a softer, country look for a traditional sofa. A ready-made beaded trim would add to the slightly exotic, Indian style of the fabric, or pleat a grosgrain ribbon for something a little crisper.

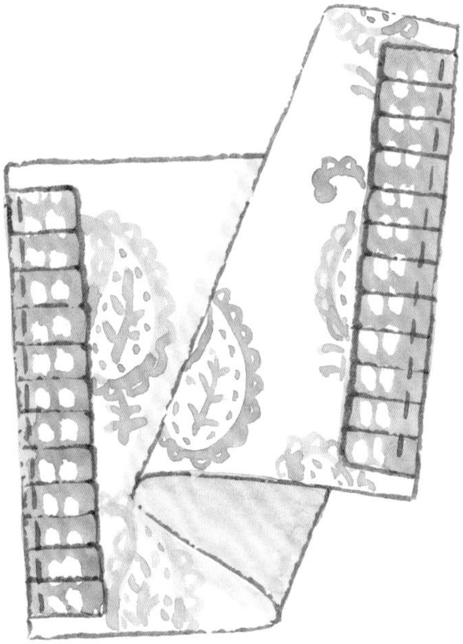

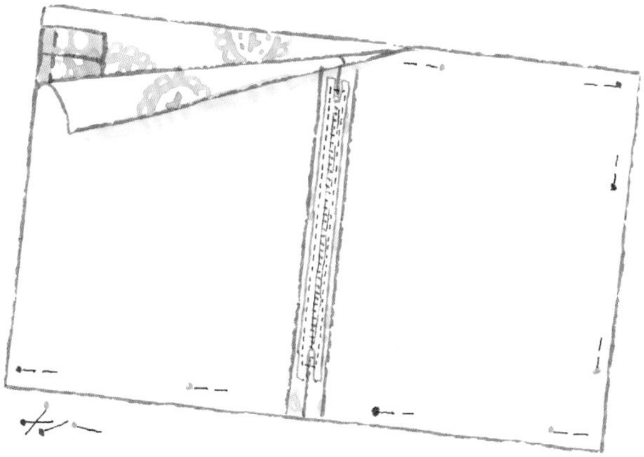

3 With right sides together and raw edges even, position each pleated strip along one short side of the front panel, centering it between the top and bottom edges. Pin and baste in place.

4 With right sides together, pin and baste the two back pieces together along one long edge, using a ⅝in (1.5cm) seam. Machine-stitch along the basting for 2in (5cm) at each end of the seam, leaving the basting stitches in the center intact. Press open the seam and insert the zipper (see page 201). Remove the basting. Complete the pillow cover as for the Piped Pillow, step 3 (see page 89), being careful not to catch the ends of the pleated strips in the long seams.

buttoned pillow

Pillows and cushions come in lots of shapes and sizes, and can be closed with zippers, ties, or buttons. They are so easy to make that you can have fun making a whole set, and piling them together on a sofa, a window seat, or a bed. Playing with different combinations of colors and patterns is made simpler as my collections have been designed to mix and match. This buttoned pillow is made from Simple Spot, in Olive and Sea Pink, a fabric that works well with Stockholm Stripe and Pretty Maids, and closed with three little loops made from the same fabric.

You will need

- Decorator fabric—see below for yardage
- Matching sewing thread
- Pillow form
- Three 1in (2.5cm) buttons

Estimating yardage

- Allow for one main-fabric piece measuring twice the length of the pillow form plus 4in (10.5cm), by the width of the pillow form plus 1in (2.5cm).
- Allow for one facing piece as long as the short edge of the main-fabric piece, by 2in (5cm).
- Allow for one strip 12 x 1½in (30.5 x 4cm) for the button loop piece.

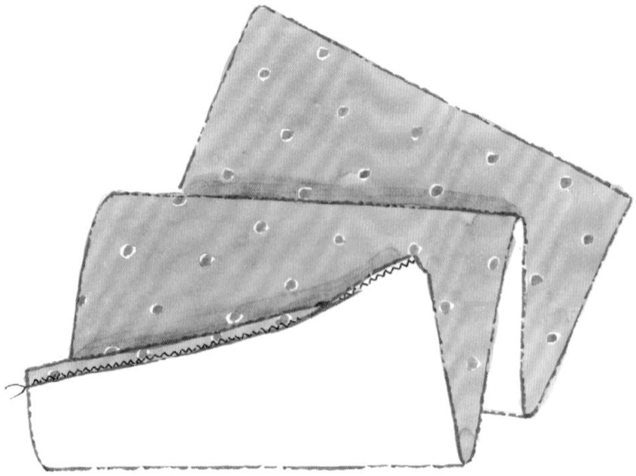

1 From the decorator fabric, cut out one main piece, one facing piece, and one strip for the button loop to the specified measurements. Finish one short edge of the main piece with machine zigzag stitch, or use a serger if you have one. Press a single ½in (1.2cm) hem to the wrong side. Pin and machine-stitch the hem in place close to the finished edge.

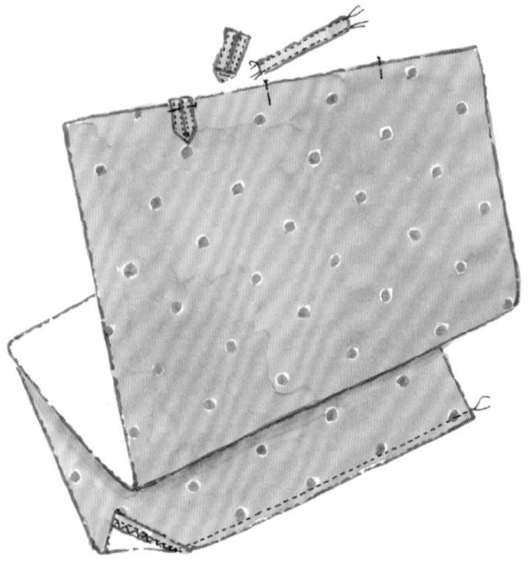

2 Make up the button-loop piece following Ties, method 1 (see page 202) without finishing the ends, but stitching along both long edges. Cut it into three equal lengths. On the raw short edge of the main piece, mark the button-loop positions with pins on the right side of the fabric, placing one in the center and the remaining two 4in (10cm) to either side. Fold each loop in half and, matching the raw ends to the raw edge of the main cover, and matching seamed edges to the pin markers, pin and baste each loop in place on the right side of the main piece.

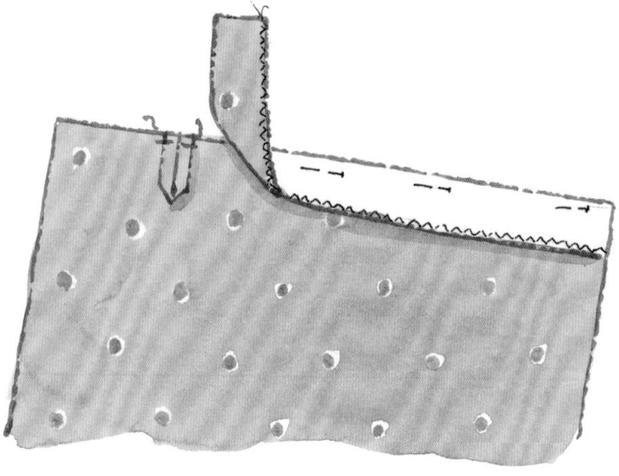

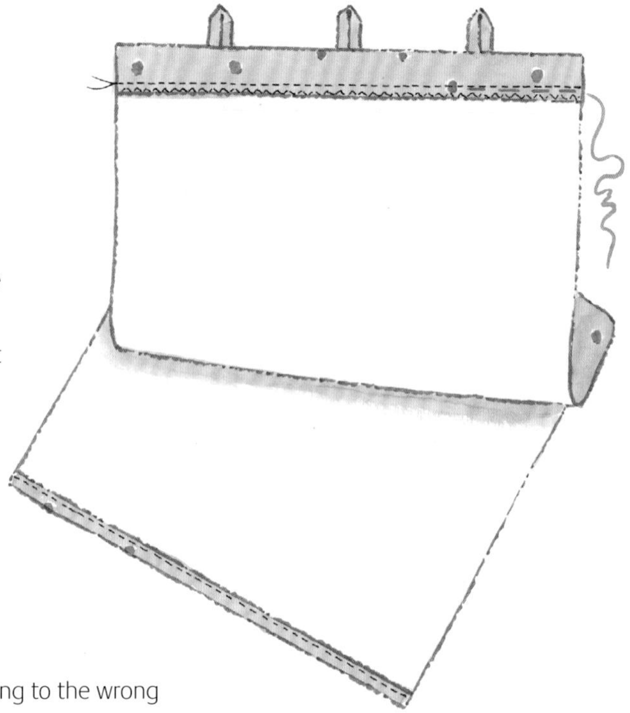

3 Finish one long edge of the facing piece using machine zigzag stitch, or a serger if you have one. With right sides together, pin the other long edge of the facing to the short raw edge of the main piece, sandwiching the button loops in between. Baste, then machine-stitch a ½in (1.2cm) seam, reverse-stitching over each loop for extra strength. Remove the basting, and press the seam toward the facing.

4 Fold the facing to the wrong side of the main piece, so that the seam lies just on the edge. Press flat, with the button loops extending beyond the seam. Pin and baste the facing in place, then machine-stitch 1in (2.5cm) in from the seamed edge. Remove the basting.

5 Lay the main piece right side up on a flat surface. With right sides together, fold over 3in (8cm) at the end that has the facing and loops. Pin and baste in place down the side edges.

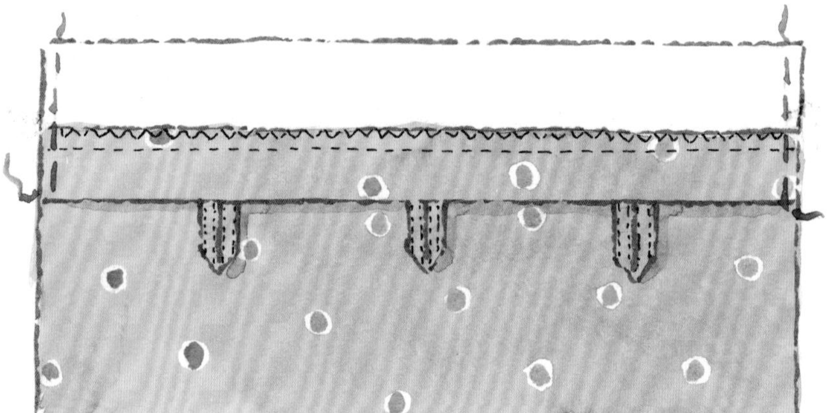

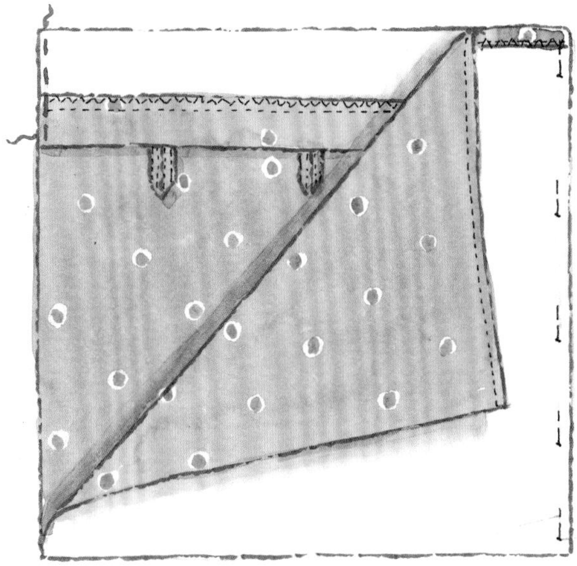

6 Now bring the hemmed edge of the main piece up and line it up with the fold of the faced end, right sides together, covering up the facing and button loops. Pin and baste in place along the side edges, then machine-stitch a ½in (1.2cm) seam down each side edge; remove the basting.

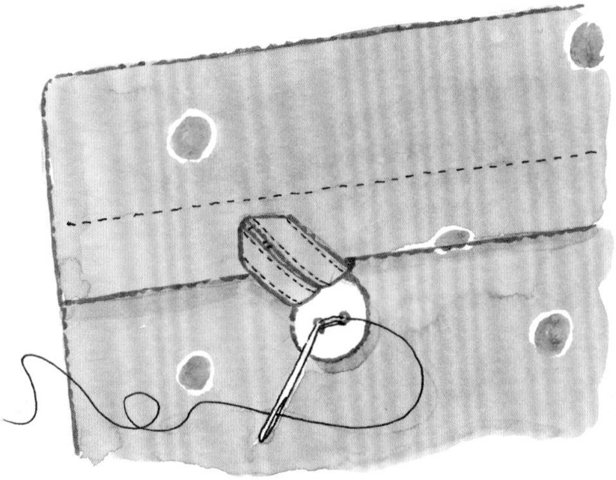

7 Turn the cover right side out and press. Hand-sew the buttons to the front of the cover in line with each button loop. Insert the pillow form into the cover underneath the flap and then fasten the loops over the buttons.

As a variation, you could use short lengths of cord or ribbon to make the button loops instead of sewing your own. These could be in a harmonizing shade, or in a contrast color for an extra design touch.

tied pillow cover

I had a wonderful time drawing the feathers I found when collecting eggs—the shapes and patterns are so graphic and lend themselves easily to the design process. Feather and Egg looks good in any of the four colorways, but Raspberry is particularly rich and vibrant. The pillow is made from three pieces, and closed with two neat ties.

You will need

- Decorator fabric—see below for yardage
- Matching sewing thread
- Square or rectangular pillow form

Estimating yardage

- Measure the length and width of the pillow form.
- For the front, allow for two pieces of fabric, each the length of the form plus 1¼in (3cm), by half the width plus 3½in (9cm).
- For the back, allow for one piece of fabric the size of the form, plus ⅝in (1.5cm) all around.
- Allow for four ties, each 1½ x 14in (4 x 35.5cm).

TIP

It's important to match the pattern repeat across the front when cutting out the two front pieces for this pillow. They will overlap each other, so take this into account when cutting out. It's a good idea to cut out the top piece first, then lay it over the fabric to see how the patterns match before cutting out the bottom piece. Don't forget that the opening edges are hemmed. Feather and Egg is a good fabric to use as the pattern has space between each row.

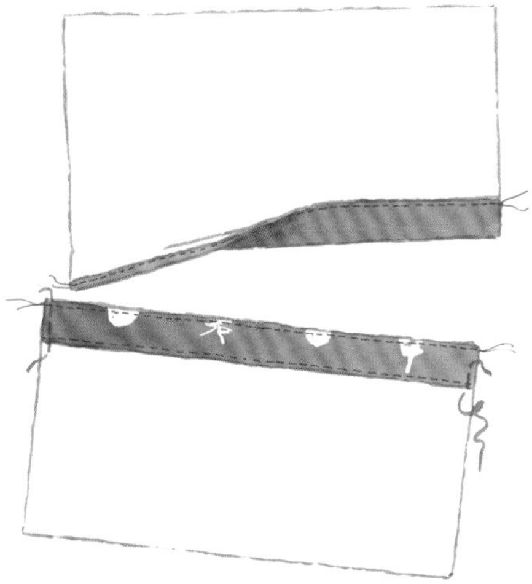

1 From the fabric, cut out two front pieces, one back piece, and four strips for the ties. Press a single ⅝in (1.5cm) hem to the wrong side along the bottom long edge of one front piece and along the top long edge of the other front piece. Machine-stitch in place. Press a further 1½in (4cm) to the wrong side along each hemmed edge to form a facing. Baste the raw ends of each facing in place. Machine-stitch along each facing edge close to the pressed edge.

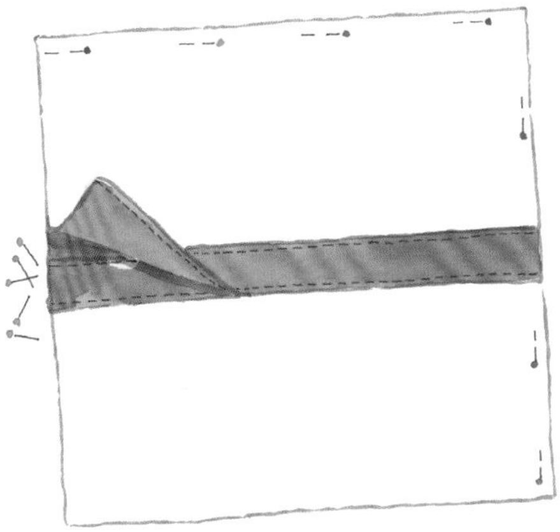

2 Lay the back piece right side up on a flat surface and place one front piece on it, with right sides together and raw edges even. Place the other front on top, right side down, with its raw edges even with those of the back piece and its facing overlapping that of the other front piece. Pin together around the outer edges and machine-stitch a ⅝in (1.5cm) seam. Snip off the corners of the seam allowances and remove the basting. Turn the cover right side out and press.

3 Make four ties using method 1 (see page 202). Lay the cover out flat and use pins to mark the edge of the overlap on the underlap. Using more pins, mark the position of the ties on the overlap, placing them roughly a quarter of the way in from each side edge of the cover. Finally, use pins to mark the positions of the corresponding ties on the underlap, in line with those on the overlap.

4 Pin the ties to the underside of the overlap and to the top side of the underlap in the marked positions, so that their ends are even with the edges. Hand-sew the ends of the ties in place as shown. Insert the pillow form through the front opening and tie the bows to close the cover.

box-edge cushion

Having old thick stone walls in our house, there are plenty of low, deep sills to be made into window seats. A box-edge cushion in Plain Check, Damson, has transformed this sill into a comfortable place to sit. The cover is closed with a zipper, which makes it easy to remove for cleaning should our cats, Pumpkin and Pickle, find it just as welcoming!

You will need

- Main decorator fabric—see below for yardage
- Medium-thick cable cord or piping cord—see below for yardage
- Matching sewing thread
- Box-edge cushion form
- Zipper 3in (7.5cm) shorter than the back boxing strip—see below for its length
- Paper for making patterns

Estimating yardage

- Measure the length, width, and depth of the cushion form.
- On a sheet of paper, draw a pattern piece to fit the top and bottom of the cushion, adding a ⅝in (1.5cm) seam allowance all around. Cut out the pattern piece.
- For the sides-and-front boxing strip, draw a pattern piece the depth of the cushion, by the length of the front plus the two sides. Subtract 6in (15cm) from the length, then add a ⅝in (1.5cm) seam all around. Cut out the pattern piece.
- For the back boxing strip, draw a strip half the depth of the cushion, by the measurement of the back. Add 6in (15cm) to the length (to allow the back boxing strip to extend around the corners) then add a ⅝in (1.5cm) seam allowance all around. Cut out the pattern piece.
- For the cable cord or piping cord, allow enough cord to go around all of the edges of the top and bottom, plus 4in (10cm).
- For covering the cord, gauge the width of your fabric strip. To do this, measure around the cord and allow an extra 1¼in (3cm) for seam allowances. Allow for enough bias strips of fabric, of this width, to fit the length of your cord.

1 Using the pattern pieces, cut out one top piece, one bottom piece, one sides-and-front boxing strip, and two back boxing strips. Also cut out the bias strips to cover the cord (see page 194). With right sides together, pin and baste the two back boxing strips together along one long edge of each, using a ⅝in (1.5cm) seam. Machine-stitch along the basting for 1½in (4cm) at each end of the seam, leaving the basting stitches in the center intact. Press open the seam, and insert the zipper (see page 201). Remove the basting.

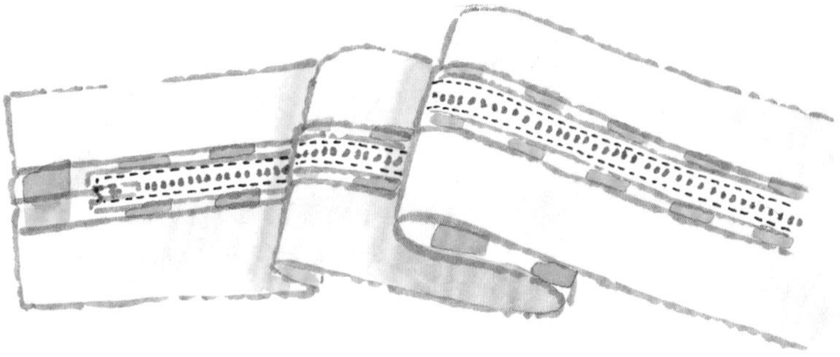

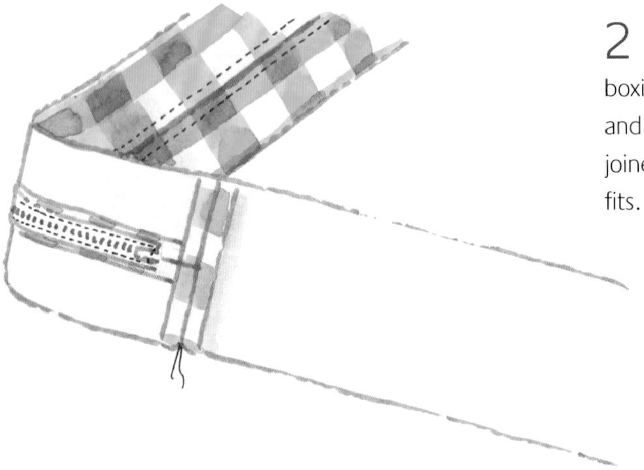

2 With right sides together, pin the ends of the back boxing strip to the ends of the sides-and-front boxing strip, and baste them together with ⅝in (1.5cm) seams. Place the joined boxing strip around the cushion form to check that it fits. Adjust it if necessary, then machine-stitch the seams.

3 Make a tailor's tack (see page 187) at the center front and another at the center back of the joined boxing strip. Mark corresponding tailor's tacks at the center front and center back of the top and bottom pieces.

4 Join the bias strips to the required length and cover the cord with them (see page 196). Pin and baste this piping to the right side of the top and bottom panels around the edges, with raw edges even. At each corner, snip into the seam allowances of the piping so it will bend around the corner. Join the ends of the piping and machine-stitch it in place (see page 197).

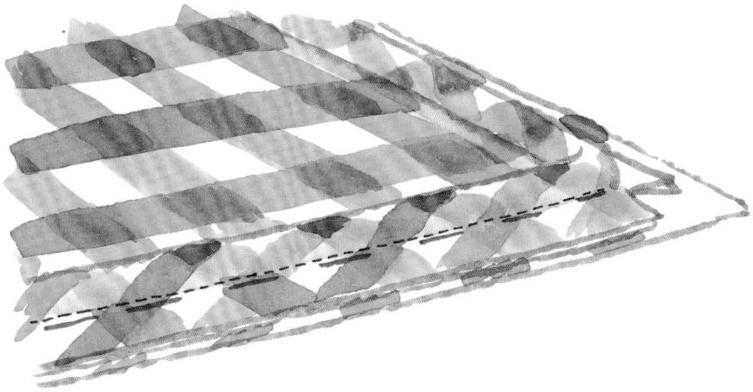

5 With right sides together and raw edges even, pin and baste one edge of the boxing strip around the piped top panel, matching the tailor's tacks and snipping into the boxing strip seam allowance at each corner to allow it to bend. Working with the top panel facing up, and using the zipper foot on your machine, stitch the pieces together along the piping stitching line. Be sure to stitch as close to the cord as possible.

6 Undo the zipper. Pin, baste, and machine-stitch the bottom panel to the remaining raw edge of the boxing strip, as in step 5. Remove all the basting stitches. Turn the cover right side out, insert the cushion form through the back opening, and close the zipper.

frilled pillow

This stylish pillow, made in Pretty Maids, is the perfect way to use up remnant pieces of coordinating fabric. It is a little more challenging to make than the easy pillow on page 76, but the finished look will be truly individual and worth the effort.

You will need

- Decorator fabric—see below for yardage
- Coordinating fabric for the frilled edge—see below for yardage
- Matching sewing thread
- Pillow form
- Zipper 3in (7.5cm) shorter than the width of the pillow form

Estimating yardage

- Measure the length and width of the pillow form.
- For the front, allow one piece of fabric that is the size of the pillow form, plus a ⅝in (1.5cm) seam allowance all around.
- For the back, divide the pillow form size into two halves. Allow for two pieces of fabric, each the size of one of these halves plus a ⅝in (1.5cm) seam allowance all around each.
- Allow 6in (15cm) for the width of the frill. For the length, allow enough fabric to go around the pillow two or three times, depending how full you want the frill to be. Shorter lengths of fabric may be joined together for this.

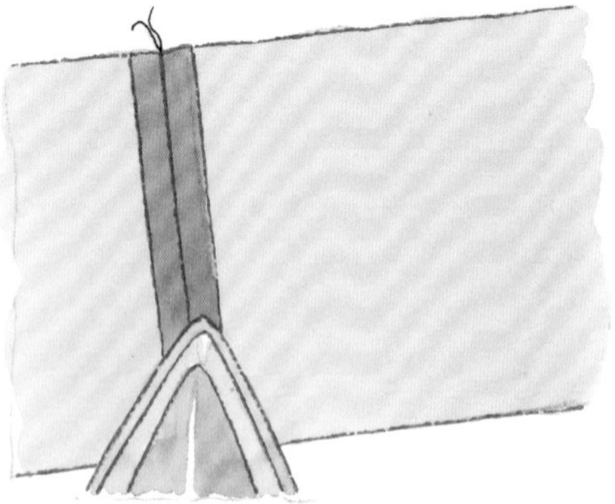

1 From the main fabric, cut the front and back pieces. Measure around the four sides of the pillow form and multiply by two or three (see estimating yardage right) and add 1¼in (3cm) for seam allowance. From the coordinating fabric, create a continuous length by cutting out strips 6in (15cm) wide. With right sides together, pin and join the ruffle pieces into a long continuous strip, using ⅝in (1.5cm) seams. Press the seams open.

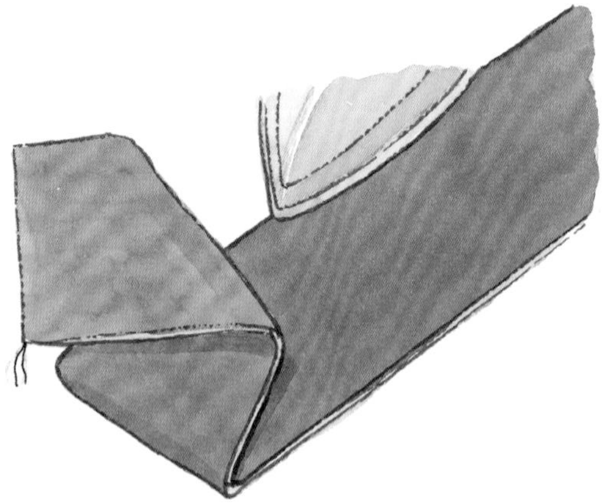

2 Fold the long strip of coordinating fabric in half lengthwise, wrong sides together. Press in half along the length so it is now half the width.

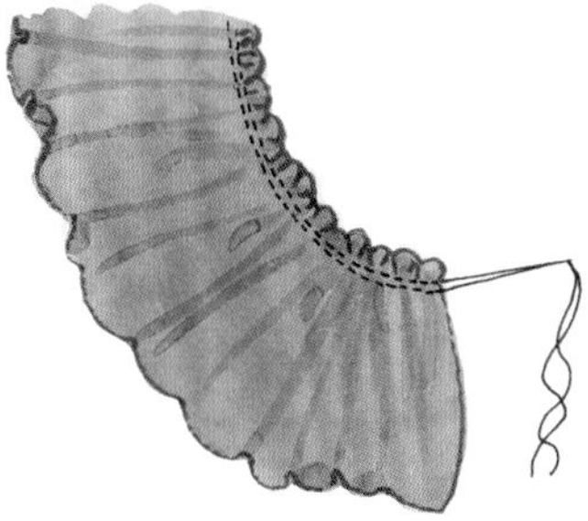

3 Fold the frill into four sections. This will give the amount of frill for each side of the pillow. Mark each of the folds with a pin or cut a small notch. With the raw edges of the frill even, sew two parallel rows of gathering stitches (see page 198) along the raw edges of the frill, spacing the rows roughly ¼in (5mm) apart. Carefully pull the threads to gather the frill evenly until it fits around the four sides of the front piece.

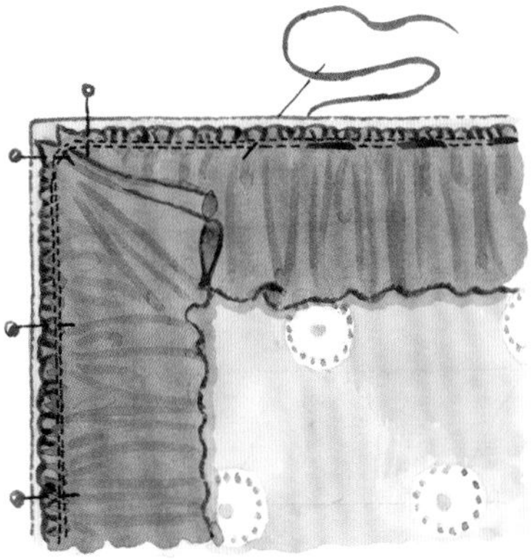

4 Place the frill on the right side of the front piece, matching up the markers on each corner. With raw edges even, pin in place along all sides of the front, allowing a seam allowance of ⅝in (1.5cm) all around. Baste the frill in place, and then machine stitch. Remove the basting stitches.

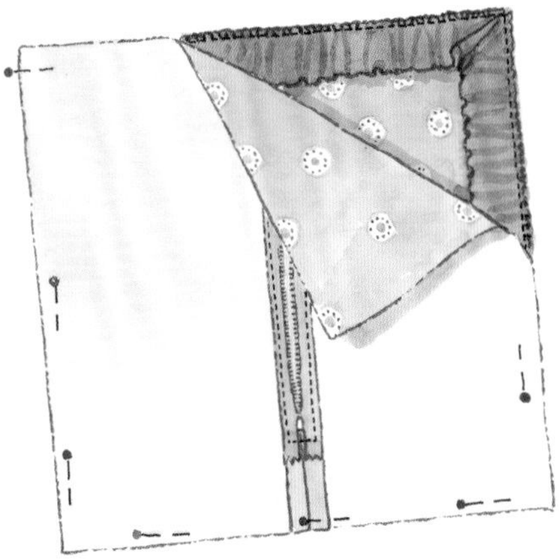

5 Insert the zipper between the two back pieces of the pillow cover following the instructions in step 5, page 80. Undo the zipper. With right sides together, pin the base to the top piece, making sure that the frill is facing towards the center of the pillow. Machine stitch around all four sides, taking care not to catch the frill in the stitching. Snip off the corners of the seam allowance. Turn the cover right side out, insert the pillow form, and close the zipper.

chapter 4

covers

upholstered dining chair cover

A perfect way to give an old dining chair new life, this tied cover, made in Up The Garden Path, in Pumpkin, fits neatly over an upholstered seat. I found the chair in a local sale room, and painted it blue, which works wonderfully well with the sharp orange.

You will need

- Main fabric—see below for yardage
- Matching sewing thread
- Small amount of cotton tape
- Hook-and-loop tape
- Unbleached muslin and paper for patterns
- Upholstery T-pins (optional)

Estimating yardage

- Make patterns for the seat and skirt (see step 1) and allow for cutting one seat and one skirt from the fabric, each twice the size of the pattern.
- Also allow for four 1½ x 14in (4 x 35cm) strips of the fabric for ties.

1 To make a muslin pattern for half the cover, start by using pins to mark a line between center back and center front.

For the seat pattern, cut out a piece of muslin as deep as the distance along the pin line from the bottom of the front edge to the bottom of the back edge plus 6in (15cm), and as wide as the distance from the pin line to the bottom of the seat at one side.

For the skirt pattern, cut out a piece of muslin to the desired depth of the skirt—anywhere from about 6in (15cm) to floor-length—and as wide as the distance around the side, from the front pin line to the back pin line, plus 5in (12.5cm).

Lay the seat pattern over half of the chair seat, aligning one long edge with the pin line and letting the extra fabric hang down at the back. Pin it to the front and side of the chair, leaving a ⅝in (1.5cm) seam allowance all around (apart from the center front edge). When pin-fitting, you can use T-pins if you have them, sticking them into the chair at right angles. Cut around the back chair support if necessary. Pin a dart (see page 197) in the muslin at the front corner.

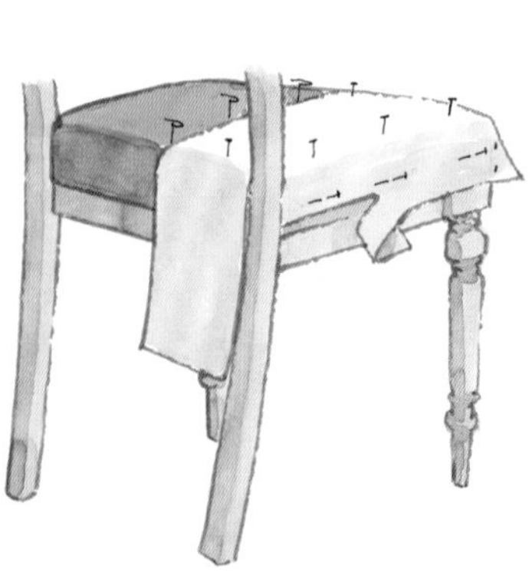

2 On the seat front and sides (but not the back), about 2in (5cm) down from the top, use pins to mark the stitching line for the skirt. Trim away the excess muslin below that, leaving a ⅝in (1.5cm) seam allowance. At the back of the seat, trim the muslin around the chair frame, again leaving a ⅝in (1.5cm) seam allowance on all edges (apart from the center back edge).

3 Pin the skirt pattern to the front and sides of the seat pattern along the pinned stitching line, with a ⅝in (1.5cm) seam allowance. The back extensions will not be attached to the seat but will meet at center back and overlap by 2in (5cm), so allow for this. Adjust the length of the back of the seat pattern so that its lower edge will align with that of the skirt, remembering to allow a ⅝in (1.5cm) seam allowance on these lower edges. Once you are happy with the cover, use a pencil to draw the seam lines and dart line on the muslin. Unpin the pieces and trim away the seam allowances following the pencil lines. Press the pattern pieces then draw around them on paper, smoothing the lines and adding ⅝in (1.5cm) seam allowances to all edges apart from the center edge.

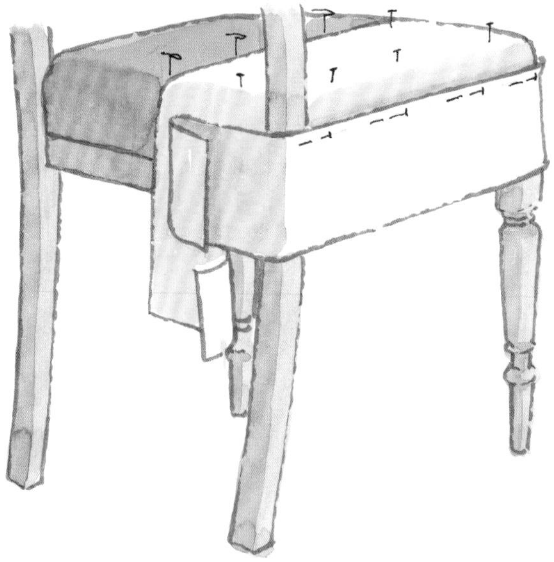

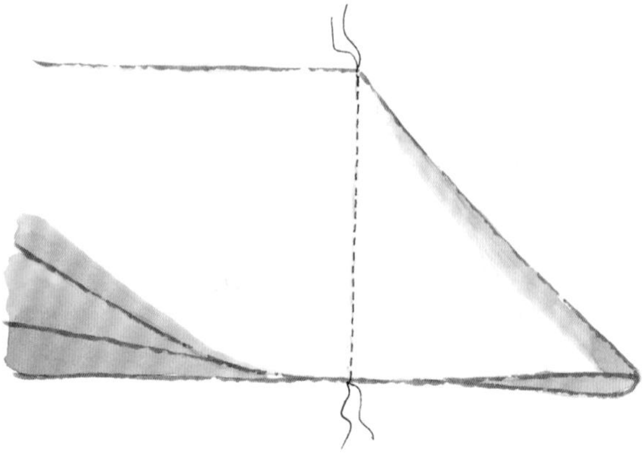

4 Fold the decorator fabric in half and place the center line of both pattern pieces on the fold. Cut out one seat piece and one skirt piece, joining fabric widths (see page 188) if necessary to achieve the required length for the skirt. Transfer the dart markings to the fabric (see page 197). With right sides together, pin and machine-stitch the darts at the front of the seat piece.

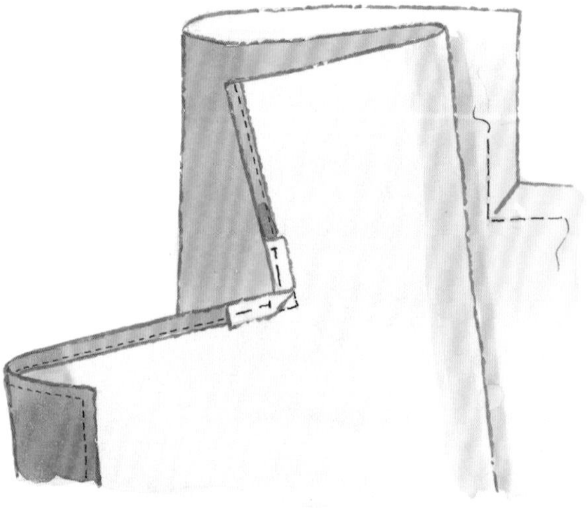

5 On the cut-away corners at the back of the seat piece, staystitch (see page 183) ⅝in (1.5cm) from the raw edge for 1¼in (3cm) each side of each corner. Diagonally clip into the corner seam allowance. Press a double-fold 5/16in (7mm) hem to the wrong side along the straight back edge and the cut-away edges. Pin and machine-stitch in place. Pin a piece of cotton tape to the wrong side of the cut-away corner, covering the raw corner edges, by folding over the tape to make a right angle. Tuck under the raw ends, and machine-stitch along all edges of the tape.

6 With right sides together, matching the center fronts of the seat and skirt, pin the top edge of the skirt around the lower front and side edges of the seat. At the back, the skirt should extend equally beyond the seat cut-away corners at both sides. Machine-stitch a ⅝in (1.5cm) seam. Clip into the curved front-corner seam allowances. Also clip into the skirt seam allowance at the beginning and end of the skirt seam where the skirt back extensions start. Press a double-fold 5/16in (7mm) hem to the wrong side along the top edge of the skirt back extensions, down the short ends, and along the lower edge of the skirt. Pin and machine-stitch.

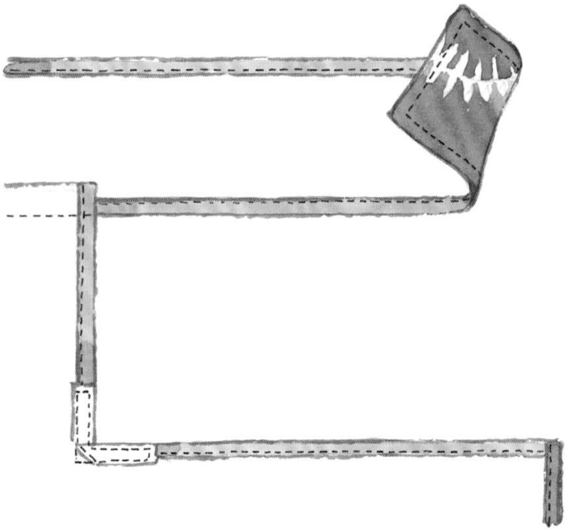

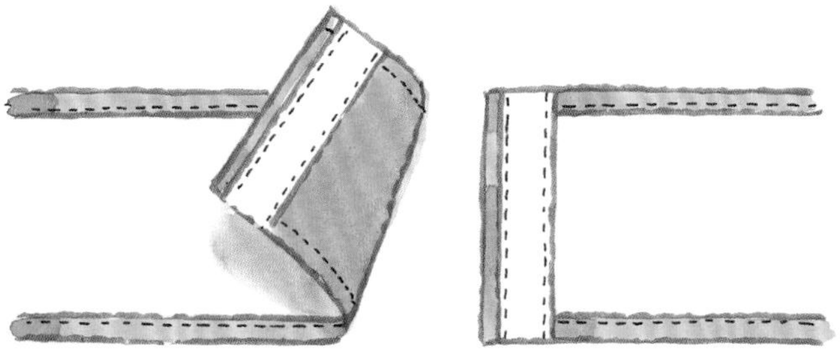

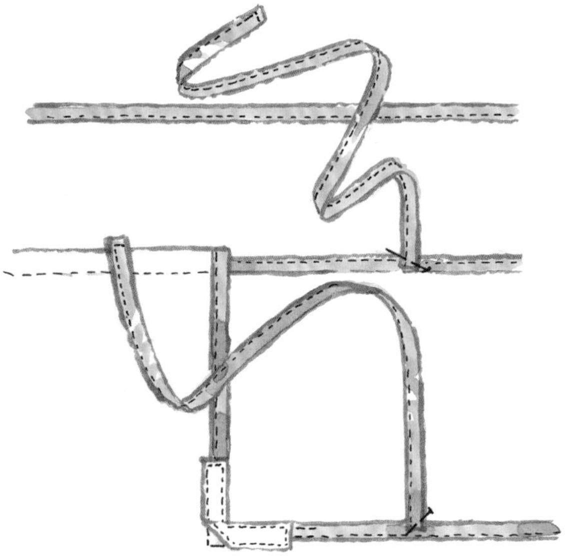

7 Cut a short length of hook-and-loop tape. Pin and machine-stitch the loop side of the tape to the wrong side of one skirt back extension, and attach the hook side to the right side of the remaining skirt back extension in the same way, making sure that the skirt extensions will fit neatly together when the tape is fastened.

8 Make up four narrow ties using method 1 (see page 202), finishing both ends on each. Place the cover over the chair seat and fasten the hook-and-loop tape. Flip the back of the seat piece over the top of the skirt extensions and use pins to mark the tie positions at either side of the back chair struts. Remove the cover and use overhand stitch (see page 186) to sew the ties in place. Replace the cover, fastening the hook-and-loop tape again, and tie the ties into bows at the back corners.

tied dining chair cover

If your high-backed dining chairs have seen better days, making a set of covers will instantly smarten them up. The large bow at the back of this cover is a lovely feature when the chair is tucked into the table. I made this one in Swallow Dive, in Sea Pink.

1 From the fabric, cut out one back, one front, and two L-shaped side pieces (one the mirror image of the other), plus two strips for the ties. With right sides together, place one side piece on one front piece, aligning the edges at the bottom and at one side as shown. Pin together and then machine-stitch a ⅝in (1.5cm) seam, stopping ⅝in (1.5cm) before the top edge of the seat side.

2 Clip into the seam allowance of the front piece at the point where the stitching ends, as shown.

You will need

- Decorator fabric—see below for yardage
- Matching sewing thread

Estimating yardage

- For the front of the chair cover, measure the chair from the rear of the top down the front of the chair back, along the seat, and down to the floor. Add 1⅜in (3.5cm) to the measurement for seam and hem allowances. Measure the width of the chair and add 1¼in (3cm) for seam allowances. Allow for one piece of fabric to these dimensions.
- For the back of the chair cover, measure the chair from the rear of the top down to the floor and add 1⅜in (3.5cm) to the measurement for seam and hem allowances. Measure the width of the chair back and add 32in (81.5cm) for the inverted pleat, plus 1¼in (3cm) for seam allowances. Allow for one piece of fabric to these dimensions.
- For each chair side, you will need one L-shaped piece of fabric. At the side of the chair, measure four dimensions: the height from the top of the chair back to the floor, the depth of the chair back from front to back, the depth of the chair seat from front leg to back leg, and the height of the chair seat to the floor. Add 1⅜in (3.5cm) to the first and last dimensions for seam and hem allowances, and add 1¼in (3cm) to the second and third dimensions for seam allowances. Allow for two L-shaped pieces of fabric in these dimensions.
- For each tie, allow one 6¼ x 27½in (16 x 70cm) strip of fabric cut on the straight grain. Allow for two of these strips.

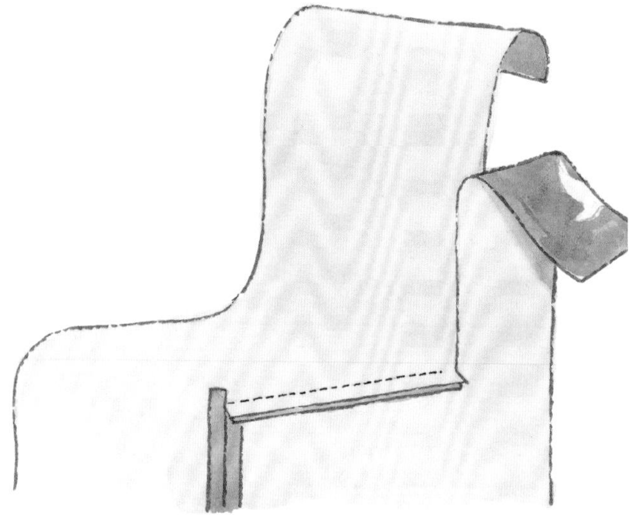

3 Fold the front piece at the clipped seam allowance and pin it along the top edge of the seat side. If there are any curves in the chair, clip into the seam allowance, in the same way as shown in step 7. Machine-stitch a ⅝in (1.5cm) seam, stopping ⅝in (1.5cm) from the back edge; clip into the seam allowance as in step 2.

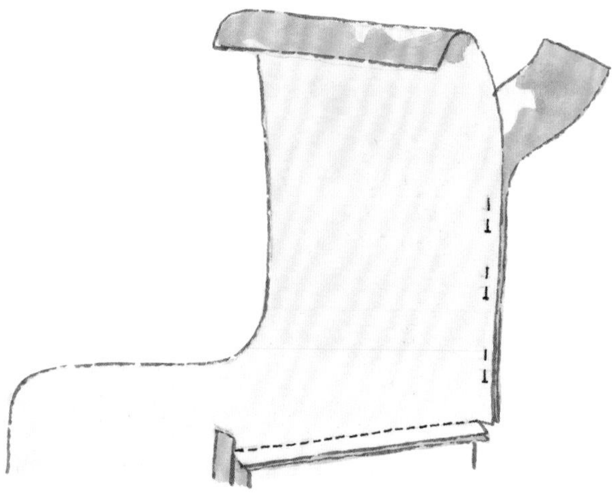

4 Pin the remaining portion of the side piece to the remainder of the front piece, and machine stitch a ⅝in (1.5cm) seam, stopping ⅝in (1.5cm) from the end. Attach the other side piece to the other side of the front piece in the same way.

5 On the back piece, use pins to mark the center point along the top and bottom edges. Press a 16in (40.5cm) inverted pleat down the center back (see page 200). Pin and baste in place at the top edge through all layers.

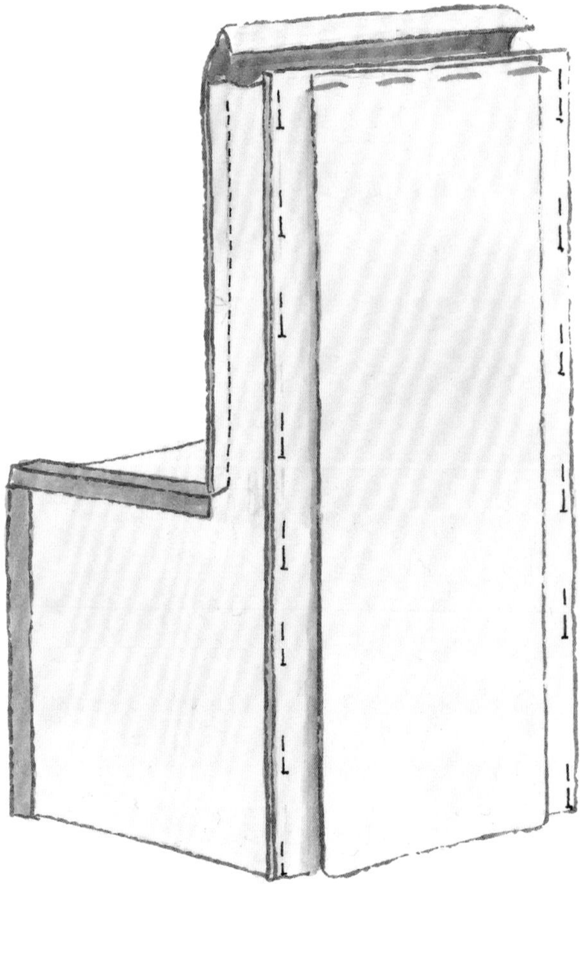

6 With right sides together, place the joined front and side pieces on top of the back piece. Pin together along the side edges as shown.

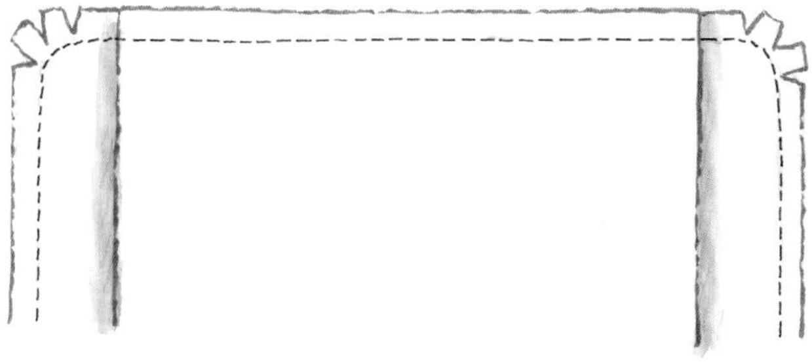

7 Pin the top edges together, curving the corners slightly to fit the chair back. Machine-stitch the pieces together around the top and side edges with a ⅝in (1.5cm) seam. Remove the basting. Clip into the seam allowances on the curved corners, no closer than ⅛in (3mm) from the stitching line.

8 Press a double-fold ⅜in (1cm) hem to the wrong side along the bottom edges of the cover. Pin and machine-stitch in place. Turn right side out and press all the seamed edges flat. On the right side, use pins to mark halfway down the back pleat on each side. Make up the two ties using method 2 (see page 203) but with the seam running down the edge rather than the middle, finishing one end of each. Press a 1in (2.5cm) hem to one side at the raw end of each. Pin this end to the pleat at the marked points, on the right side of the chair cover. Machine-stitch as shown. Place the cover over the chair and make a bow from the ties.

The deep inverted pleat on the back is held together with a wide bow made in the same fabric.

director's chair cover

Refurbish a shabby director's chair with a new back and seat, using the old ones as a pattern. I've used two different fabrics—on the back, Stockholm Stripe in Lime, Teal, and Winter, and for the seat, Pretty Maids in Mushroom, Teal, and Winter.

You will need

- 1yd (1m) of canvas-type fabric
- Matching sewing thread
- Tacks or staples (optional)

Estimating yardage

- Follow step 1 to find the size of the new cover, based on the old one, adding extra for any side channels, plus ½in (1.2cm) for each side hem and 1in (2.5cm) for each top/bottom hem.
- Allow for one back panel and one seat panel in the fabric.

TIP

If you wish, reinforce the stitching lines by stitching along them twice, and reverse-stitch two or three times at the beginning and end of each row. This will give extra strength, especially on the seat, which will be taking the strain.

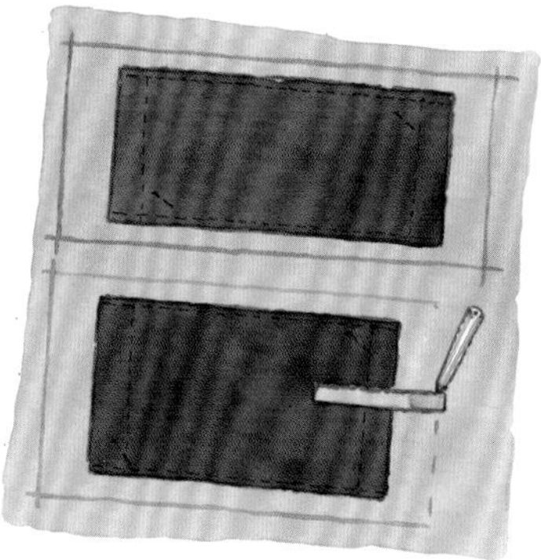

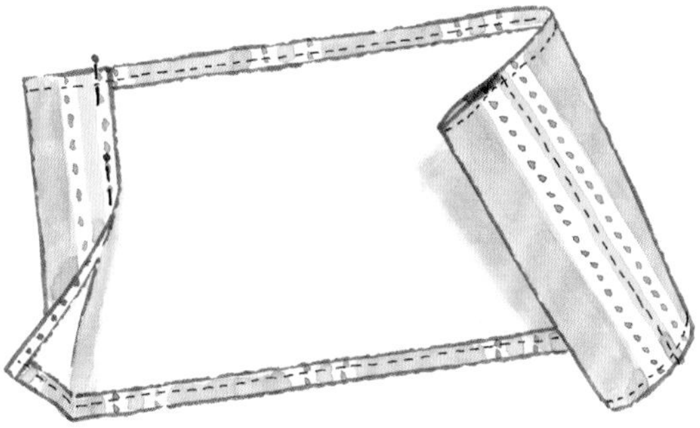

1 For the back, slide the old back off the poles and use it as a pattern for the new one, adding extra for the side channels, plus ½in (1.2cm) for each side hem, 1in (2.5cm) for the top hem, and 1in (2.5cm) for the bottom hem. For the seat, slightly fold the chair to make the seat fabric go slack, then carefully slide the old seat out of the wooden grooves, where it is held in place by plastic or wooden rods—or, if it is held in place by tacks or staples, remove them to release the seat cover. Use the old seat as a pattern for the new one, adding extra for the side channels, if any, plus the same hem allowances as for the back. From the fabric, cut out one back panel and one seat panel.

2 For the back, press a double-fold ½in (1.2cm) hem to the wrong side along the top and bottom edges of the back panel. Machine-stitch close to the first pressed edge of each hem. Press a single ½in (1.2cm) hem to the wrong side along each side edge, and then fold over the channel amount, using the old back as a guide. Pin, baste, and machine-stitch close to the first pressed edge of each hem.

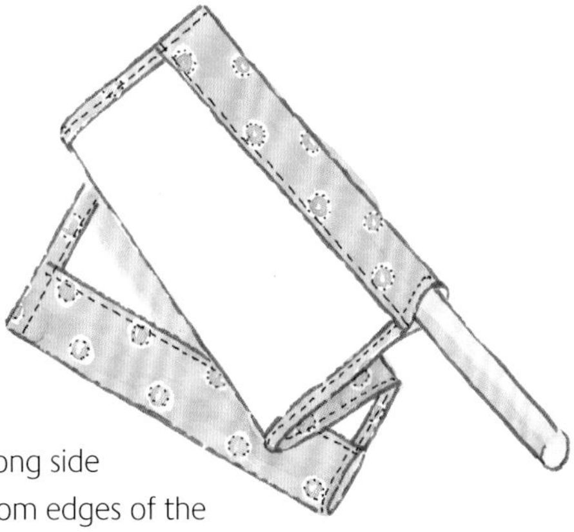

3 For the seat, press a double-fold ½in (1.2cm) hem to the wrong side along the top and bottom edges of the back panel. Machine-stitch close to the first pressed edge of each hem. If the seat panel is held in place within grooves, press a single ½in (1.2cm) hem to the wrong side along each side edge, and then fold over the amount you need for each channel, using your old cover as a guide. Pin, baste, and machine-stitch the channel in place close to the first pressed edge. Insert a rod into each seat-panel channel. (If the seat is only stapled or tacked in place, omit the channels and the rods.)

4 With the chair frame slightly folded, either slide the rods of the new seat into each wooden groove or staple/tack the new seat to the underside of the seat frame using the old staple/tack holes as a guide. Slide the new back cover onto the frame.

easy tablecloth

There's nothing we like more than having tea in the garden on a sunny day at the weekend, and this simple tablecloth, in Feather & Egg, in Sky Blue, brightens up the faded top of our metal table. Each corner is weighted with a small curtain weight to hold down the tablecloth in a breeze.

1 Cut out the fabric. Press a ⅝in (1.5cm) double-fold hem to the wrong side all around. Pin and machine-stitch in place.

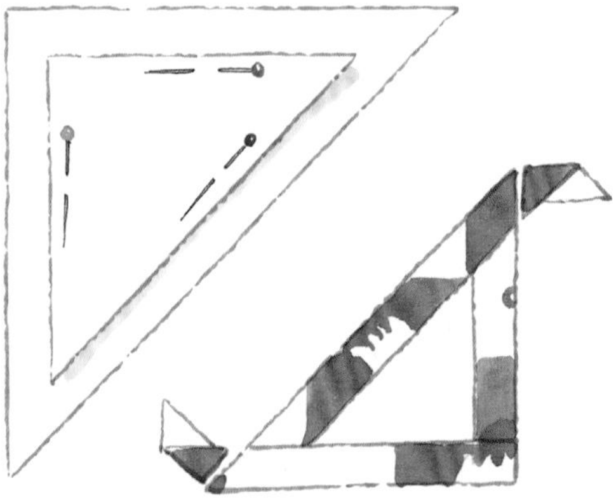

2 Using a ruler and carpenter's square (set square) or similar right-angled object, draw a right-angled triangle on the paper, making the two lines forming the right angle 3in (7.5cm) long. Cut out the pattern, then pin it onto a piece of the remaining fabric. Leaving a ⅜in (1cm) hem allowance all around, cut out four triangles of fabric. Press a ⅜in (1cm) hem to the wrong side on all three edges of each triangle, trimming the excess fabric at the corners.

You will need

- Fabric—see below for yardage
- Matching sewing thread
- Four curtain weights
- Paper for making a pattern
- Carpenter's square (set square) or similar right-angled object

Estimating yardage

- Measure the length and width of the tabletop and decide on the depth of the overhang at the sides.
- Add twice the overhang depth to both the length and width measurements, plus a 1¼in (3cm) hem allowance all around.

TIP

If your table is large, you may need to join fabric widths to get the right size of tablecloth. If so, position a full width in the center, and add a half width either side, joining the pieces with French seams (see page 189).

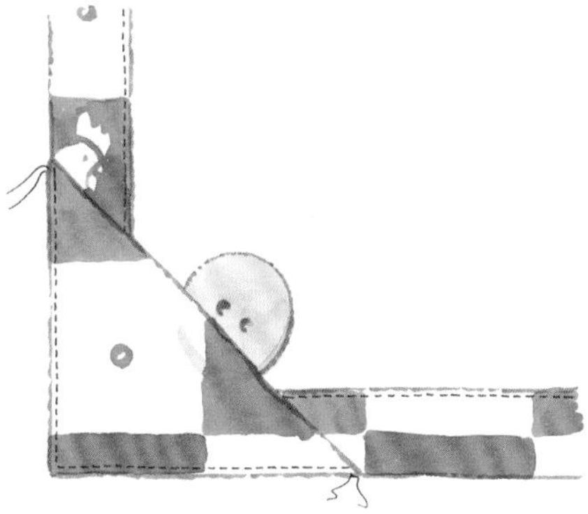

3 Place one triangular piece over one corner of the tablecloth, with wrong sides together and the edges forming the right angles even. Pin and machine-stitch close to these edges. Slip a curtain weight into the triangular pocket at the corner, through the open diagonal edge.

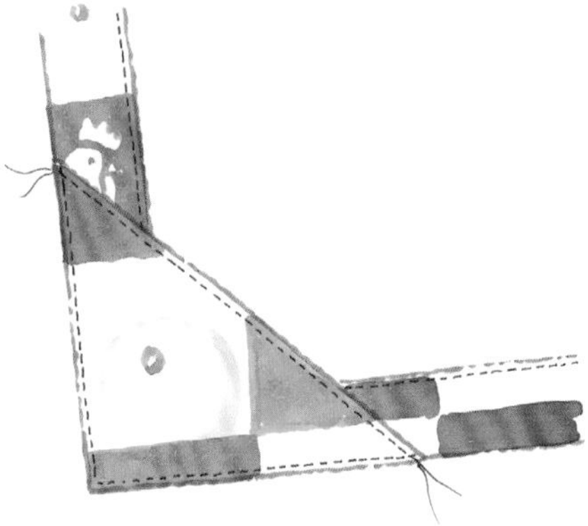

4 Pin and machine-stitch close to the diagonal edge of the triangle to enclose the weight. Repeat steps 3 and 4 for the remaining tablecloth corners, fabric triangles, and weights.

circular tablecloth

Garden tables can become quite weatherworn over the years, so give yours a new lease of life by covering it with a pretty cloth. This one has been made in Acorn and Leaf, Cranberry, and echoes the warm colors of the terra-cotta pots.

1 Cut out a square of fabric to the required measurements, joining widths if necessary, using French seams (see page 189). Fold the fabric square in half, and then again so it is folded in quarters. Cut a square of paper that is slightly larger than the folded fabric and place it on a large, flat surface. Cut a length of twine 8in (20cm) longer than one of the folded edges. Tie one end of the twine to a pencil and attach the other end to the corner of the paper with a push pin or thumbtack (drawing pin).

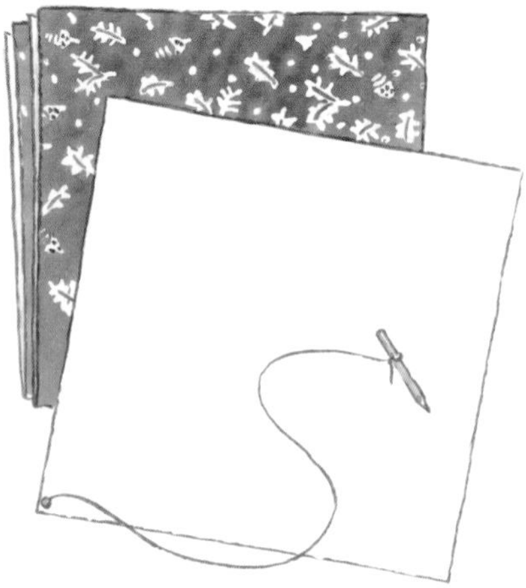

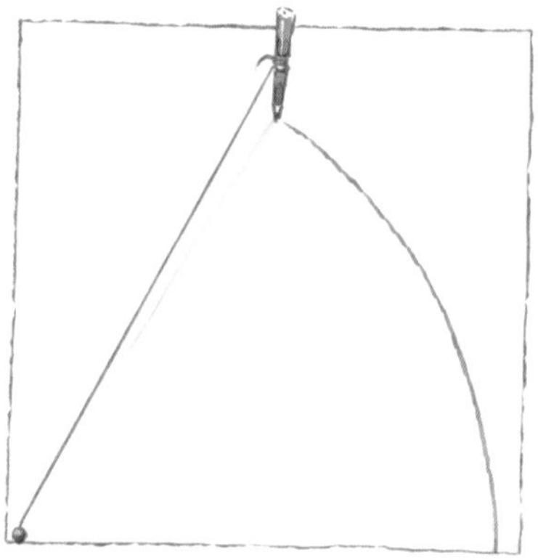

2 Wrap the twine around the pencil until it is exactly the same length as one folded edge of the fabric. Keeping the twine taut, draw an arc from one edge of the paper to the other using the pencil. Cut out the paper pattern along the curved line.

3 Place the paper pattern on the folded fabric, with the pattern's straight edges along the fabric's folds and the center points matching. Pin the pattern in place, and cut along the curved edge through all thicknesses of fabric. Remove the pattern and open out the fabric to form the complete circle.

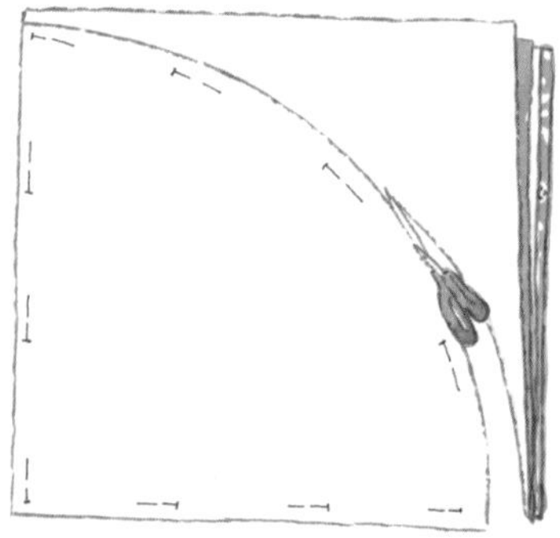

You will need

- Decorator fabric—see below for yardage
- Matching sewing thread
- Paper for pattern
- Twine
- Plastic push pin or brass thumbtack (drawing pin)

Estimating yardage

- Take the measurement from the center of your tabletop to the floor, or to the desired tablecloth length, and add ⅜in (1cm) for a hem allowance.
- To estimate your fabric yardage, double this measurement to find the finished size of your tablecloth and allow for a square of fabric this size. For a large table, you will need to join widths (see page 188), in which case position a full width in the center and add a half width on each side.

4 Using matching thread, staystitch (see page 183) all around the edge of the tablecloth ⅜in (1cm) from the edge. Zigzag-stitch the raw edge, or use a serger if you have one. Press a single ⅜in (1cm) hem to the wrong side, making sure the staystitching is just inside the hem allowance. Pin and machine-stitch the hem in place all around the edge.

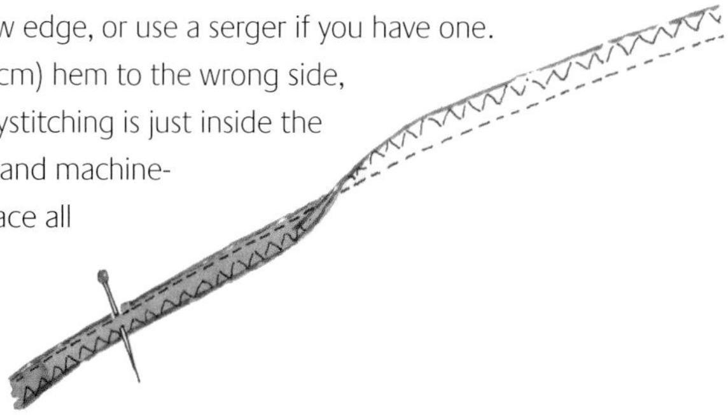

TIP

To enjoy leisurely outdoor meals, why not make comfortable tie-on seat cushions for your garden chairs? See pages 78 and 82 for ideas. You may even be able to use up scraps left over from the circular tablecloth.

bordered tablecloth

If you have a battered table that is better covered up, this bordered tablecloth will give it an instant update. The tablecloth has been made from two different colorways of my Simple Ticking fabric—the main fabric is Dormouse, while the border uses Brick. Both colorways work well with the darker wood furniture, the weathered wooden bench seat, and the plain plaster walls in this country kitchen, while the understated fabric pattern allows the glassware and china to take centerstage. You can make the contrast border to whatever size you like, but remember that the deeper the border, the more striking the effect.

You will need

- Main decorator fabric—see below for yardage
- Contrast decorator fabric for borders—see below for yardage
- Matching sewing thread

Estimating yardage

- Measure the length and width of the tabletop and decide on the depth of overhang at the sides. Remember this will be affected by how deep you would like the border to be. Typically, the overhang of a tablecloth stops just above the lap of a seated person. Add a ⅝in (1.5cm) seam allowance all around.
- Decide how wide you would like your borders to be. Consider the pattern of the fabric and how the design will orient on the cloth. You will need two side pieces the same length as the main fabric, plus two end pieces the width of the main fabric plus the width of the side borders. To all border pieces add a hem and seam allowance of 1¼in (3cm).

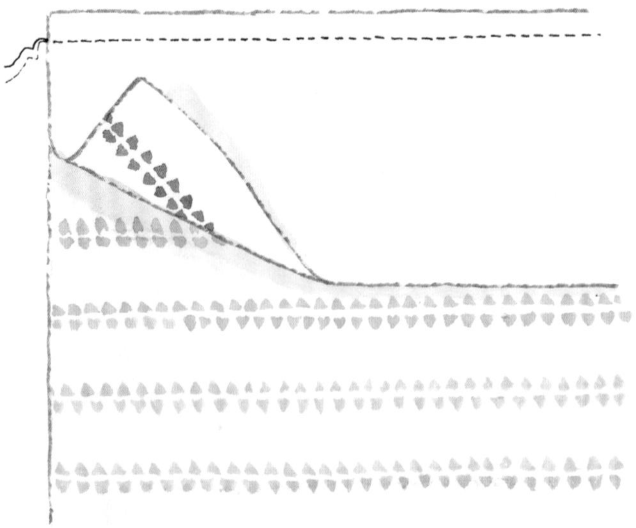

1 From the main fabric, cut out the top piece of the tablecloth. From the contrasting fabric, cut out both long side border pieces and the two end pieces. With right sides together and raw edges even, pin a side border piece along the length of the main fabric. Machine stitch a ⅝in (1.5cm) seam. Repeat on the other side. Press the seams away from the main body of the cloth.

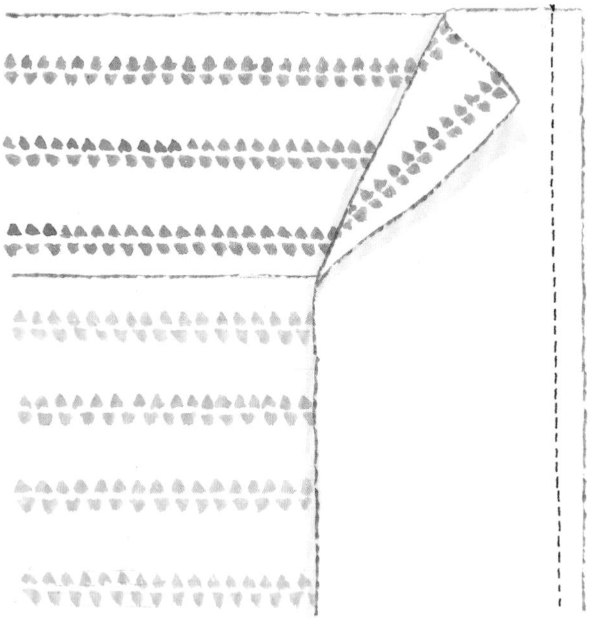

2 Repeat step 1 to attach the two end border pieces, pinning, stitching, and pressing the seams.

3 To hem the tablecloth, press a ⅝in (1.5cm) double-fold hem to the wrong side all around. Pin and machine stitch in place, then remove the pins and press.

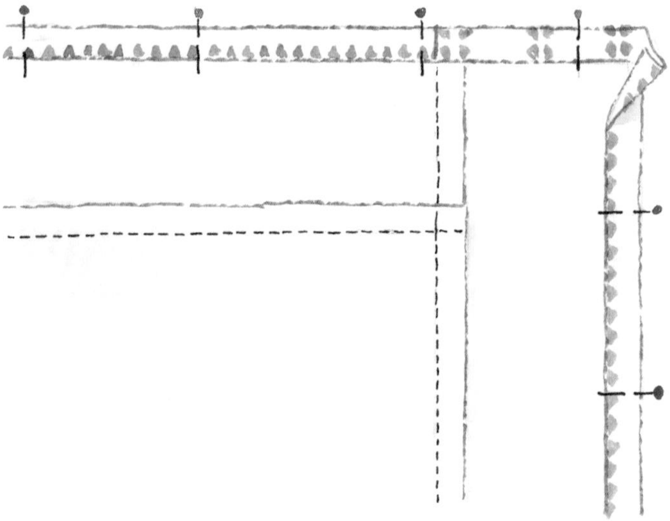

TIP

If you wish, make a set of matching napkins from the border fabric—see the simple instructions on page 148.

padded headboard

A beautiful padded, patterned headboard can completely transform a bedroom. For the Love of Rose, in Saffron and Charcoal, looks stunning as a bedroom centerpiece. The contrast of the charcoal piping gives the look a contemporary feel.

You will need

- Main decorator fabric—see right for yardage
- Contrast decorator fabric—see right for yardage
- Matching sewing thread
- Medium-sized cable cord or piping cord—see right for yardage
- Sew-on hook-and-loop tape—see right for yardage
- Sheet of ¾in (2cm-) thick MDF (medium-density fiberboard) or plywood
- Lightweight batting (wadding)—see right for yardage
- Unbleached muslin—see right for yardage
- Staple gun
- Two 35in (89cm-) long pieces of 2 x 1in (5 x 2.5cm) wood (such as pine) with a vertical ⅜in (1cm-) wide slot cut up the center of each—the length of the slots will depend on the height of the fixing bolts on your bed. If the bed does not have fixing bolts, these pieces are not necessary.
- 1¼in (3cm-) long wood screws (not needed if the bed does not have fixing bolts)

Estimating yardage

- For the board length, if your bed has fixing bolts for a headboard, measure from the top of the bed base to the desired height. If it does not, then measure from the floor to the desired height. For the board width, measure the width of the bed base.
- For the batting, allow for enough to cover the board plus 2in (5cm) all around. You may need to join widths.
- For the muslin, allow for a front piece that is the same size as the batting and a back piece the same size as the board. You may need to join widths.
- For the front and back panels, allow for one panel of main fabric and one panel of contrast fabric, each the height measurement—measuring only down to 4in (10cm) above the bed base, as you don't need to cover the board below that—by the width measurement, plus ⅝in (1.5cm) all around for the seam allowances. You may have to join fabric widths to obtain your correct panel widths. When estimating the yardage, allow a further ⅜in (1cm) all around for the thickness of the padding. (The headboard is measured again after step 1, to make sure the cover will fit perfectly.)
- For the cable cord or piping cord, you will need to allow enough to go all around the top, plus 4in (10cm).
- For covering the cord, first gauge the width of your fabric strip. To do this, measure around the cord and allow an extra 1¼in (3cm) for seam allowances (see page 194). Allow enough bias strips of contrast fabric of this width to fit the length of your cord.
- You will need enough hook-and-loop tape to fit down the straight part of one side edge of the headboard cover.

TIP

For a country-style headboard cover, instead of using hook-and-loop tape, leave the straight part of both sides open and finish the edges with plain tape. Attach four sets of narrow ties (see page 202) down both sides and tie the back and front pieces together with bows.

1 Cut out the batting (wadding) and muslin pieces, and join widths if necessary (for the batting use lapped seams, in which one raw edge overlaps the other). Place the board in the center of the batting and wrap the batting over onto the back of the board. Staple in place. Place the padded board, batting side down, on the wrong side of the muslin front piece, and repeat the procedure, gently pulling the muslin as you work. Press under a ¾in (2cm) hem on the muslin back piece, then center it on the back of the board and staple in place, covering the edges of the front piece.

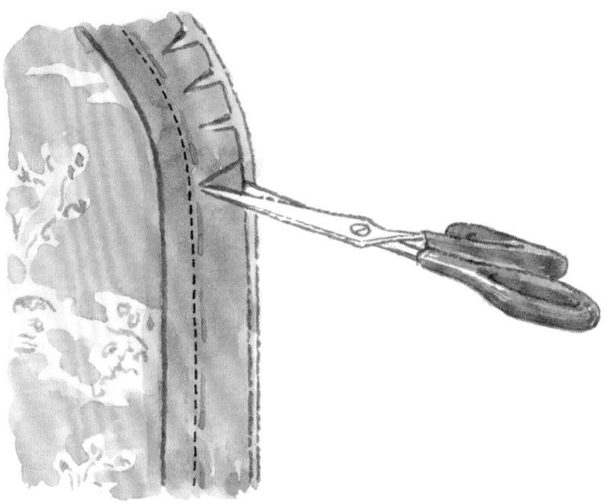

2 Measure the padded headboard to calculate the exact sizes of the front and back panels. From the main fabric, cut out these panels. Join fabric widths, if necessary, to obtain the correct widths, positioning the full width in the center. From the contrast fabric, cut out the bias strips, seam them together to obtain the correct length for covering the cord, and make up the piping (see page 196). With right sides up and raw edges even, pin and baste the piping all around the front panel. To help the piping go around the curve, snip into the piping seam allowance, as shown.

3 To finish the ends, cut the piping to about ½in (12mm) below the bottom edge of the front panel. Undo a little of the basting and the stitching on the piping, and trim the cord itself even with the bottom edge. Fold the excess covering strip over the end of the cord, then pin the piping in place. Using a zipper foot on your machine, stitch the piping to the front panel, stitching as close to the cord as possible.

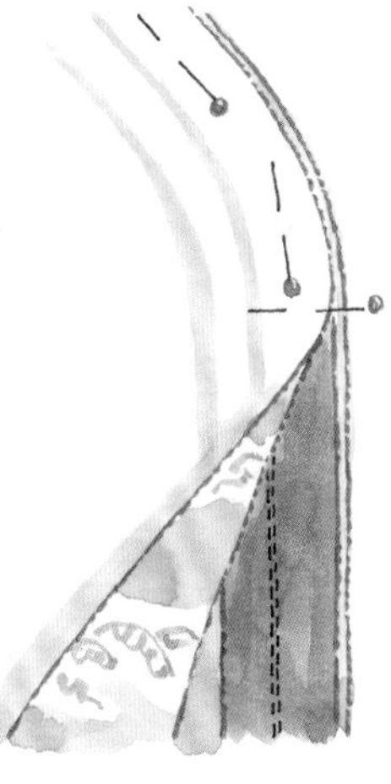

4 With right sides together and raw edges even, place the back panel on top of the front, sandwiching the piping in between. Pin the pieces together up one side and across the curve, but do not pin the straight part of the opposite side, which will be the opening.

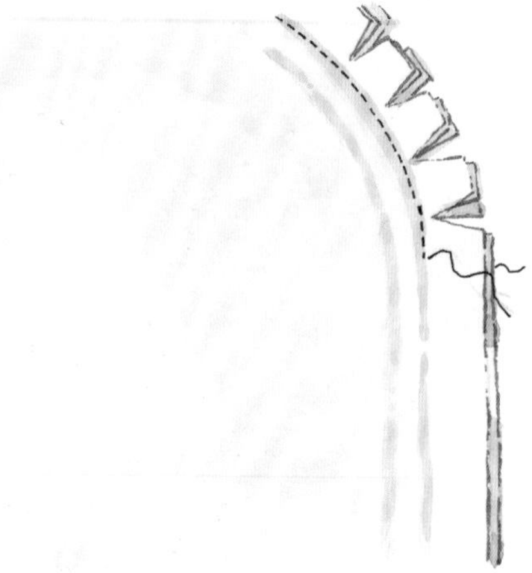

5 Using a zipper foot on your machine, machine-stitch the back panel to the front panel along the pinned edges, restitching over the piping stitching line and making sure you get as close to the cord as possible. Snip into the seam allowance around the curve. Do not stitch the unpinned side where the opening will be.

6 Finish the bottom raw edges of both the front and back panels with a machine zigzag stitch, or use a serger if you have one. Turn the cover right side out and press the cover flat.

7 Open the two sides of the hook-and-loop tape and pin the loop section to the wrong side of the opening on the front panel, butting the edge of the tape against the piping. Machine-stitch the tape in place around all edges of the tape. Repeat on the other edge of the opening, stitching the hook side of the tape to the right side of the back panel.

8 Pull the cover over the headboard and smooth it down until it fits snugly. Press the two sections of the hook-and-loop tape together to close the opening edge. If using the two lengths of wood, screw them to the back of the headboard in line with the fixing bolts on the bed, and then attach the headboard to the fixing bolts. Otherwise, rest the headboard on the floor and push the mattress up to it, concealing the lower edge of the cover.

reversible bed cover

On winter nights we all sometimes need a bit of extra warmth, and this reversible bed cover is just the thing to throw across the bed. It's also a great way to introduce extra color into the bedroom. For this bed cover I used Four Seasons, in Speedwell, for the top, and backed it with Wild Rose, in Buttercup, Clay, and Charcoal. The room is painted in a soft yellow, and coordinated with more fabrics from the Earth and Sky collections.

You will need

- Main decorator fabric for the top—see right for yardage
- Contrast decorator fabric for the back and the piping—see right for yardage
- ¼in- (5mm-) thick cotton batting (wadding)—see right for yardage
- Matching sewing thread
- Preshrunk cable cord or piping cord—see right for yardage
- ¼in- (5mm-) wide Quilters' Tape (a special tape used for marking quilting lines, which does not leave adhesive residue on the fabric when removed)

Estimating yardage

- To find the size of your bed cover, decide how far you wish the cover to overhang the bed at the base and sides. With the mattress and bedding in place, measure the length and width including the overhang.
- Allow for one top panel from the main fabric and one back panel from the contrast fabric. The panels should each measure the calculated finished length and width, plus ⅝in (1.5cm) all around for seam allowances. You may have to join lengths to obtain the required width (see step 1).
- To find the length of cord required, add together the calculated length and width measurements of your cover and double the total, then add 8in (20cm).
- For covering the cable cord or piping cord, allow enough contrast-fabric bias strips to fit the length of your cord (see page 194).
- For the cotton batting (wadding), you should be able to purchase a single piece to fit the length and width of your cover. It can be bought from quilting stores in single, double, and king-sized pieces.

The fabrics are machine-stitched together through all layers to stop them from slipping.

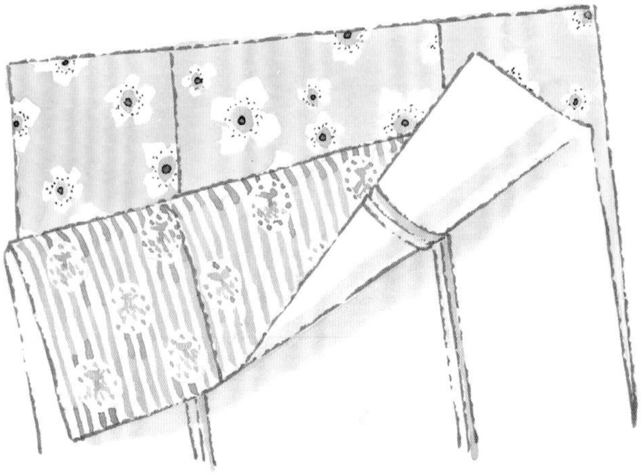

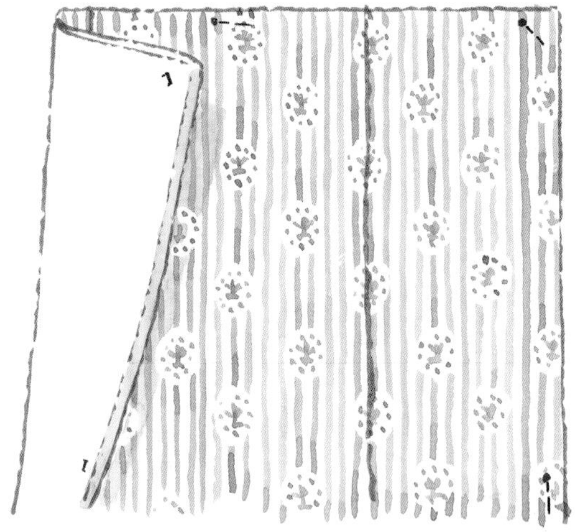

1 Cut out the top panel and the back panel. If necessary, join fabric lengths with ⅝in (1.5cm) seams, placing full fabric widths down the center and part-widths down each side. Also from the contrast fabric, cut out and join the bias strips (see page 194).

2 Cut the batting (wadding) to the calculated size of your cover, including the seam allowance all around. On a large work surface lay out the batting. Lay the top panel, right side up, on top of it, and smooth it out gently until there are no wrinkles. Use weights around the edges to keep the fabric taut. Pin the layers together at the corners and midpoint of each side, close to the edges.

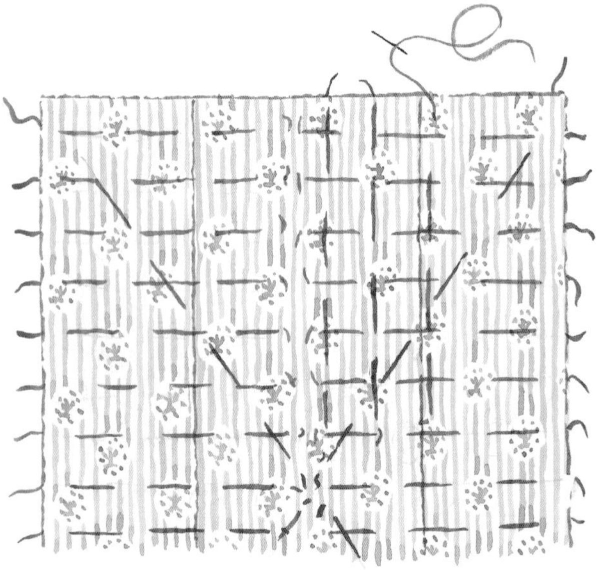

3 Beginning at the center, baste diagonal lines outward toward the corners, making your stitches about 3in (7.5cm) long. Then, again starting at the center, baste horizontal and vertical lines out to the edges, creating a grid of lines roughly 4in (10cm) apart over the entire cover.

4 Cover the cord with the bias strips (see page 196). With right sides together, pin and then baste it around the edges of the top panel. Now place the back cover on top, right sides together and raw edges even; pin and baste around all sides. Using a zipper foot on your sewing machine, machine-stitch the front and back covers together, close to the piping cord, leaving a 12in (30.5cm) opening along one side edge. Remove the basting from the piped seam.

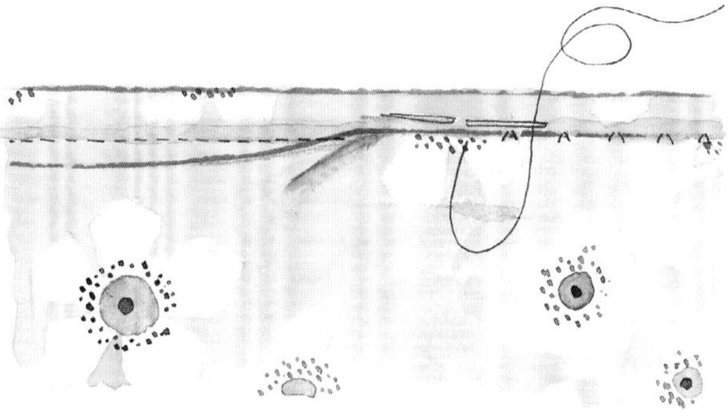

5 To reduce bulk, trim away the seam allowance of the batting close to the stitching line, then snip off the corners of the seam allowances. Turn the cover right side out through the opening.

6 Press the ⅝in (1.5cm) seam allowances of the opening to the wrong side and pin the opening edges together. Slipstitch (see page 185) the opening edges together, close to the piping.

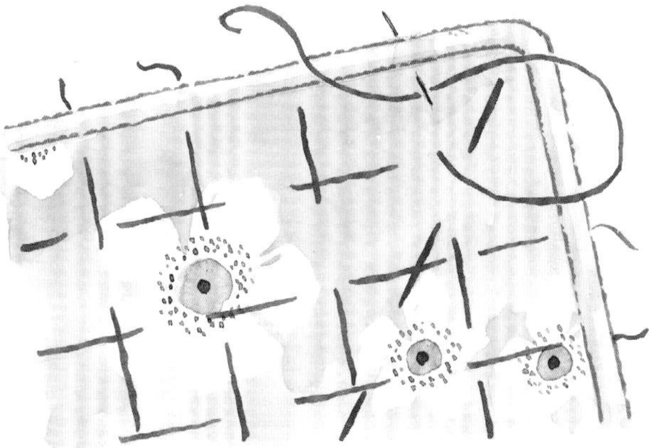

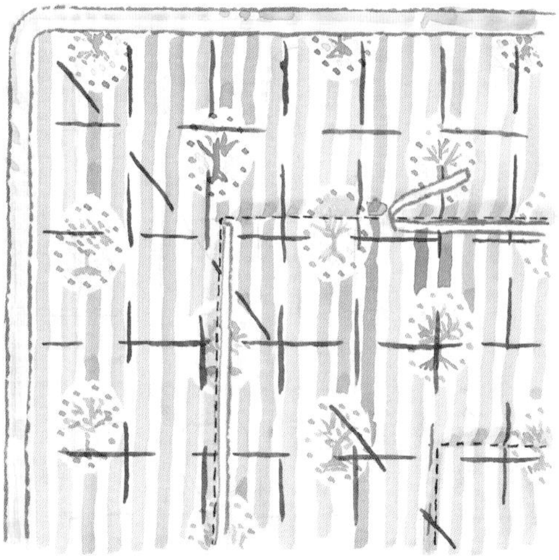

7 Carefully press the piped edges of the cover flat. Working on a large work surface again, lay out the bed cover with the back panel facing up. Gently smooth out the fabric until there are no wrinkles, then baste all three layers together, as in step 3.

8 Working with the top panel facing up, measure and mark the quilting lines 9in (23cm) from each edge of the bed cover, using the Quilters' Tape. Carefully machine-stitch along the edge of the tape, through all layers of fabric. If the cover is for a double bed, repeat the process a further 9in (23cm) in from that stitching. Peel off the tape and remove the basting stitches.

ruffled quilt

I loved the old eiderdowns we had on our beds as children so much that I had to design my own paisley fabric, and then make it into a quilt. Paisley Ground, in Apple Green, is backed with Plain Check in Raspberry and looks great with the French Ticking Pleated Bed Skirt (see page 136), in Raspberry, and the shaped headboard.

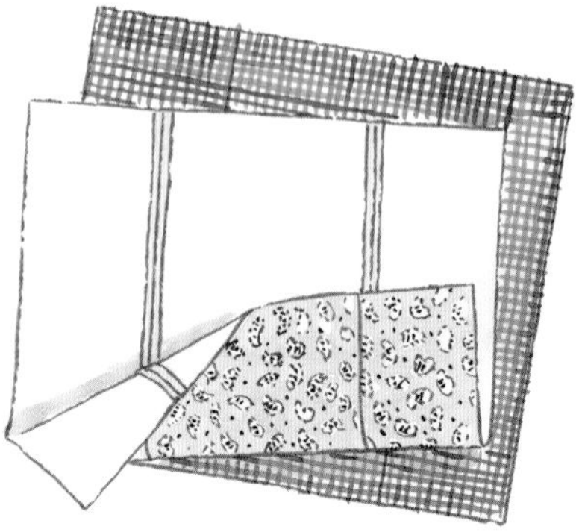

1 Cut out the top panel from the main fabric and the back panel from the contrast fabric, each to the length and width calculated. If necessary, join fabric lengths (see page 188), placing full fabric widths down the center and part-widths down each side. Also from the contrast fabric, cut out the correct number of pleating strips to obtain the required length, and join the lengths.

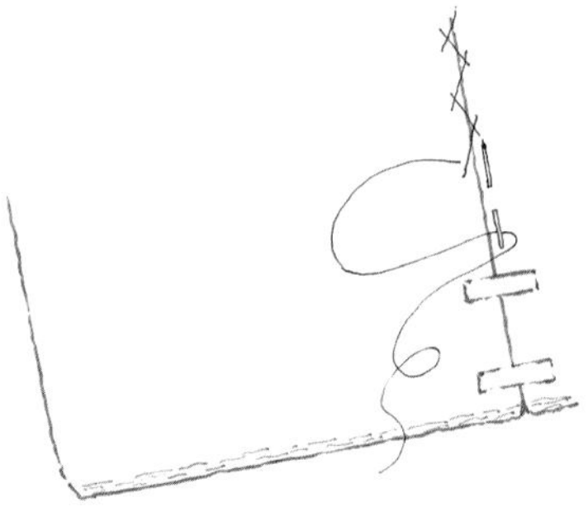

2 Cut the batting (wadding) to the calculated size, including the seam allowance all around. If you need to join lengths, butt the edges together to avoid unsightly ridges. Hold the batting edges together temporarily with strips of low-tack masking tape. Hand-sew them together on both sides of the batting using large herringbone stitches (see page 187); remove the masking tape strips as you sew. Baste the batting panel to the top panel as for the Reversible Bed Cover, step 3 (see page 132).

TIP

This quilt has a pleated edge which gives a tailored finish to the quilt. If you want a more country-style look, simply make a gathered ruffle (see step 2, page 141) instead of the pleats in step 3.

You will need

- Main decorator fabric for the top—see below for yardage
- Contrast decorator fabric for the back—see below for yardage
- 4oz (135g) polyester batting (wadding)—see below for yardage
- Matching sewing thread
- Low-tack masking tape
- ¼in- (5mm-) wide Quilters' Tape (a special tape used for marking quilting lines, which does not leave adhesive residue on the fabric when removed)

Estimating yardage

- To find the size of your quilt, decide how far you wish the cover to overhang the bed at the base and sides. With the mattress and bedding in place, measure the length and width including the overhang.
- The front and back panels should each measure the calculated finished length and width, plus ⅝in (1.5cm) all around for seam allowances. You may have to join lengths to obtain the required width (see step 1).
- For the ruffle strip, allow for a fabric depth of 5¼in (13.5cm) deep. To find the cut length of your ruffle strip, add together the calculated length and width measurements of the cover and multiply the total by six, and then add 1¼in (3cm) for seam allowances. You will need to join lengths to achieve the required length (see page 188).
- Polyester batting (wadding) can be bought in single- and double-bed widths. Allow enough for the finished length of your cover including the overhang. If you have to join lengths to obtain the correct width, allow for the correct number of lengths.

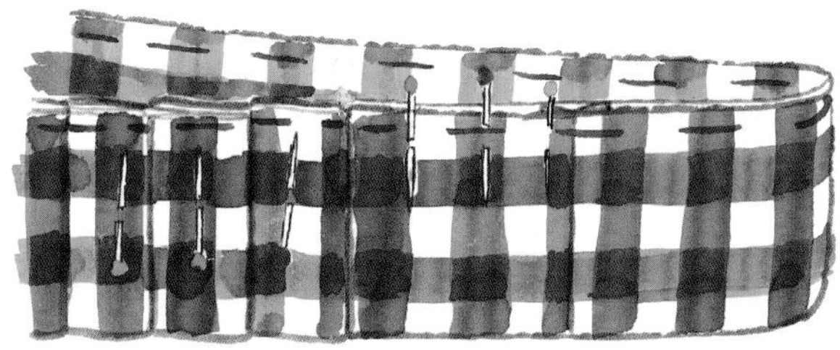

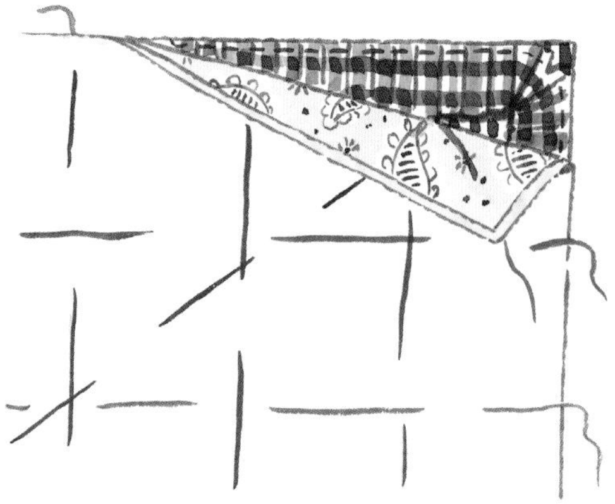

3 With right sides together, pin the ends of the pleating strip together to form a ring; machine-stitch a ⅝in (1.5cm) seam. With wrong sides together and raw edges even, press the pleating strip in half lengthwise, then baste the raw edges together. Using pins for markers, divide the long, raw, basted edges into 1in (2.5cm) sections and pleat the entire strip, as for the Pillow with Knife Pleats, step 2 (page 92).

4 Pin and baste the pleated ruffle around the edge of the top panel, with right sides together and raw edges even. If necessary, adjust the size of a few pleats slightly in the least noticeable spot so it fits exactly. Machine-stitch a ⅝in (1.5cm) seam, snipping into the ruffle seam allowances at each corner. With right sides together and raw edges even, pin and baste the back panel to the top panel around all sides. Machine-stitch, following the ruffle stitching line and leaving a 12in (30.5cm) opening along one side edge. Remove all the basting from the seam. Complete the quilt following steps 5–8 of the Reversible Bed Cover (see page 133).

pleated bed skirt

I love combining stripes and checks with other patterns, and we have a good variety of colors in the range to coordinate with any design you choose. These classic fabrics are wonderful for underpinning a patterned design—select one of the colors from the main print for other fabrics in the room. This traditional pleated skirt for a bed is made in French Ticking in Raspberry and coordinates with the Ruffled Quilt (see page134).

You will need

- Main decorator fabric—see below for yardage
- Plain cotton sheeting fabric—see below for yardage
- Drapery lining fabric—see below for yardage
- Matching sewing thread

Estimating yardage

- To find the size of the deck (top piece), measure the width and length of the bed base (without the mattress), and add ⅝in (1.5cm) all around for seam and hem allowances. Allow one piece of plain sheeting to these measurements.
- To find the depth of the side panels and end panel, measure the height of the bed base from the top to the floor (without the mattress), and add 1½in (4cm) to the measurement for seam and hem allowances.

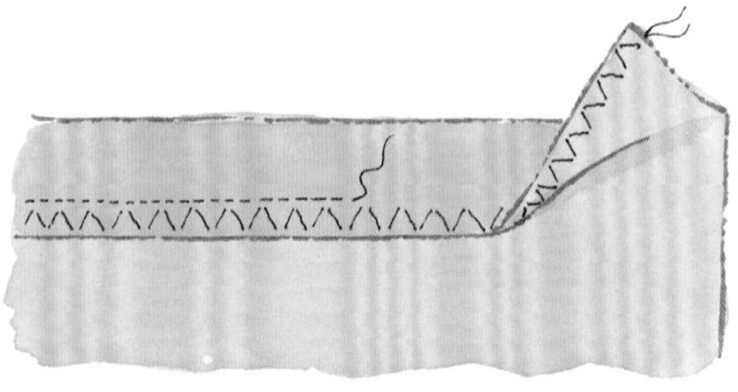

1 From the main fabric and the lining fabric, cut out the side and end panels and the pleat backings. From the sheeting fabric, cut out one deck (top piece). Finish the edge at the head end of the deck with machine zigzag stitch, or a serger if you have one, and then press ⅝in (1.5cm) to the wrong side along this edge. Machine-stitch in place.

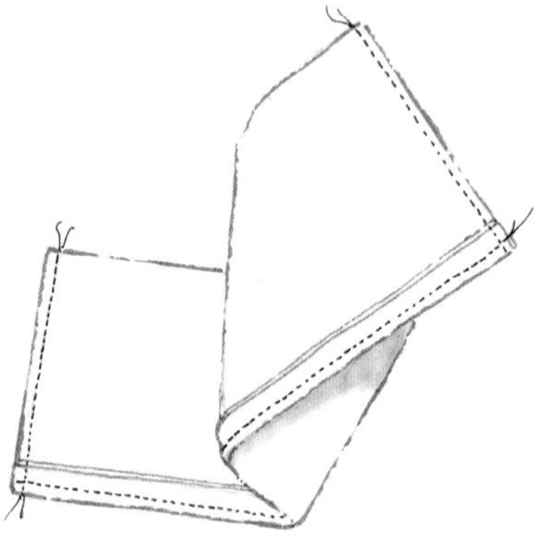

2 With right sides together and the lower raw edges and side edges even, lay a lining side-panel piece on top of a main-fabric side-panel piece. Pin and machine-stitch a ⅝in (1.5cm) seam along the lower edge. Press the seam toward the lining. With right sides together, reposition the lining on top of the main fabric, so that the raw edges are even at the top and sides. Very lightly press the folded edge so that a strip of main fabric shows along the bottom edge of the lining. Pin and machine-stitch a ⅝in (1.5cm) seam down both short sides of the panel. Trim the corners and turn the panel right side out. Press the seamed edges flat.

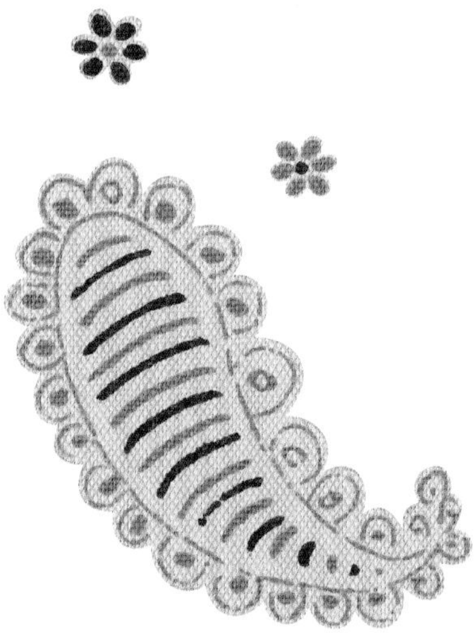

- Each side is made up of two separate panels for ease of access under the bed. For each of the four side panels allow a piece of the main fabric half the length of the bed, plus 7in (18cm) for the pleats and 1¼in (3cm) for seam allowances, by the depth calculated.
- For the end panel, allow a piece of the main fabric the width of the bed, plus 7in (18cm) for the pleats and 1¼in (3cm) for seam allowances, by the depth calculated. (If the bed skirt is for a double bed, allow for the end to be two panels rather than one, each half the width of the bed plus the same amounts as for a single end panel.)
- For the pleat backings, allow four pieces (or five if there are two end panels) of the main fabric, each 8¼in (19.5cm), by the depth calculated.
- For the lining, allow for four side panels, one end panel (or two if it is for a double bed), and four pleat backings (or five if there are two end panels) to the same width as the main fabric, but ¾in (2cm) shorter.

3 Repeat step 2 for the remaining side and end panels and pleat backing pieces. Along both side edges of each panel, press 3½in (9cm) to the lined side to form the front of the pleat. Pin the pleats in place along their top edge.

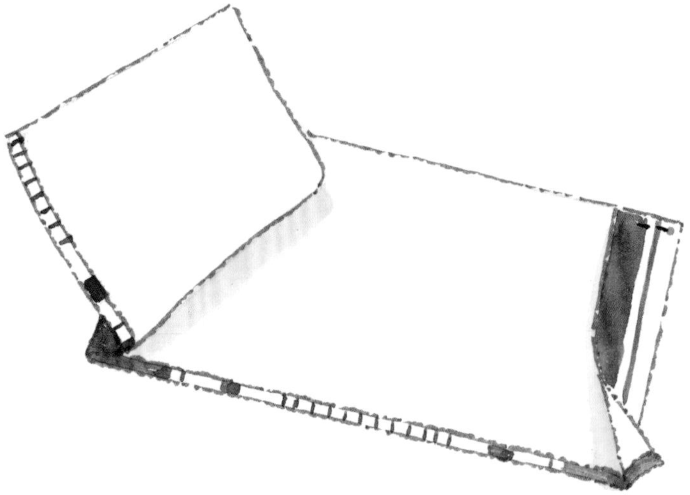

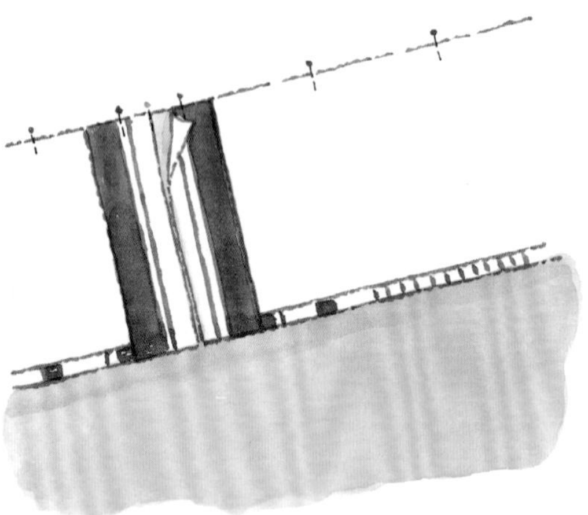

4 Fold the deck in half, bringing the finished edge at the head end to lie ⅝in (1.5cm) from the raw edge at the foot end. Mark the fold at both side edges with pins, then open out the deck so it is right side up. Place two side panels along one side edge of the deck, with raw edges even, and with the pleat edges meeting at the pinned center point. At the foot end of the deck, the pleat edge of the side panel should finish ⅝in (1.5cm) in from the raw edge. At the head end of the deck, the pleat edge of the other side panel should be even with the hemmed edge of the deck. (The "pleat edge" at each side of the head end of the deck will not actually be a pleat but simply a finished edge.) Pin and machine-stitch the side panels to the deck with a ⅝in (1.5cm) seam. Repeat with the other two side panels on the remaining side edge of the deck.

5 At the foot end of the deck, fold the side panels back out of the way. With raw edges even, pin the end panel(s) to the deck along this edge. The pressed pleat edges should sit ⅝in (1.5cm) from the sides. Machine-stitch a ⅝in (1.5cm) seam. Fold the side panels back over the end panel(s).

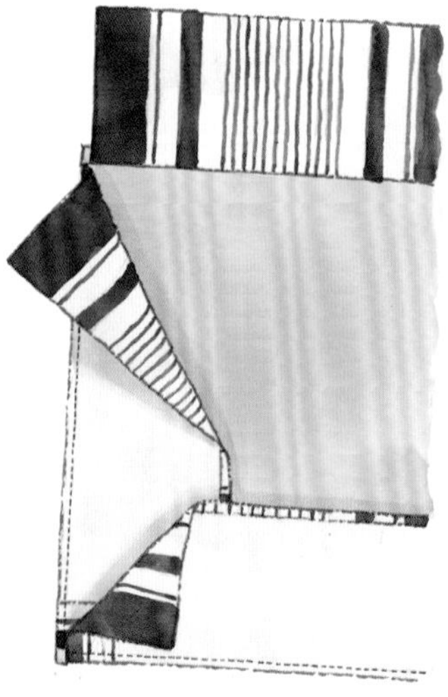

TIP

To ensure that the side and base panels will fit correctly, fold and temporarily pin the pleats in place. Then try them against the deck for size. Adjust the pleat depths, if necessary, before pressing and stitching them permanently in place.

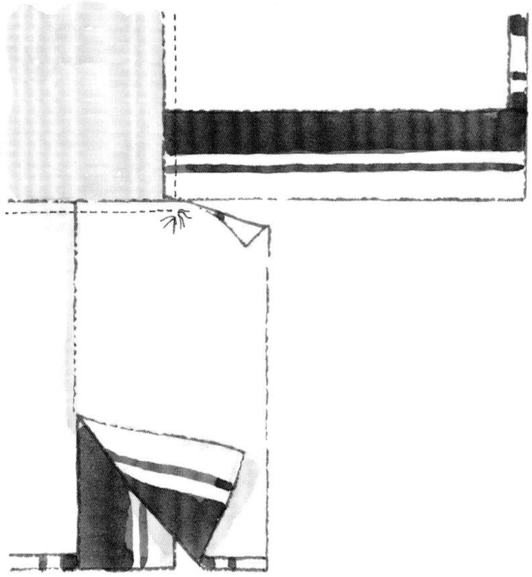

6 Fold one pleat backing in half, mark the center of the top raw edge with a tailor's tack (see page 187), and then unfold it. With the lining side of the pleat backing on top and raw edges even, lay half the pleat backing over the pressed pleat of a side panel at the foot end, matching the tailor's tack to the corner, ⅝in (1.5cm) from the edge. Pin and machine-stitch the pleat backing in place, through all layers of fabric, with a ⅝in (1.5cm) seam, ending at the tailor's tack.

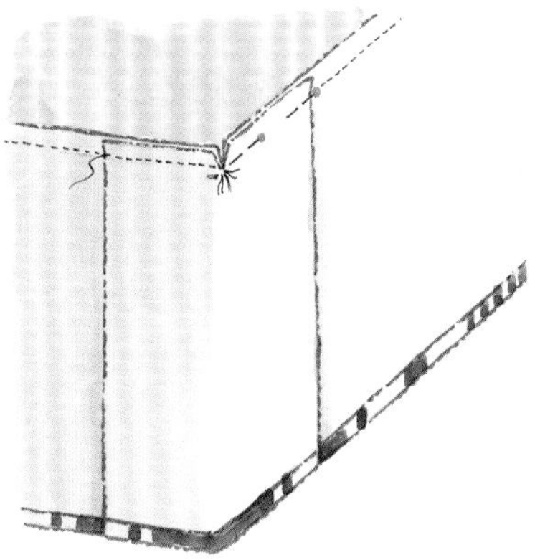

7 Snip into the seam allowance of the lining and main fabric of the pleat backing at the tailor's tack, to allow the pleat backing to turn the corner. Pin and machine-stitch the remaining top edge of the pleat backing in place along the end panel. Repeat steps 6 and 7 for the other corner at the foot end of the deck.

8 Mark the center of another pleat backing with a tailor's tack and place it over the central pressed pleats on one side, matching the tailor's tack to the center. Pin and machine-stitch the pleat backing in place. Repeat for the pleats on the other side, and on the end if you are using two end panels. Turn the finished bed skirt right side out and press. Place it over the bed base, and then replace the mattress.

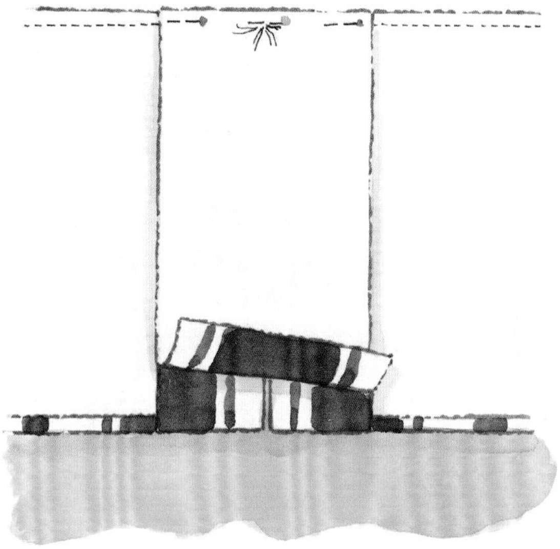

dust ruffle

Blue-and-white check is an all-time classic, suggesting the summer freshness of a Swedish Gustavian country house. A gathered dust ruffle in Plain Check, Smoke, hits just the right note with bare bleached floorboards in the guest bedroom.

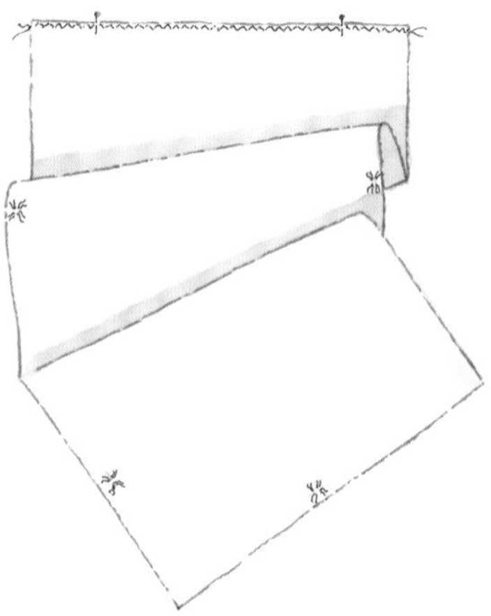

1 From cotton sheeting cut out one deck (top piece). Finish the edge at the head end of the deck using zigzag stitch, or a serger if you have one. Still at the head end, measure in 6½in (16cm) from each side of the deck, and mark with pins. The section between the pins will be hemmed later. The ruffle will be attached to the remaining edges, so measure the distance from one pin all the way around the edge of the deck to the other pin, and divide this distance by six. Mark six sections of this length on the edge of the deck with tailor's tacks (see page 189), starting and finishing with the pins.

2 From the main fabric, cut out enough pieces of the required depth and join them with French seams (see page 189) until the ruffle is the length you calculated in Estimating Yardage. Press a double-fold ½in (1.2cm) hem to the wrong side along the lower edge of the ruffle. Pin and machine-stitch close to the first folded edge. Do the same along the ends of the ruffle. Divide the raw top edge of the ruffle into six equal sections and mark the positions with pins. Using the largest straight stitch on your sewing machine, sew two parallel rows of stitching within the ⅝in (1.5cm) seam allowance, between the pin markers, finishing and then restarting the stitching at each pin.

You will need

- Main decorator fabric—see below for yardage
- Plain cotton sheeting—see below for yardage
- Matching sewing thread

Estimating yardage

- To find the size of the deck (top piece), measure the width and length of the bed base (without the mattress), and add ⅝in (1.5cm) all around for seam and hem allowances. Allow one piece of plain sheeting to these measurements.
- To find the depth of the ruffle, measure the height of the bed base from the top to the floor (without the mattress), and add 1⅝in (4cm) to the measurement for seam and hem allowances.
- To find the length of the ruffle, measure the length and width of the bed base. Add together the bed width plus twice the bed length, plus 13in (33cm) for hems and returns at the head of the bed, and then double the total, which will give you the right amount of fabric fullness.

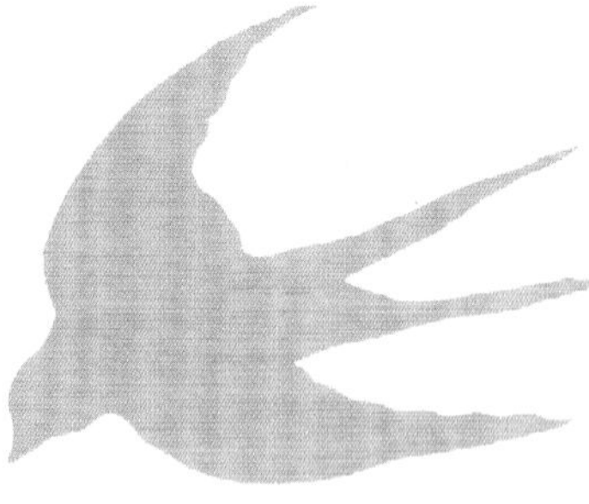

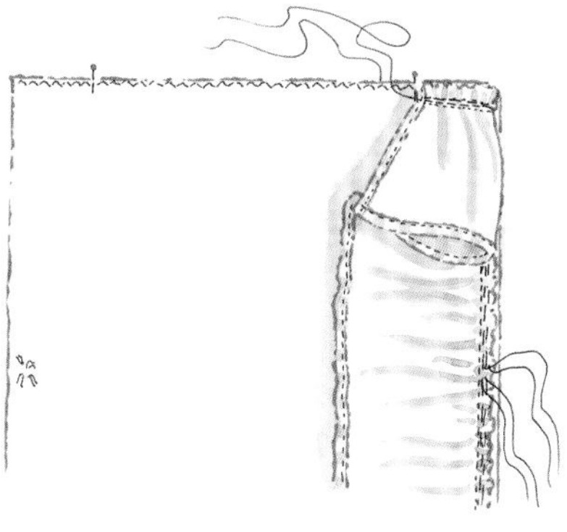

3 Gently pull on the bobbin threads to gather up the top edge of the ruffle. Lay the deck out on a flat surface, right side up. With right sides together and raw edges even, pin the gathered edge of the ruffle to the deck, placing the hemmed ends of the ruffle to the pin markers at the head end of the deck, and matching the pins at the end of each gathered section to the tailor's tacks on the deck. Distribute the gathers evenly and baste the ruffle in place. Machine-stitch the ruffle to the top piece with a ⅝in (1.5cm) seam. Zigzag-stitch the edges together and remove the basting and tailor's tacks. Cut off the long ends of the gathering threads.

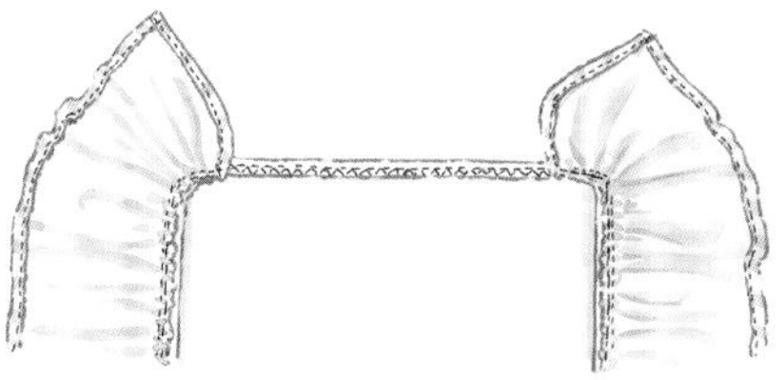

4 Press a ⅝in (1.5cm) hem to the wrong side along the remaining edge at the head end of the deck, and machine-stitch in place, close to the finished edge.

chapter 5

accessories

table runner

If you have a lovely old wooden table like this one, it's a shame to cover it completely, but if you are laying the table, it makes it a bit more special to add a fabric runner down the center. The pattern on Song Birds is perfect for a project like this as it has a strong vertical design. I made this runner in Mushroom and Raspberry, with a strip of Plain Linen Union, in Cream, along each edge, and piled up the table with red and white china and napkins (see page 148 for instructions).

You will need

- Main decorator fabric—see below for yardage
- Contrast decorator fabric—see below for yardage
- Matching sewing thread

Estimating yardage

- Decide how wide you wish the runner to be and how far you want it to overhang the table at the ends. Allow for two pieces of main fabric to the desired length plus 1¼in (3cm), by the desired width minus 1¾in (5cm).
- Allow for two pieces of contrast fabric the same length as the main fabric by 4¼in (11cm) wide.

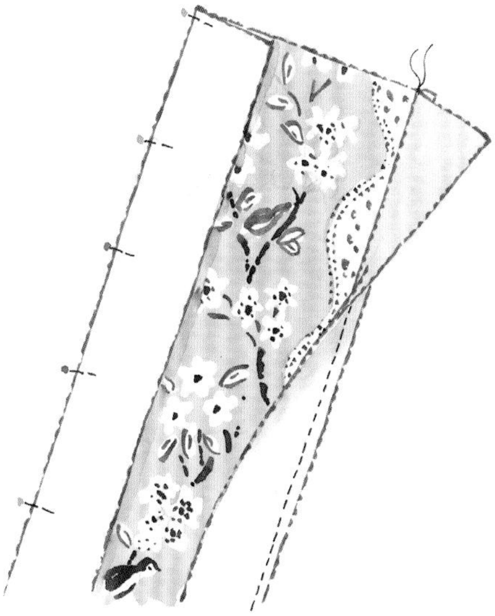

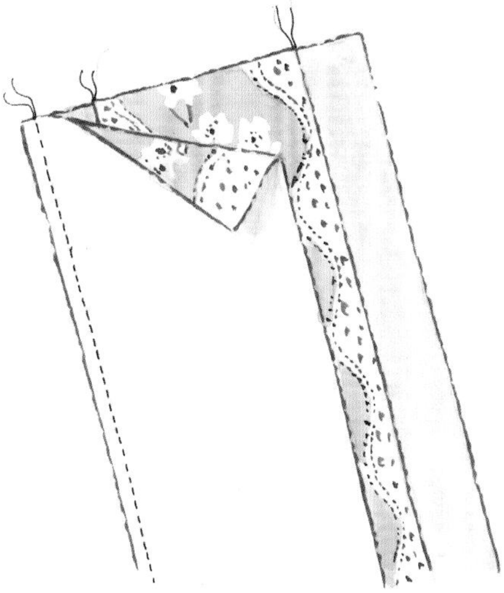

1 Cut out two pieces of main fabric and two strips of contrast fabric to the calculated dimensions. With right sides together, pin one contrast strip to one of the main-fabric pieces along one long edge. Machine-stitch a ⅝in (1.5cm) seam. Join the other contrast strip to the remaining long edge of this main-fabric piece in the same way. Press the seams open.

2 With right sides together, pin and machine-stitch one long edge of the second main-fabric piece to the remaining raw edge of one of the contrast strips.

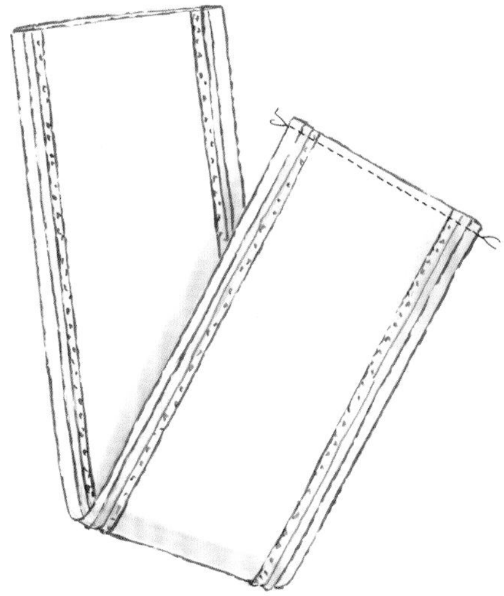

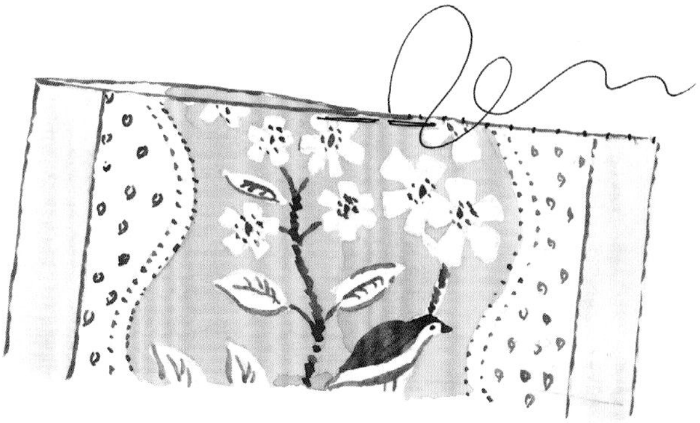

3 Repeat to join the other long edge of this main-fabric piece to the remaining long edge of the other contrast strip, forming a tube. Press the seams open. With right sides together and with the seams aligned so that you have an even-sized border of contrast fabric on each side of the main-fabric piece, pin across one short end of the runner. Machine-stitch a ⅝in (1.5cm) seam along one end of the runner.

4 Turn the runner right side out. At the open end, press ⅝in (1.5cm) to the wrong side on both raw edges. Pin the folded edges together and slipstitch the opening closed (see page 185). Press.

reversible placemat

Placemats make an informal table setting and are useful for protecting a polished surface or for making a scrubbed wooden table top look less bare. I used two fabrics for these mats, which means they can be reversed. They are simplicity itself to make—just stitch two pieces together, turn right side out, slipstitch the opening. They are perfect for beginners to try out their new sewing skills, and they make a lovely gift for a friend.

You will need

- Main decorator fabric—see below for yardage
- Contrast decorator fabric—see below for yardage
- Matching sewing thread

Estimating yardage

- Decide on the size of your placemat and add ⅜in (1cm) all around for seam allowances. The placemat shown here is cut to 11½ x 19in (29 x 48cm).
- Allow for a front cut to these dimensions in the main fabric and a back cut to the same dimensions in the contrast fabric.

TIP

Make a decorative edging by adding a length of coordinating rickrack. Pin and stitch it in place around the edge of one piece of the placemat before stitching the two pieces together. Alternatively, topstitch the rickrack around the edges of the finished mat.

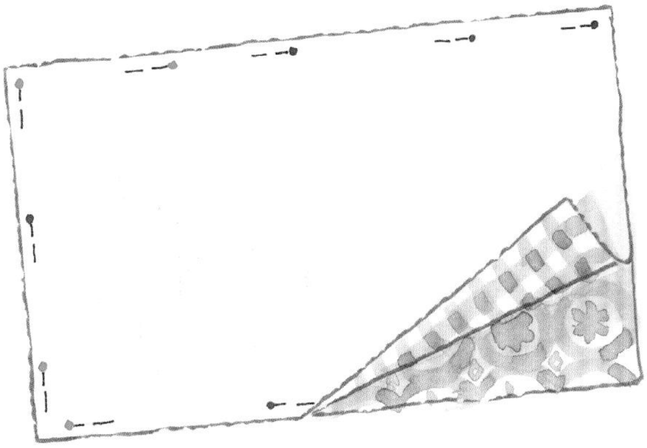

1 Cut out a front and a back. With right sides together, pin the front to the back around the outer edges. Machine-stitch a ⅜in (1cm) seam down all four edges, leaving a 4in (10cm) opening along one short edge. Snip off the corners of the seam allowances.

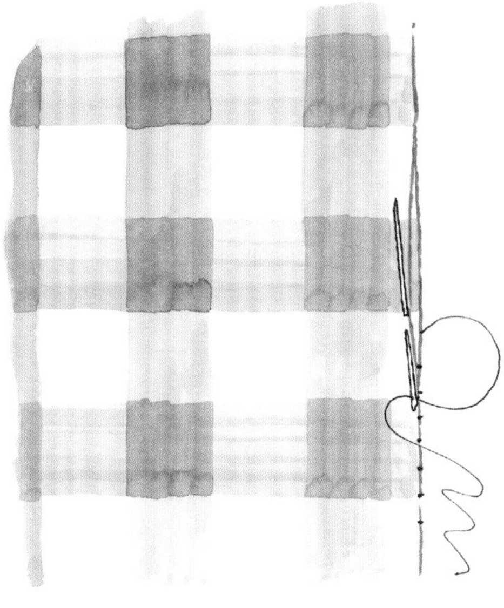

2 Turn the placemat right side out through the opening. Press the seamed edges flat. On the edges of the opening, press ⅜in (1cm) to the wrong side. Slipstitch the edges of the opening together (see page 185).

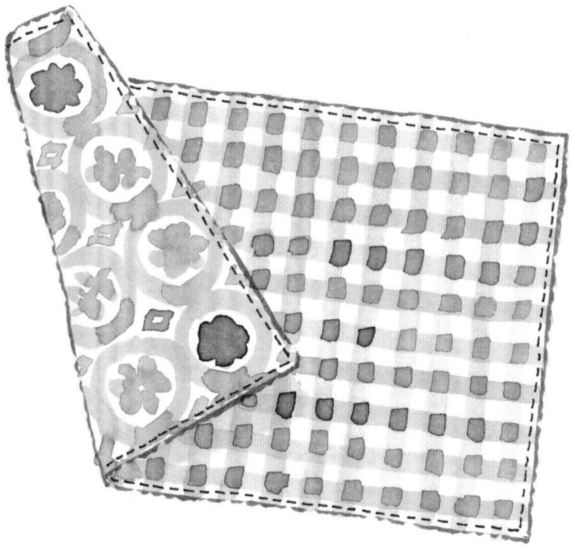

3 Thread your sewing machine with a different colored thread in the needle and on the bobbin, to match the two fabrics of your placemat, then machine-stitch around all sides, close to the edge.

quick and easy napkins

What could be simpler than making a set of napkins? They make such a difference to a lunch or supper table, adding color and atmosphere. Speedy to sew, the napkins simply have a hem turned all the way around, with mitered corners giving the perfect finish. This set is made from Dandelion Trellis, in Stone and Forget-me-not, which coordinates well with the Plain Dotty tablecloth in Stone.

You will need

- Decorator fabric—see below for yardage
- Matching sewing thread
- Paper for making a pattern
- Carpenter's square (set square) or similar right-angled object

Estimating yardage

- Decide on the size of your napkins, which should each be about 18–20in (46–51cm) square, and add ½in (1cm) all around for a hem allowance.
- Allow one square of fabric to this size for each napkin.

TIP

If you have a hemmer foot for your machine, you can make a very narrow double hem.

1 Use a long ruler and a carpenter's square (set square) or something with a right-angled corner to draw on the paper a square of the desired size, including ½in (1cm) all around for a hem allowance. Cut out and use this as a pattern to cut out one square of decorator fabric for each napkin.

TIP

These napkins must be the easiest thing to make in this book, so make two sets and use them every day. Dandelion Trellis is the only cotton fabric in the collections, and is just right for napkins as it's so soft and easy to launder. With two colorways to choose from, this one in Stone and Forget-me-not, or the warmer shades of Cranberry and Stone, you could make a set to mix and match.

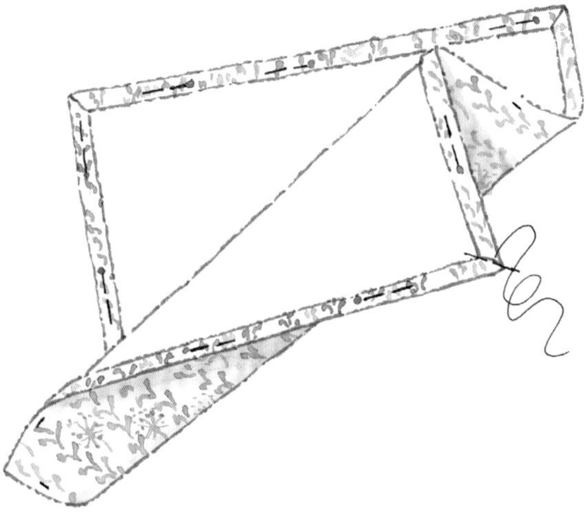

2 Press a double-fold ¼in (5mm) hem to the wrong side on each edge; pin in place, and miter the corners (see page 192).

3 Machine-stitch or slipstitch (see page 185) the hem in place along the first pressed edge on each side.

tea cozy

A tea cozy might seem an old-fashioned item in this world of tea bags, but there's no doubt that tea tastes better made in a pot. So make yourself this easy, padded tea cozy, in Dawn Chorus, in Duck Egg, Pumpkin, and Winter, and keep the pot warm. We painted the alcove wall of our kitchen to match the brightness of Pumpkin, and it's amazingly cheerful first thing in the morning, especially teamed with the colors of the painted chairs.

You will need

- Main decorator fabric—see below for yardage
- Contrast fabric for lining—see below for yardage
- Medium-weight batting (wadding)—see below for yardage
- Matching sewing thread
- Paper for pattern
- Template (see page 220)

Estimating yardage

- Use your paper pattern (see step 1) to calculate the amount of fabric you need. Allow for two pieces from the main fabric, the lining fabric, and the batting. You'll also need a 1¼ x 3¼in (3 x 8cm) strip of main fabric for the hanging loop.

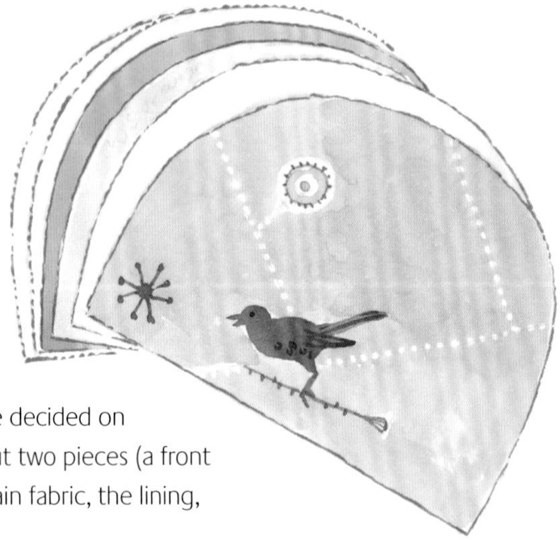

1 Enlarge the template on page 220 to make a paper pattern. A ⅝in (1.5cm) seam allowance is included in the template. You may wish to adjust the size, as the tea cozy pictured, which is 14 x 10½in (35.5 x 26.5cm), fits a large teapot. Once you have decided on the size, use the pattern to cut two pieces (a front and a back) each from the main fabric, the lining, and the batting (wadding).

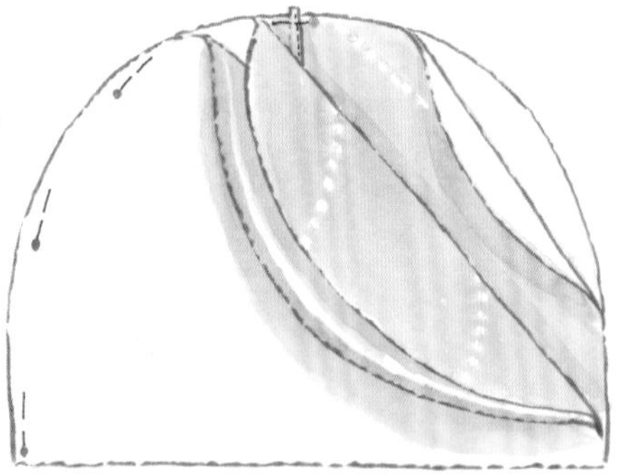

2 To make the hanging loop, cut a 1¼ x 3¼in (3 x 8cm) piece of main fabric, and make it up using Ties, method 1 (see page 202)—you do not need to finish the ends. Lay one piece of batting on your work surface, and place the main-fabric front, right side up, on top. Fold the hanging loop in half and, with raw edges even, pin and baste the loop in place at center top. Lay the main-fabric back, right side down, on top, followed by the remaining piece of batting. Pin all around the curved edge, then machine-stitch a ⅝in (1.5cm) seam through all thicknesses. Trim away the seam allowances of the batting, and snip into the fabric seam allowances on the curve. Turn right side out.

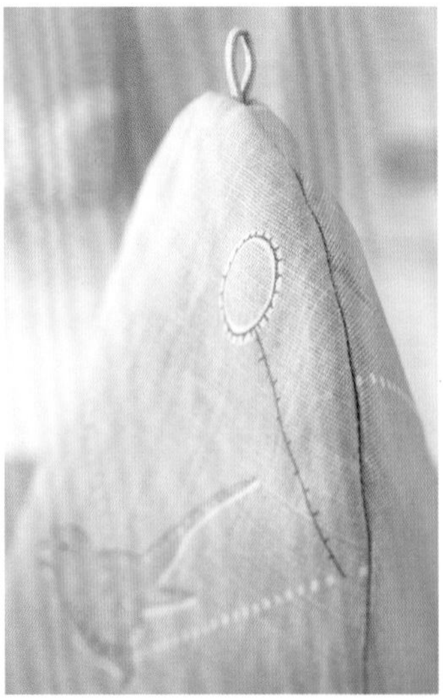

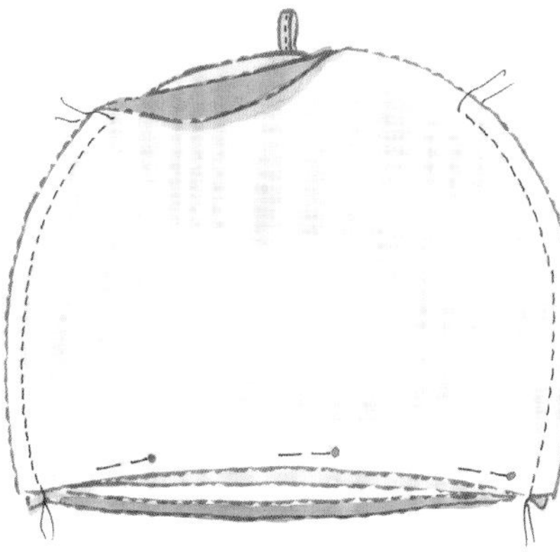

3 With right sides together, pin the lining front to the lining back around the curved edge. Machine-stitch a ⅝in (1.5cm) seam, leaving an 8in (20cm) opening along the top; press. With the lining wrong side out, place it over the tea cozy, so the right sides of the main fabric and lining are together. Pin around the bottom edge of the front and the back, and machine-stitch a ⅝in (1.5cm) seam all the way around. Trim away the seam allowances of the batting.

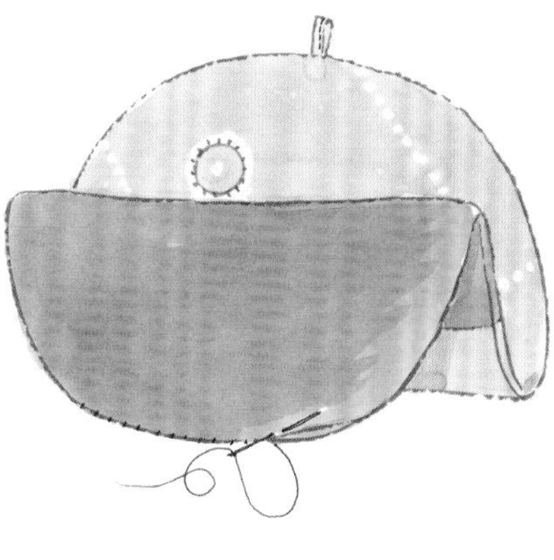

4 Turn the lining right side out and slipstitch (see page 185) the opening closed, then push the lining inside the cozy.

lampshade cover

A quick makeover for a bedroom lamp, this gathered lampshade fits over the original, so is ideal for updating a slightly old-fashioned or grubby cardstock shade. Keep the old one in place as you will need it to support the folds. I made this in Dandelion Trellis, in Cranberry and Stone, which is ideal for this project as the softness of the cotton falls easily into pleats all around. Once it's in place, gently tease the fabric down to evenly distribute the folds.

You will need

- Cotton decorator fabric—see below for yardage
- Matching sewing thread
- Narrow two-cord curtain heading tape—see below for yardage
- Plain lampshade

Estimating yardage

- Measure the depth of the lampshade (from the top of the shade to the bottom, with your tape measure on the shade) and the circumference around the base.
- For the fabric piece, allow for a piece the depth of the lampshade plus 6in (15cm) for hems, by the circumference multiplied by 1.5. If necessary, adjust the latter fabric dimension a little so that any pattern will match across the seam. (Adjusting it slightly will make the shade just a little looser or tighter.)
- For the curtain tape, allow enough to fit around the circumference, plus 4in (10cm).

TIP

When you fit the cover over the shade, hold it in place over the top and gently pull the folds down to arrange them evenly around the base. They will stay in soft folds as you arrange them.

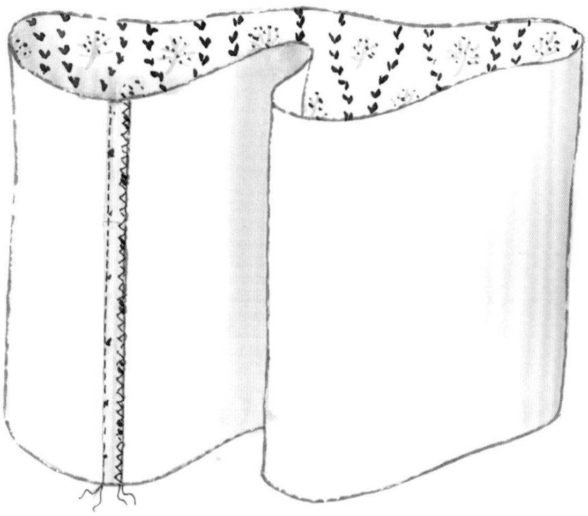

1 With right sides together, pin the short ends of the fabric together. Machine-stitch a ⅝in (1.5cm) seam, forming a fabric ring. Press the seam allowance to one side and zigzag-stitch the raw edges of the seam together.

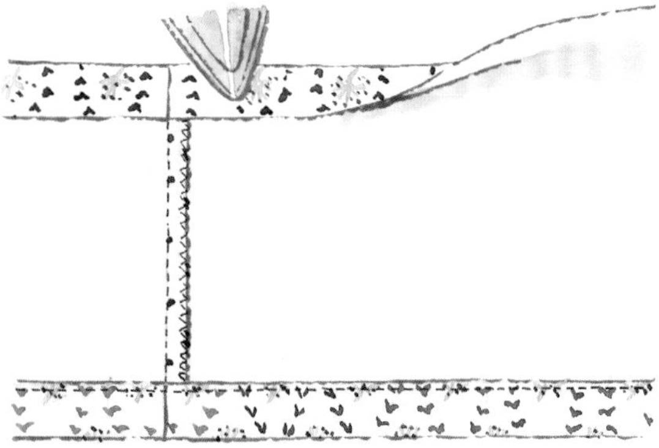

2 Along the lower edge of the ring, press ⅜in (1cm) and then a further 1½in (4cm) to the wrong side to form a hem. Machine-stitch close to the first folded edge. Along the top edge of the fabric, press 1½in (4cm) to the wrong side.

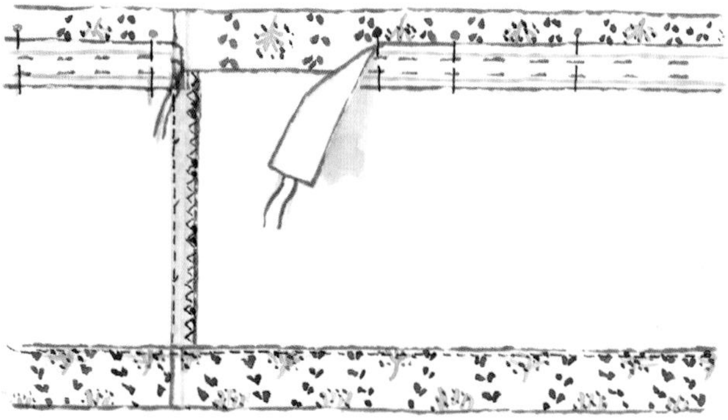

3 Starting and finishing at the side seam, pin the curtain heading tape to the top hem, with the tape covering the raw edge of the hem. The closer you put the tape to the top edge, the less of a ruffle effect there will be at the top. Machine-stitch the tape in place along its top and bottom edges.

4 Pull up the tape draw-cords and gather the fabric to fit the top of your lampshade. Tie the cords. Turn right side out and place on top of the lampshade.

ironing board cover

Ironing is not always the most popular household chore, but it has to be done, so make your ironing as pleasant as possible with this pretty ironing board cover. This one is made in Paisley Ground, in Limestone and Raspberry, and has a tape threaded through the edge that is pulled up to fit the board. Fit it over a padded cover to provide plenty of softness underneath.

You will need

- Linen or linen union fabric—see below for yardage
- Matching sewing thread
- Thin cotton batting (wadding)
- 3yd (3m) of 2in- (5cm-) wide ready-made bias binding
- 4yd (4m) of ¼in- (5mm-) wide cotton tape
- Paper for pattern
- Bodkin or safety pin

Estimating yardage

- Use your paper pattern (see step 1) to calculate the amount of fabric you need. Allow for one piece in the fabric and one piece in the batting.

1 Make a pattern by tracing the shape of your ironing board onto paper and adding 1⅜in (3.5cm) all around; cut out the paper shape. Using the pattern, cut out one piece each from the fabric and the batting (wadding). Lay the fabric piece flat, wrong side up, and place the batting on top, with the edges even. Pin and baste the batting to the fabric around the edges.

2 Open out the folds on the edge at one end of the bias binding and press ⅜in (1cm) to the wrong side at the end. With the right side of the binding against the batting, and starting at the center of one end of the cover, pin the binding around the edge of the cover, opening out the binding as you go and pinning the opened-out press line 1in (2.5cm) from the edge of the cover. To finish, cut off the working end of the binding, leaving ⅜in (1cm) extra. Fold the end to the wrong side by this amount, and pin in place with the two folded ends of the binding butting together.

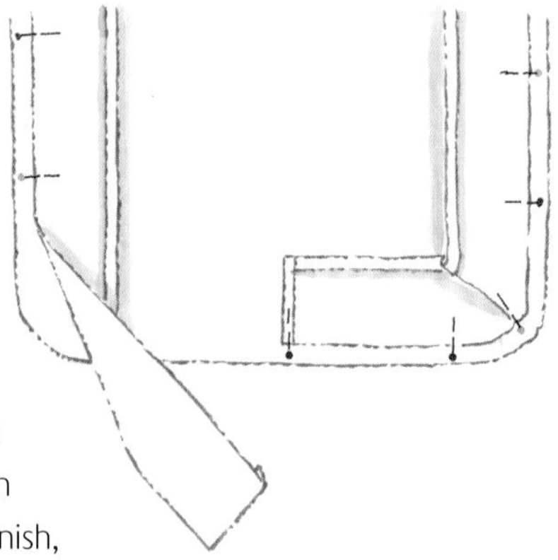

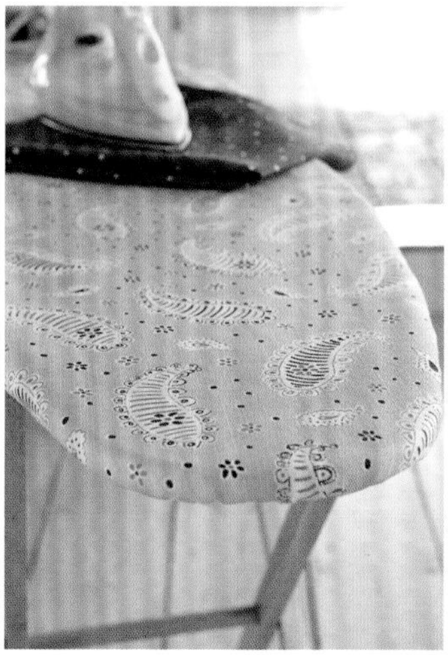

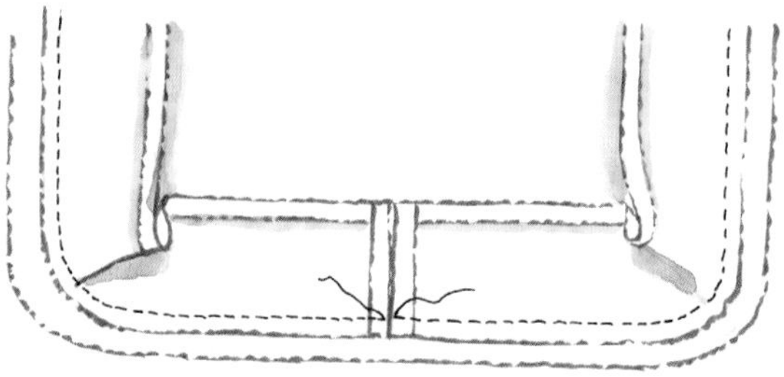

3 Machine-stitch the binding in place all around the outer edge, stitching along the opened-out binding press-line.

4 Press the binding over to the right side of the cover, aligning the folded edge of the binding with the stitching line. Pin and baste the folded edge of the binding to the right side of the cover all around the machine-stitched line.

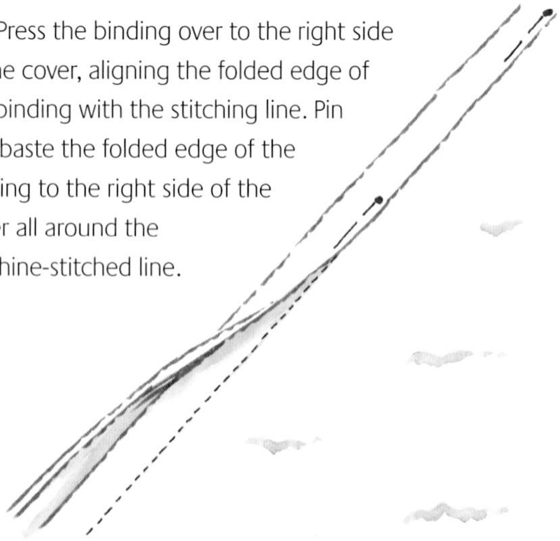

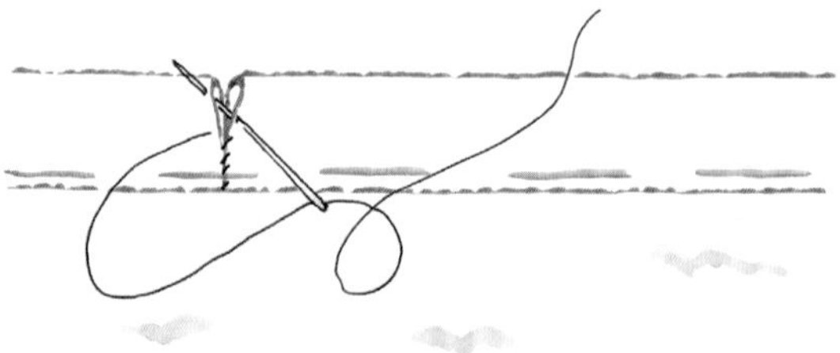

5 Working from the wrong side of the cover, use overhand stitch (see page 186) to join the ends of the binding together up to the folded edge only. Machine-stitch the binding in place, then remove the basting stitches.

6 Thread one end of the cotton tape into a bodkin or attach it to one end of a safety pin. Thread the tape through the opening in the bias binding, through the casing, and back out through the opening, leaving approximately 8in (20cm) of tape showing at each end. Place the cover over the ironing board and pull up the tape so the cover folds underneath and fits tightly. Tie the tapes into a double bow and tuck the ends underneath the edges of the cover.

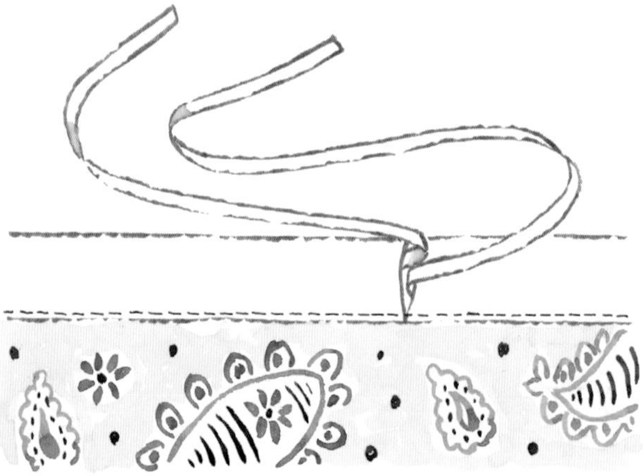

gathered sink skirt

I am so pleased with this combination of fabrics from the Swedish Collection. The skirt is made from Stockholm Stripe, in Clay and Sweet Pea, and the ruffle from Pretty Maids, in Sweet Pea. The skirt hides the ugly plumbing under the large sink and also creates a storage space for spare soap and towels. In our house, the window sill is a lovely sunny spot for flowers and plants, which bring wonderful colors and scents to the room.

You will need

- Main decorator fabric—see below for estimating yardage
- Contrast decorator fabric—see below for estimating yardage
- Matching sewing thread
- Curtain hardware—vinyl-coated wires, hooks, and eyes
- Wire cutters

Estimating yardage

- For the depth of the skirt, measure from the floor to the required height on the sink, and add 2½in (6.5cm) for hem and seam allowances.
- For the width of the skirt, measure the sink from the back wall on one side, around the front, and to the back wall on the other side, and multiply this measurement by two. You may need to join lengths to achieve the required width (see page 188).
- For the contrast-fabric ruffle, allow for a ruffle piece the same width as calculated for the main fabric, by 6⅜in (16.5cm) deep. This will produced a finished ruffle that is 2½in (6.5cm) deep. You may need to join lengths to achieve the required width (see page 188).

TIP

Before installing the hooks in the wall, you may need to attach small blocks of wood to ensure a stronger hold.

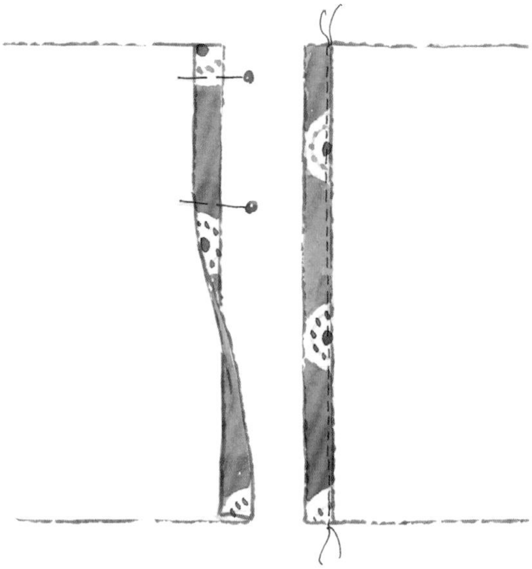

1 From the main and contrast fabrics cut out the required pieces. Join fabric lengths, if necessary, to achieve the required widths (see page 188). Press a double-fold ⅜in (1cm) hem to the wrong side along the two short side edges of the contrast piece. Pin and machine-stitch the hems in place. Repeat along both side edges of the main-fabric panel.

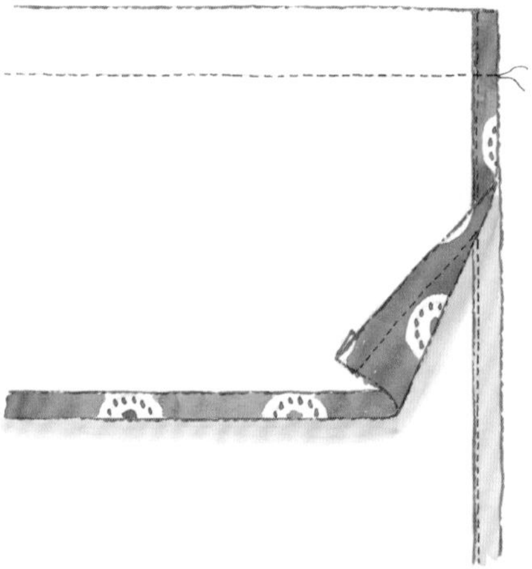

2 On one raw long edge of the contrast ruffle piece, press ⅜in (1cm) to the wrong side. With the right side of the ruffle piece to the wrong side of the skirt, pin the other long edge of the contrast ruffle to the top edge of the panel, with raw edges even and matching the hemmed side edges. Machine-stitch a 1in (2.5cm) seam.

TIP

If the edges of your sink or basin slope down, you'll have difficulty holding the skirt in place. In addition to the wire and screw eyes, use small lengths of hook-and-loop tape, sticking the hook side of the tape to the front edges of the sink and hand-sewing the loop side to the wrong side of the gathered skirt top casing. Attach the skirt to the hooks and press the two sides of the tape together.

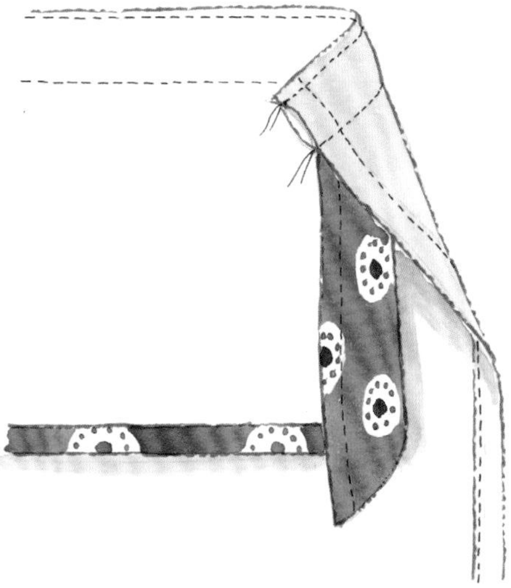

3 Now stitch again, ¼in (5mm) from the raw edges, forming a ¾in- (2cm-) wide casing within the seam allowance.

4 Fold the contrast ruffle piece over to the right side of the skirt, and pin the pressed-under edge along the seam line. Slipstitch in place (see page 185) from the right side. Press the top fold. Slipstitch the ends of the ruffle closed above the casing.

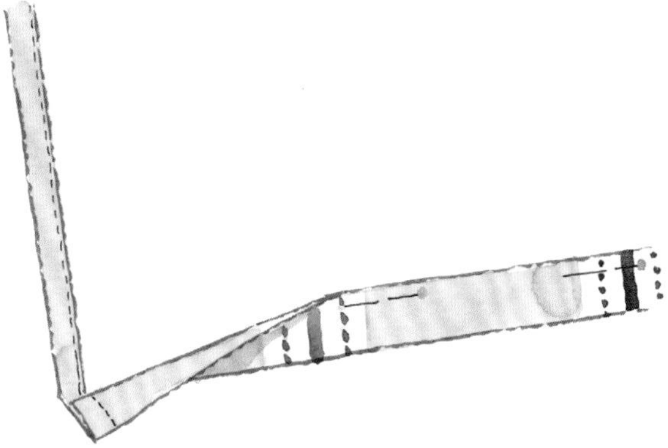

5 Press a double-fold ¾in (2cm) hem to the wrong side along the lower edge of the main panel, pin, and machine-stitch in place.

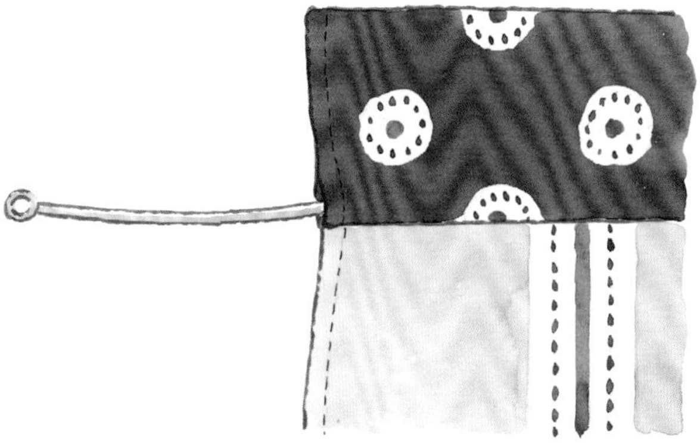

6 Install the hooks into the wall on either side of the sink at the required height. Attach a screw eye to one end of the wire and hook it onto one of the hooks. Pull the wire so that it stretches tightly around the sink and cut it to fit. Fix another screw eye into the cut end of the wire. Thread the wire through the casing at the top of the panel and gather it up to fit. Place the eyes over the hooks, stretching the wire as before.

drawstring bag

There is something enlivening about the colors and prints in the Swedish Collection, and they lend themselves very well indeed to making small things. These simple drawstring bags help keep the bathroom tidy, and each member of my family has one for their bits and pieces. These are all made from my Stockholm Stripe design in three different colorways.

You will need

- Decorator fabric—see below for yardage
- Matching sewing thread
- 1⅓yd (120cm) cotton cord

Estimating yardage

- For the decorator fabric, allow for a front and a back, each measuring 16in (41cm) wide by 24in (61cm) deep, plus a casing strip measuring 30¼in (78cm) wide by 2in (5cm) deep.

TIP

To thread the cord through the top casing, attach the end of the cord to a large safety pin. Close the pin and push it into an opening in the casing. Gathering the fabric in your hand, and smoothing it as the safety pin moves through, push the safety pin through the casing until it reappears at the opening. Pull the cord through until the two ends are a matching length, before tying the ends together.

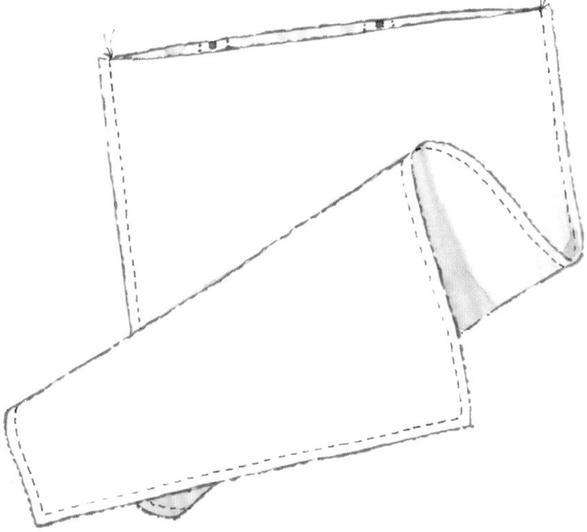

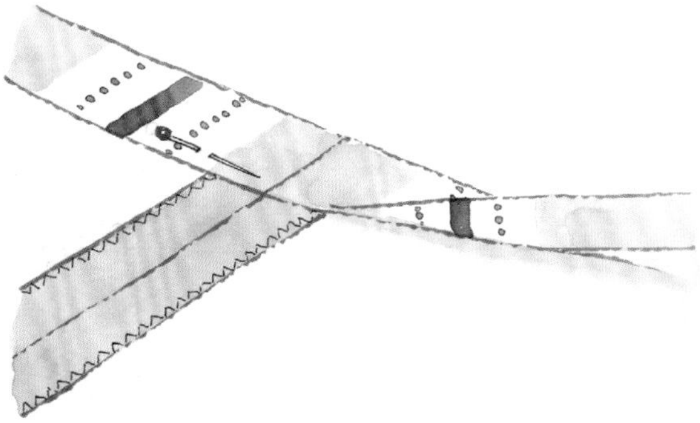

1 From the fabric, cut out one front, one back, and one casing strip. With right sides together, pin the front to the back along the two side edges and the bottom edge. Machine-stitch a ⅝in (1.5cm) seam. Zigzag-stitch the seam allowances individually and press the seam open. Turn the bag right side out, and press.

2 Press ⅜in (1cm) and then a further 1in (2.5cm) to the wrong side around the top edge of the bag; pin in place. Machine-stitch close to the first pressed edge.

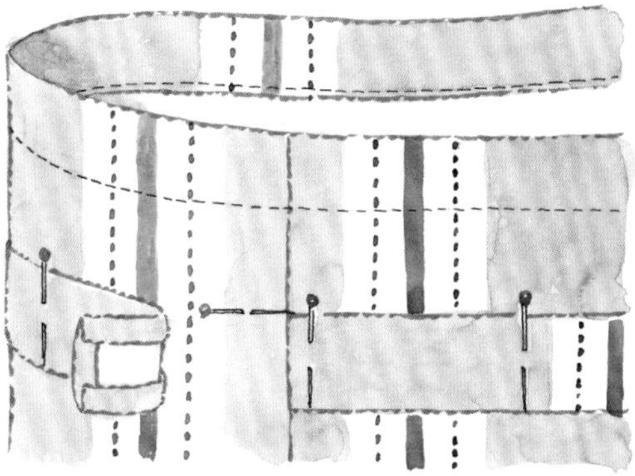

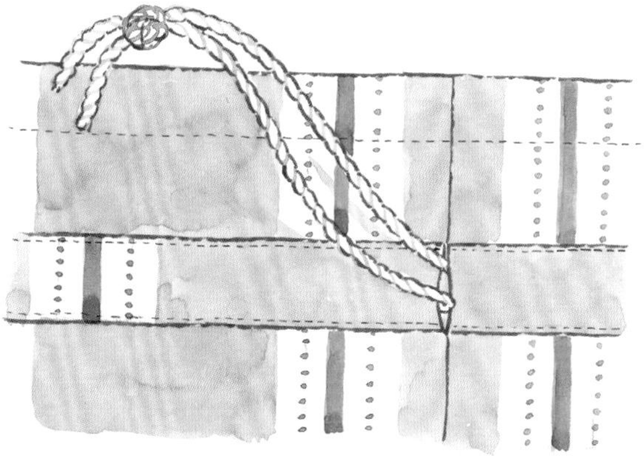

3 Using pins for markers, mark points 2in (5cm) down from the top edge of the bag, all the way around. Press ⅜in (1cm) to the wrong side on both ends of the casing strip and then on both long edges. With the wrong side of the strip to the right side of the bag, pin the strip around the bag, starting and finishing at a side seam and lining up the top edge with the pins. Stitch in place close to both long edges of the strip, leaving the ends open, to form a casing.

4 Attach a safety pin to the cord and thread it through the stitched channel around the top of the bag and knot the ends securely together.

clothespin bag

I hang my clothespin bag on the washing line every dry day when I hang out the laundry in the garden to dry. It helps me save money (and the environment) by foregoing the tumble dryer. Instead I have fresh-smelling clothes and linen that remain wrinkle-free.

You will need

- Decorator fabric—see right for yardage
- Matching sewing thread
- Child's wooden coat hanger
- Paper for patterns
- Template (see page 221)

Estimating yardage

- Use your paper patterns (see step 1) to calculate the amount of fabric you need. Allow for two top fronts, two bottom fronts, and two backs.
- You will also need a 6 x 1½in (15 x 4cm) fabric strip (cut on the bias) for covering the hook, and a 19 x 1in (48 x 2.5cm) fabric strip (cut on the straight grain) for the bow.

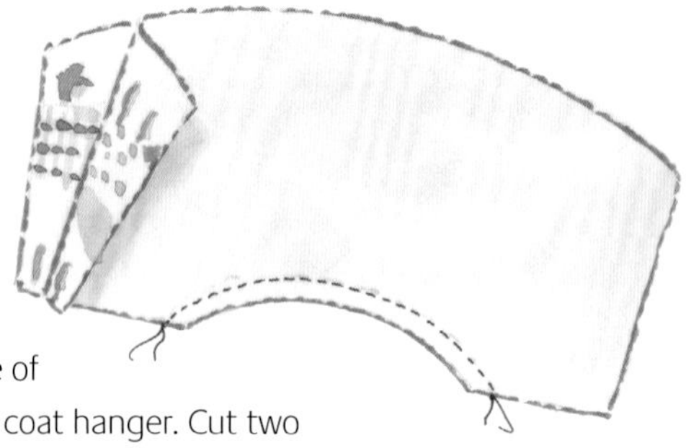

1 Enlarge the template on page 221 to make paper patterns for the back, top front, and bottom front. A ⅝in (1.5cm) seam allowance is included in the template, but you may need to adjust the size of the template to make it fit your coat hanger. Cut two fabric pieces from each of the three pattern pieces; one of each will be used for the lining. With right sides together, pin the two top-front pieces together along the curve at their bottom edge. Stitch a ⅝in (1.5cm) seam. Trim the seam allowance, turn right side out, and press.

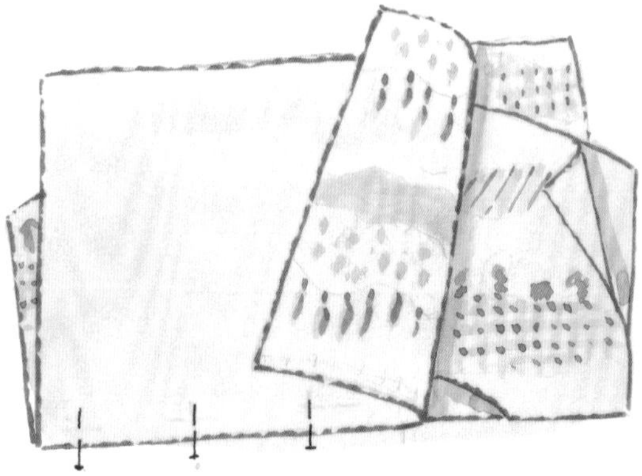

2 Lay one bottom-front piece (which will be the lining) right side up on your work surface. Place the top front right side up on top of it and the remaining bottom-front piece wrong side up on top of that. Pin together along the edge as shown. Machine-stitch a ⅝in (1.5cm) seam through all layers.

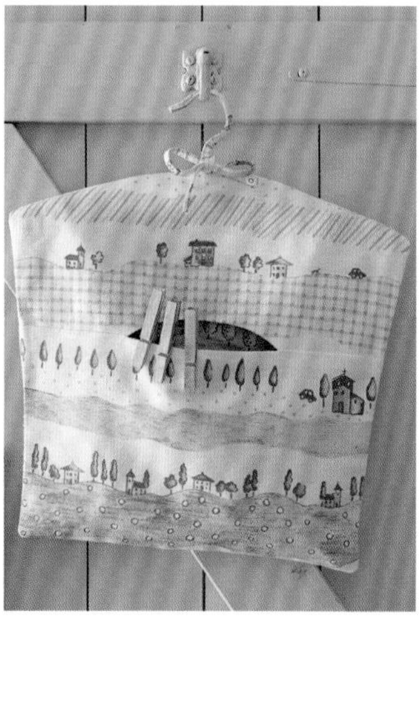

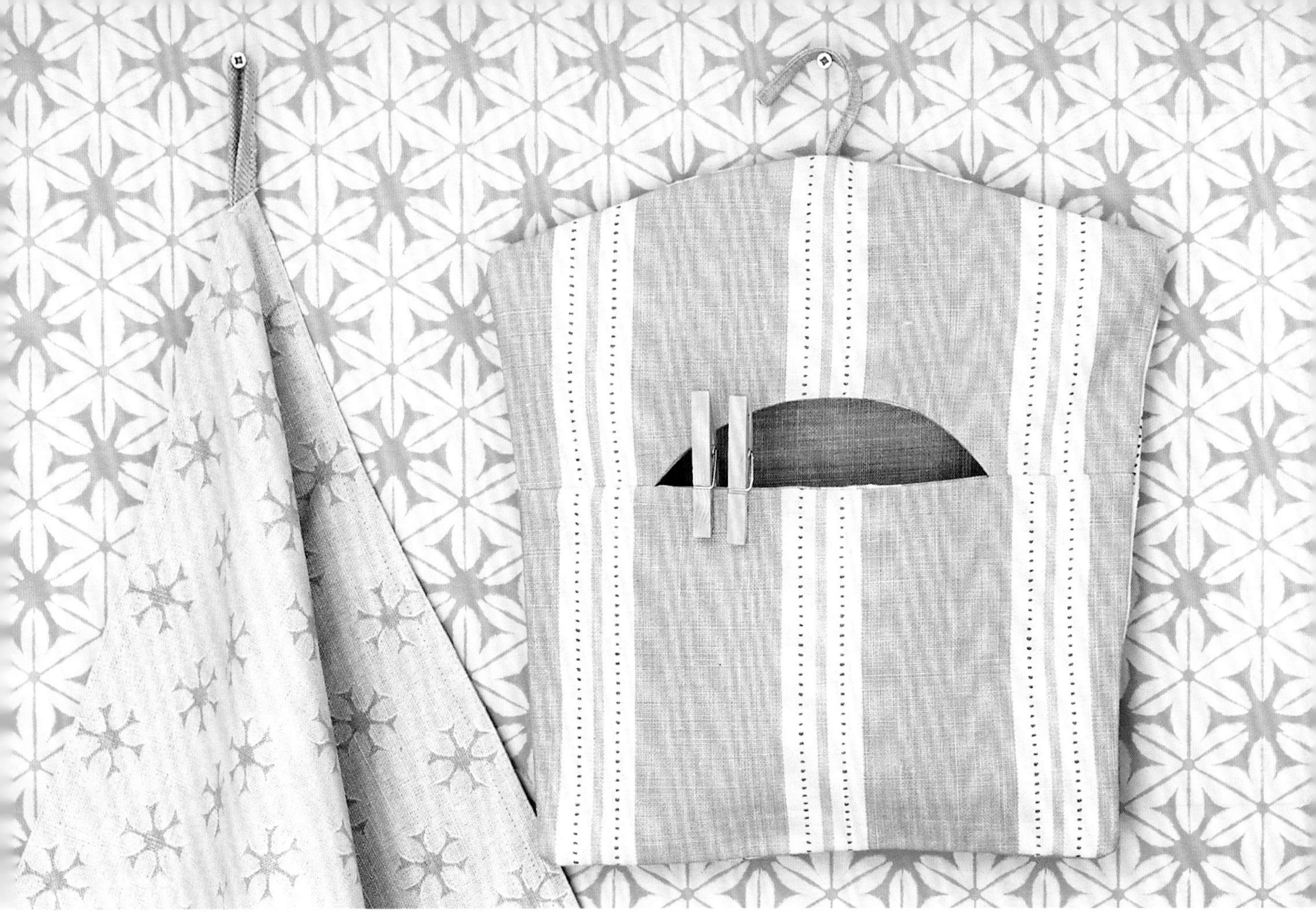

3 Turn the front right side out and press. Lay it, lining side down, on your work surface. Place one back piece, wrong side up, on top of it. Place the other back piece (which will be the lining) right side up on top. Pin all around the edge. Machine-stitch a ⅝in (1.5cm) seam, leaving a gap of about ¾in (2cm) at the center top for the hook.

4 Turn right side out through the opening in the front. Cut a 6 x 1½in (15 x 4cm) fabric strip on the bias and make a cover for the hook, as for the Padded Coat Hanger, step 3 (see page 169). Insert the covered coat hanger into the bag. Cut a 19 x 1in (48 x 2.5cm) strip on the straight grain and make a tie following method 1 (see page 202), finishing both ends. Tie this in a bow around the covered hook.

hot water bottle cover

No matter how much we rely on central heating, we still need a hotty to take with us at bedtime in this house. Pretty Maids, with its small, all-over polka-dot repeat, is a really good choice for a hot water bottle cover, and having a contrast lining means you can use two colors. I chose Lime, Teal, and Winter for the outside, and lined it with the same design in Winter.

You will need

- Main decorator fabric—see below for yardage
- Contrast decorator fabric—see below for yardage
- Matching sewing thread
- Paper for making pattern

Estimating yardage

- For the main fabric, make a paper pattern following step 1. Allow for two pieces. Also allow for four ties measuring 1½ x 10in (4 x 25cm).
- For the contrast fabric, allow for two pieces the same size as the main-fabric pieces.

1 To make a pattern, draw around the hot water bottle onto paper and add ¾in (2cm) all around, for a seam allowance and so it will fit inside easily. Because of the thickness of the stopper, add an extra ¼in (5mm) to each side at the throat. Fold the shape in half and cut out the pattern from the folded paper to create a symmetrical shape. Open the pattern out flat and check that it still fits. Using the pattern, cut two pieces from the main fabric for the outer cover and two from the contrast fabric for the lining.

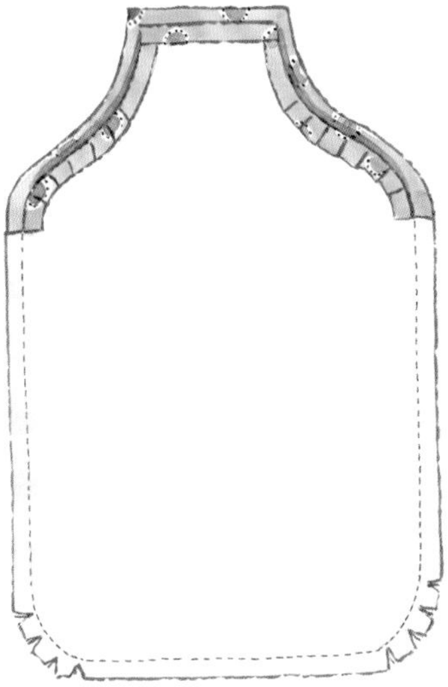

2 With right sides together, pin the two outer-cover pieces together around the side and lower edges. Machine-stitch a ⅜in (1cm) seam, leaving the shaped edges at the top open. Clip into the seam allowance on the curves around the lower stitched edge. Press under ⅜in (1cm) on the unstitched edge of both the front and the back part of the cover. Clip into the pressed-under seam allowances, taking care not to clip beyond the pressed crease. Repeat this step for the lining pieces.

3 Turn the outer cover right side out, but leave the lining wrong side out. Put the lining inside the outer cover, wrong sides together, with the side seams and the top pressed edges even. Pin the top edges of the outer cover and the lining cover together at both the front and the back.

4 Cut out four 1½ x 10in (4 x 25cm) tie pieces from the main fabric, and make up the ties using method 1 (see page 202), finishing one end of each. At the neck of the cover, insert the unfinished ends of the ties between the outer cover and lining, positioning two on the front (one at each side) and the other two opposite them on the back. Baste in place. Slipstitch the top pressed edges of the cover together (see page 185), catching in the ties at the same time. Remove the basting.

lavender heart

These pretty and useful lavender bags can be made from the tiniest scraps. They are perfect for tucking into a drawer to keep your linen smelling sweet, or they could be trimmed with ribbon loops and hung from a coat hanger, such as the ones on page 168. If you grow lavender in your garden as we do, harvest it on a hot day and dry the heads upside down in a paper bag before shaking it and collecting the flowers. I had scraps of Four Seasons, in Sea Pink and Olive, and also Lazy Daisy, in Cranberry and Sea Pink, left over from making pillows and placed the motifs in a central position on the hearts.

You will need

- Main fabric—see below for yardage
- Lining fabric—see below for yardage
- Matching sewing thread
- Paper for patterns
- Dried lavender flowers, feathers, fiberfill stuffing, or other stuffing of your choice
- Snaps

Estimating yardage

- Make paper patterns for the front piece and two back pieces (see steps 1 and 3) and allow for one piece of main fabric ⅝in (1.5cm) larger all around than the pattern for each of the three pieces.
- For the lining, allow for two pieces of lining fabric the same size as the front pattern.

1 Decide on the desired size of your heart pillow, ideally a little wider than it is high so the heart is nice and fat. Cut a rectangle of paper ½in (1cm) less than the desired finished width and depth measurements. Fold it in half vertically, draw half a heart shape all the way to the edges of the paper, and cut out through both layers. Open out the heart pattern and use this to cut out two pieces from the lining fabric.

2 With right sides together, pin the two lining-fabric hearts together around the edges. Machine-stitch a ⅜in (1cm) seam, leaving a 4in (10cm) gap on one side. Trim the corners and clip into the seam allowance on the curves, then turn right side out. Fill with the stuffing of your choice, using the handle of a wooden spoon to pack the stuffing in if necessary. If including dried lavender flowers, pour them in using a funnel. Turn in the seam allowances on the opening and slipstitch them together (see page 185).

3 Use the pattern to cut from the main fabric one piece ⅝in (1.5cm) larger all around than the pattern. Now draw a line on the pattern 1in (2.5cm) from the center fold. Fold the pattern to the line and cut two back pieces from the main fabric, each ⅝in (1.5cm) larger all around than the pattern.

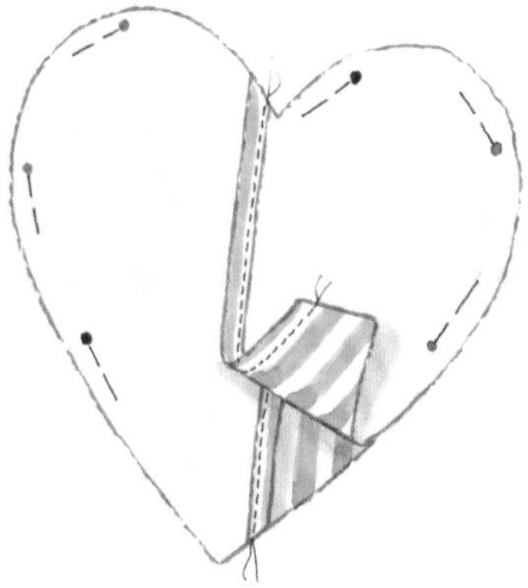

4 Press under and machine-stitch a narrow double hem on the raw straight edge of each back piece. Pin the back pieces to the front piece, right sides together and raw edges even, with the hemmed straight edges overlapping. Machine-stitch a ⅜in (1cm) seam all around the outside edge. Snip off the corners and clip the curves of the seam allowances. Turn the cover right side out and press. Sew snaps along the opening, and insert the stuffing.

TIP

If you wish, you could scale up the heart to make a larger pillow for the bed. Fill it with a fragrant mixture of dried lavender and dried hops, both of which are reputed to have sleep-inducing qualities.

padded coat hanger

This is another creative way of using up leftover fabrics. Rather than throwing scraps away, why not spend a rainy afternoon making some covered coat hangers? They come in handy for hanging up small, lightweight clothes with thin straps that tend to slide off conventional wooden hangers. These two are made from my small polka-dot print, Pretty Maids.

You will need

- Decorator fabric—see below for yardage
- Batting (wadding)
- Matching sewing thread
- Wooden coat hanger
- Paper for pattern
- Template (see page 222)

Estimating yardage

- Use your paper pattern (see step 1) to calculate the amount of main fabric you need. Allow for one piece for each coat hanger.
- Also allow for a 6 x 1½in (15 x 4cm) fabric strip (cut on the bias) to cover the hook.

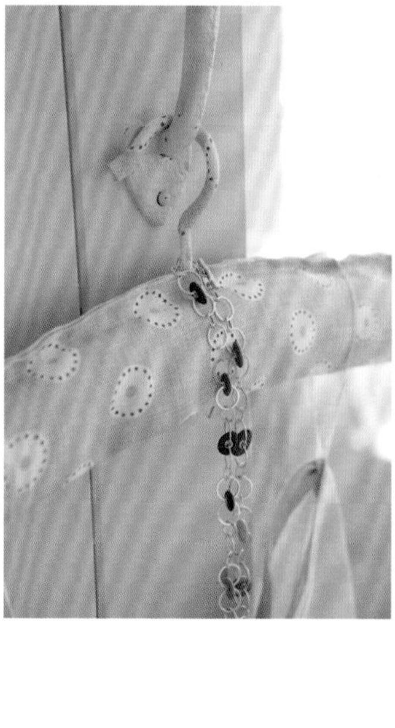

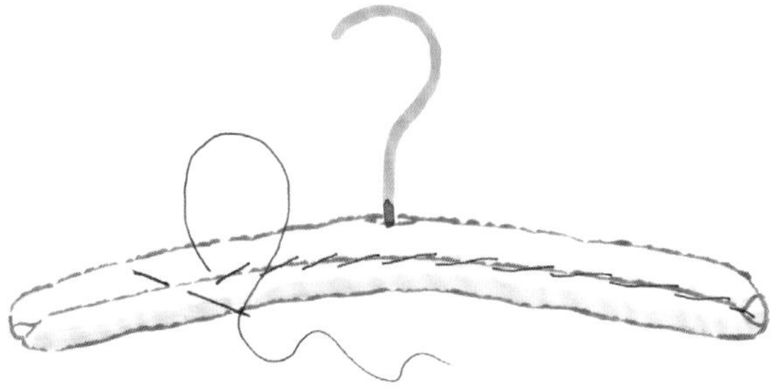

1 Cover the coat hanger with batting (wadding), hand-sewing it securely in place, and trim off any excess. Enlarge the template on page 222 to make a paper pattern for the fabric cover. A ⅜in (1cm) seam allowance all around is included in the template, but you may need to adjust the size of the pattern to make it fit your padded coat hanger. Use the pattern to cut out one shape from the fabric.

2 Press ⅜in (1cm) to the wrong side all around the fabric cover. Snip into the seam allowance on the curves. Lay the cover wrong side up on the work surface, and place the padded coat hanger on the top half. Fold up the bottom half to cover the hanger. Pin in place.

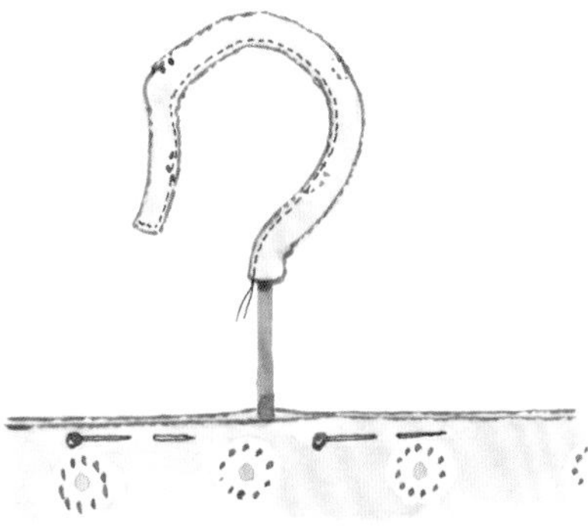

3 Cut a 6 x 1½in (15 x 4cm) strip of fabric on the bias. Make it up using Ties, method 1 (see page 202), finishing just one end. Slide this tube over the hook from the open end, and insert the open end into the top edge of the cover.

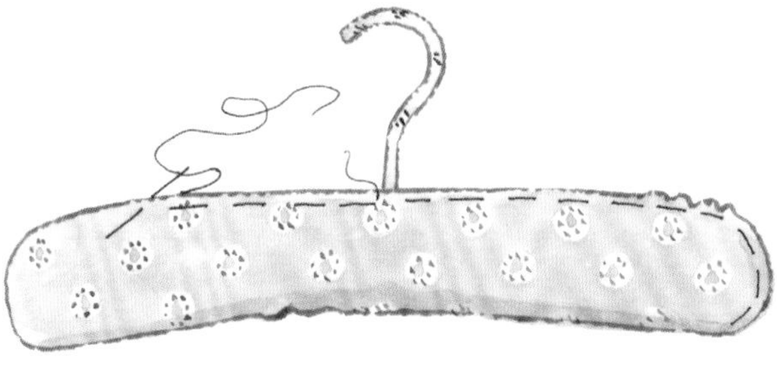

4 Using double thread, work a row of large running stitches (see page 185) along the top of the hanger, starting at the center and securing the fabric covering the hook at the same time. Work outward from the center on each side, gathering the fabric slightly as you go. Secure the thread at each end.

simple shopper

I made this shopper very quickly but have found it really useful. It saves using plastic carrier bags, and is washable too. I used Butterfly Dance fabric here and think it looks lovely. It is really very easy to make, so this is a good project for a novice. Why not make one for yourself and a second one for a friend? Anything that helps to save the planet!

You will need

- Decorator fabric—see below for yardage
- Matching sewing thread

Estimating yardage

- Decide on the size of the bag, and add 1¼in (3cm) to the width for seams, and 2⅝in (6.5cm) to the height for seams and hems. Allow for two pieces of this size—one for the front and one for the back.
- Allow additional fabric for the two handles, each of which is cut to 27 x 3in (68.5 x 8cm).

TIP

The seams might have to take a lot of strain, so, if you wish, reinforce them with extra lines of stitching.

1 From the fabric, cut out one front and one back, and two 27 x 3in (68.5 x 8cm) strips for the handles. With right sides together, pin the front to the back around the side and bottom edges. Machine-stitch a ⅝in (1.5cm) seam. Zigzag-stitch the seam allowances together, turn the bag right side out, and press. Press a double 1in (2.5cm) hem to the wrong side around the top edge of the bag. Pin in place.

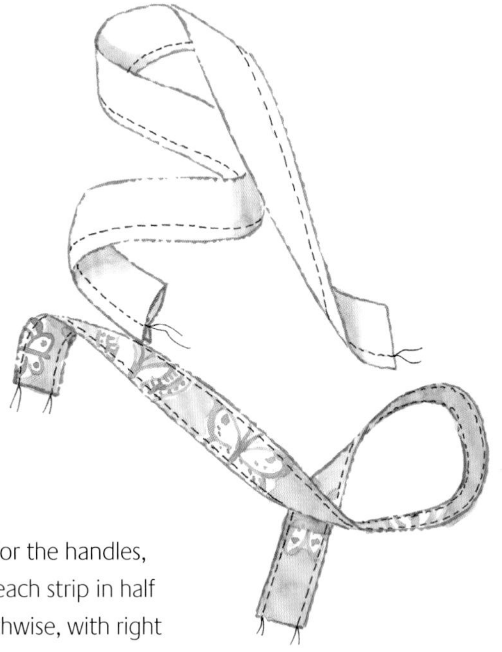

2 For the handles, fold each strip in half lengthwise, with right sides together. Pin and stitch the long edges (but not the ends) with a ⅜in (1cm) seam. Trim the seam allowances on the long edges to ¼in (5mm). Turn each strip right side out and press flat, with the seam running exactly along the pressed edge. Machine-stitch close to both long edges of each handle.

3 Using pins, mark the handle positions on the bag's top hem, 3in (7.5cm) in from the side seams on both the bag front and back. Press under ⅝in (1.5cm) on both ends of each handle. Slip one end of one handle under the loose hem edge at the marked point on the bag front, with the pressed fold on the handle aligning with the bag's hem. Pin in place. Pin the other end of the handle at the other marked point on the front, making sure the handle isn't twisted. Pin the remaining handle to the back in the same way. Machine-stitch around the bottom edge of the hem, anchoring the handles at the same time.

4 Now fold the handles upward so they extend beyond the top of the bag, and stitch around the top of the bag again, very close to the top edge.

kitchen apron

You'll really brighten up your kitchen when you make an apron in Up The Garden Path, especially if you choose Sweet Pea as I did. The linen fabric makes it a sturdy cook's apron, and it has a usefully large pocket to keep the odd wooden spoon close at hand. But, you never know, it looks so good you may just want to leave it hanging on the cupboard just to add a splash of color to your kitchen.

You will need

- Cotton print fabric—see below for yardage
- Contrast cotton fabric—see below for yardage
- Matching sewing thread
- 2¾yd (2.5m) of 1½in- (4cm-) wide white cotton webbing
- Paper for patterns

Estimating yardage

- Use your paper patterns (see step 1) to calculate the amount of main fabric you need. Allow for one apron piece in the main fabric and one pocket piece in the contrast fabric.

1 Use your favorite apron to make paper patterns for the apron and pocket. To ensure the apron pattern is symmetrical, fold the apron and the paper in half lengthwise, place the apron fold on the paper fold, and draw around the edge. Add ¾in (2cm) all around the outside for hems, then cut through both layers of paper and unfold. Also cut out a pattern for the pocket, adding 1⅛in (3cm) to the depth and ¾in (2cm) to the width for hems. Using the patterns, cut out one apron piece from the main fabric and one pocket piece from the contrast fabric.

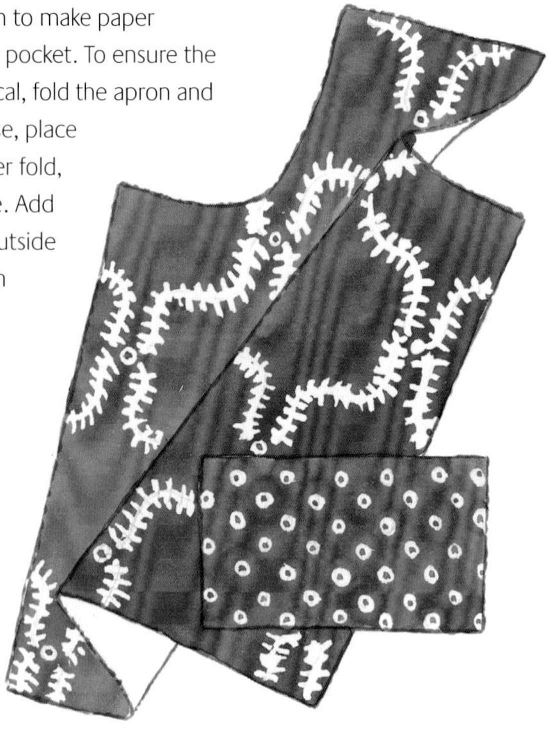

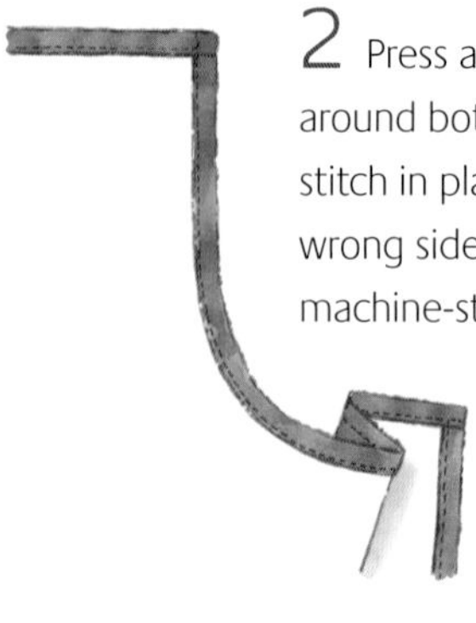

2 Press a double-fold ⅜in (1cm) hem to the wrong side around both curved edges of the apron front and machine-stitch in place. Press a double-fold ⅜in (1cm) hem to the wrong side along the remaining edges of the apron front; machine-stitch in place.

MATCHSTICK
Campbell's
ROYAL

3 Press a double-fold ⅜in (1cm) hem to the wrong side along the top edge of the pocket; pin and machine-stitch in place. Now press ⅜in (1cm) to the wrong side around the remaining edges of the pocket.

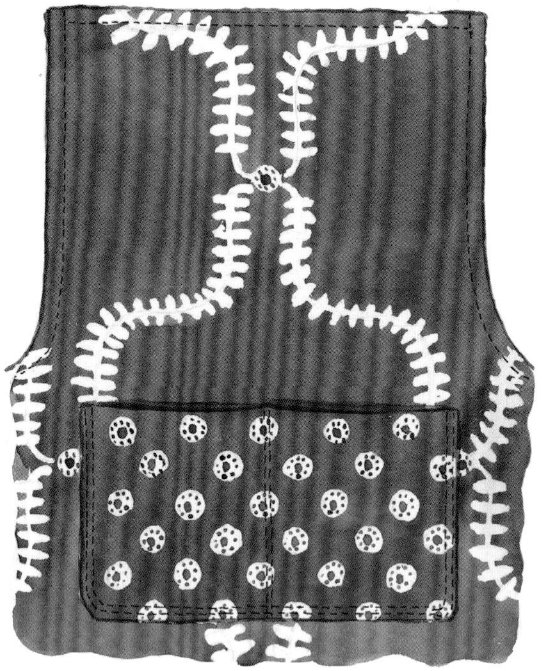

4 With right sides up, center the pocket between the side edges of the apron. The pocket should be parallel to the lower edge and in the same position as on the original apron. Pin in place. Machine-stitch close to the edge along the sides and bottom of the pocket, and then again ¼in (5mm) inside the first stitching. Stitch vertically down the center of the pocket with two rows of stitching ¼in (5mm) apart, to divide the pocket in two.

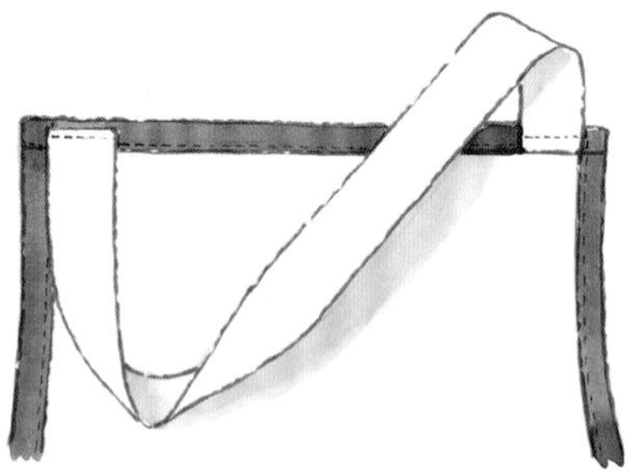

5 For the neck loop, cut a 22½in (57cm) length of cotton webbing. Place one cut end on the wrong side of the apron, even with the top hemmed edge and ⅜in (1cm) in from one curved edge. Stitch it in place following the hem stitching line. Now fold the webbing upward so it extends above the apron, and stitch across it again, close to the top edge of the apron. Repeat with the other end of the webbing at the opposite side, being careful not to twist the webbing.

6 For the waist ties, cut the remaining webbing into two equal lengths. Attach one end of each length to the top of the straight side edges in the same way as for the neck loop in step 5.

beanbag seat

This beanbag chair is a good, plump seat for drawing up to the fire, and children and teenagers will love it. To make it totally robust, I made this one in Plain Linen Union, in Charcoal—a good color for not showing the dirt. It's bound to spend much of its time rolling about the floor, so, if you wish, reinforce the seams with a couple of rows of stitching to stop them splitting.

You will need

- Decorator fabric—see below for yardage
- Unbleached muslin fabric—the same quantity as the decorator fabric
- Matching sewing thread
- A zipper 3in (8cm) shorter than the diameter of the base
- Polystyrene pellets
- Paper for making a pattern
- Twine
- Plastic push pin or brass thumbtack (drawing pin)

Estimating yardage

- Decide on the diameter (width) and height of your beanbag seat.
- For the top, allow for one square of decorator fabric, as long and as wide as the diameter, plus a ⅝in (1.5cm) seam allowance all around.
- For the base, allow for two semicircular pieces, each the size of half the top plus a ⅝in (1.5cm) seam allowance on the straight edge.
- For the sides, measure around the circumference of the top pattern piece, and allow for a rectangle of main fabric as long as the circumference measurement plus 1¼in (3cm) for seam allowances, by the finished height plus 1¼in (3cm) for seam allowances.

1 Make a paper pattern for the top and cut out one top piece from the decorator fabric, as described for the Circular Tablecloth, steps 1–3 (see page 120), but adding a ⅝in (1.5cm) seam allowance all around. Fold the top fabric piece in half and use it to cut out two semicircular base pieces from the decorator fabric, each the same size as the folded top except for an additional ⅝in (1.5cm) seam allowance on the straight edge. Also cut out one side piece from the decorator fabric to the calculated dimensions. Finally, cut out one top, two base pieces, and one side piece from the muslin to the same dimensions as the decorator fabric.

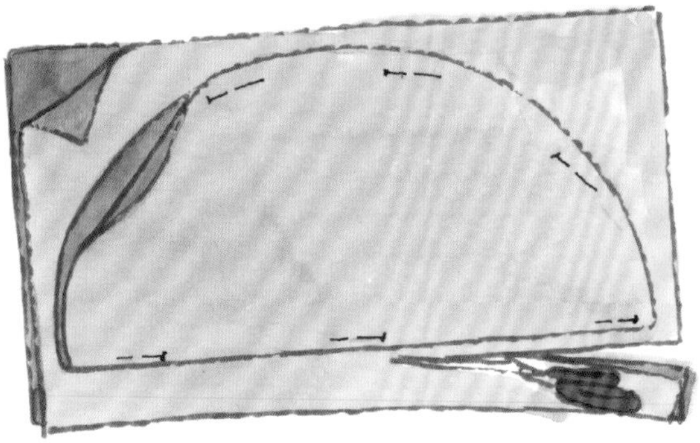

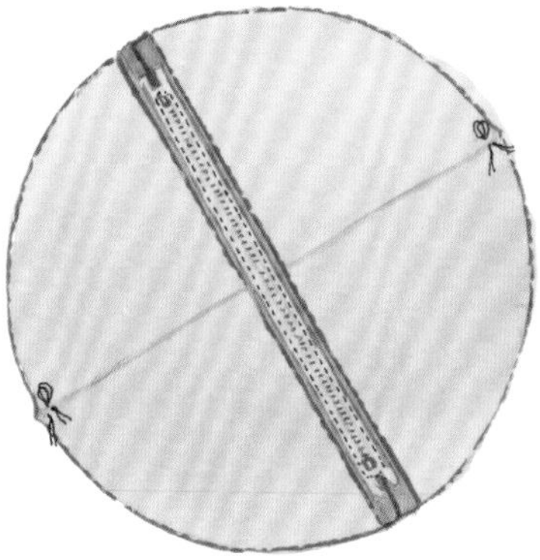

2 With right sides together, pin and baste the two base pieces together along the straight edge. Machine-stitch a ⅝in (1.5cm) seam for 1½in (4cm) at each end of the basted seam, leaving the center just basted. Press the seam open, and insert the zipper (see page 201). Remove all the basting stitches. Matching the seams, fold the base in half across the zipper, and sew a tailor's tack (see page 187) to mark the fold at each side.

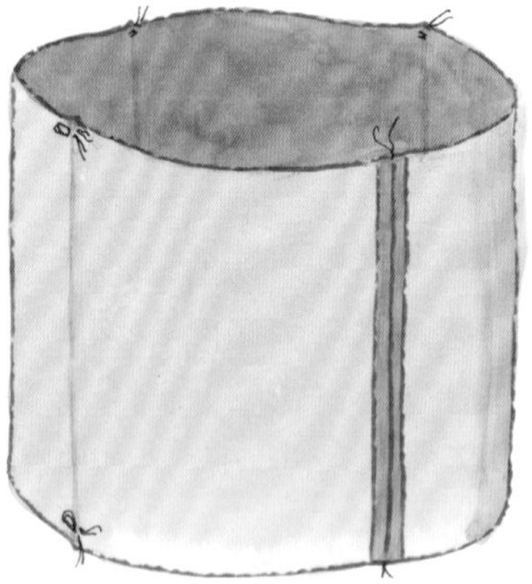

3 With right sides together, pin the ends of the side piece together to form a ring. Machine-stitch a ⅝in (1.5cm) seam. Press open the seam. Lay the side piece on a flat surface with its seam running down one edge. Mark the opposite fold with a tailor's tack on the bottom edge and another on the top edge. Refold the side piece, lining up the tailor's tacks with the seam, and mark the two new folds with tailor's tacks on the top and bottom edges.

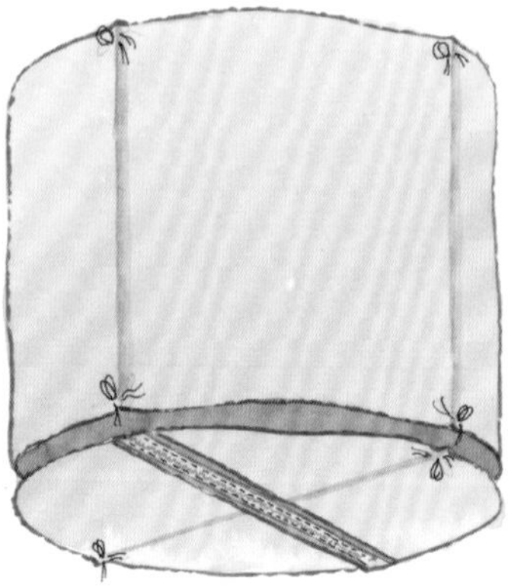

4 With right sides together, match the seam in the base to the lower end of the seam in the side piece, and match the other end of the seam in the base and the two tailor's tacks in the base to the three tailor's tacks on the lower edge of the side piece.

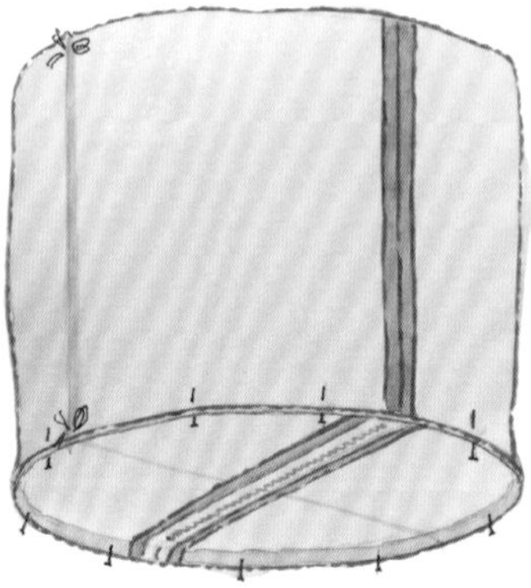

5 Pin the pieces together all around, placing the pins at right angles to the seam, and easing the fabric between the pins. Baste the pieces together, and then machine-stitch a ⅝in (1.5cm) seam.

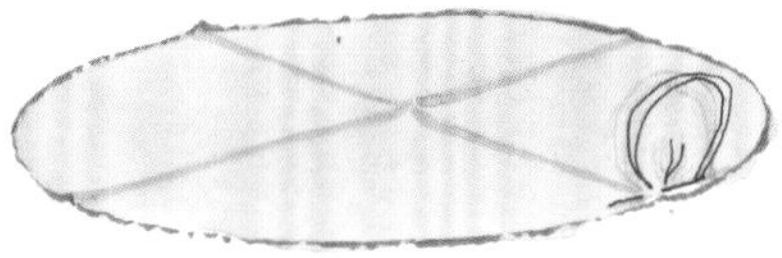

6 Fold the top piece in half and work two tailor's tacks opposite each other on the edge at the fold. Unfold and then fold the top piece the other way, lining up the tailor's tacks. Make two more tailor's tacks on the fold in the same way.

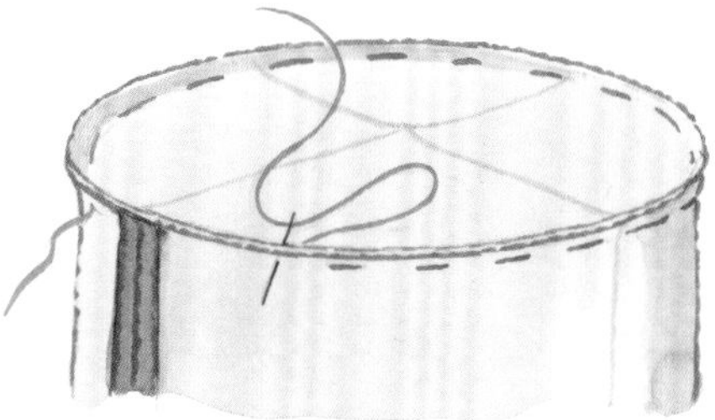

7 Open up the zipper. With right sides together and matching the three tailor's tacks and the seam on the side piece to the four tailor's tacks on the top piece, pin and baste the top to the sides. Machine-stitch a ⅝in (1.5cm) seam, as for the base. Turn the cover right side out, and press.

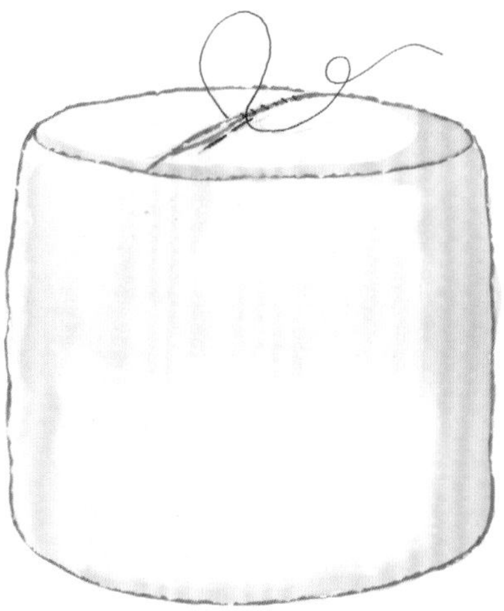

8 Make the inner shell as for the outer cover, but omitting the zipper. Remove some of the basting in the base seam and fill the shell with the polystyrene pellets through the opening until about three-quarters full. Firmly slipstitch the opening edges (see page 185). Push the muslin beanbag inside the outer cover through the zipper opening, lining up the top and base panels, and close the zipper.

TIP

Making the inner shell from unbleached muslin ensures that polystyrene pellets don't spill out, and the linen cover can be removed for cleaning. If the pellets become impacted over time and the bag begins to sag, carefully slit open a side seam in the shell and add more pellets. Slipstitch the seam to close.

chapter 6

basic techniques

choosing fabrics

Fabric choice is a matter of taste, but with so many decorator fabrics on the market today, it is difficult to know where to start. There are heavy linens, textured weaves, lustrous silks, thick velvets, fine sheers, and many more.

The real starting point for choosing any fabric is to make sure it is right for the job. Consider the wear and tear the final article will receive. Obviously seat cushions and slipcovers in busy living areas will get a lot of use, so they should be made in a fabric with a firm weave. Velvet, brocade, corduroy, and heavy-weight cotton are all suitable, while linen and linen-and-cotton blends, such as linen union, are the most hard-wearing fabrics available. For slipcovers, a medium-weight, firmly woven decorator fabric is best—avoid thick or very heavy material. Avoid rough textures, which will wear out more quickly and attract more dirt.

Accent pillows are not exposed to the same amount of wear, so you can use any type of fabric for these. They also use very little fabric, so you could perhaps choose a more expensive one than for, say, curtains.

I am a passionate advocate of organic cotton. Non-organic cotton is the world's dirtiest crop to grow, as it relies on the heavy use of pesticides which harm the cotton pickers and the environment. I use a unique cloth which combines organic cotton with eco-friendly linen.

Choose fabrics for tablecloths and bed covers that can take frequent washing, checking the fabric's care label before purchasing it. If there is no label attached to the end of the roll, ask a salesperson. If you are not sure, buy a small sample and do a laundry test (see page 212). If it doesn't hold up to the process, choose something else or resign yourself to dry-cleaning bills.

For curtains you need to consider how well the fabric will drape.

- Natural fibers include cotton, linen, wool, and silk. They are resistant to dirt but may shrink when washed. Cotton, linen, and silk will wrinkle, and silk is prone to fading and rotting in direct sunlight.
- Manmade fibers, such as acetate and rayon, have been regenerated from natural materials and chemically treated. They do not shrink and are easy-care and resistant to mold. Their silkiness, luster, and draping qualities make them a good substitute for silk.
- Synthetic fibers such as acrylic and polyester are stronger than natural fibers and will not shrink or crease, but they can attract dirt and never look as beautiful as natural fibers.
- Blends of fibers can give you the best of both worlds. For example, acrylic blended with cotton or wool gives a material that hangs well but resists sunrot. Linen blended with cotton, as in linen union, is hard-wearing and less prone to wrinkles.

If you want a soft, billowing look for your curtains, you could consider silk taffeta or a synthetic equivalent. Silks, satins, taffetas, and the various synthetic varieties possess excellent draping qualities and are available in a wide range of colors and patterns. However, natural silk is expensive and it can rot over time if exposed to strong sunlight, unless it is properly lined, so a look-alike may be a better choice.

Decorator fabrics are often given special finishes to make them look, feel, or perform better. Glazing is used to give chintz a sheen, and there are also finishes to improve resistance to sun, mildew, dirt, stains, wrinkles, or flames.

Pattern is, of course, another important factor. Do you want a traditional floral print such as a chintz, a modern abstract pattern, or perhaps a cozy check gingham? Or maybe you like stripes, which can vary from fine and delicate through ticking to wide and bold stripes. Don't forget to consider solid colors, too—these not only show off the texture to full advantage, but can look fabulous set off by a contrast border or piping.

Once you have made a preliminary selection, take several small samples home with you. When you have decided on your favorite, either borrow a large sample from the shop or invest in a large piece of it. Look at it in both natural and artificial light, and think about the size of any pattern repeats. Bear in mind that patterns can look totally different when viewed from a distance and also when pleated. For curtains, roughly pleat or gather up the sample and hang it in the window to see how it looks.

patterned fabrics

Patterns often have a direction, so think about which way a pattern will run. Striped fabric can be cut to run in different directions on, say, a box cushion or a pillow with panels to add graphic impact. For most projects, if fabrics have large motifs these will look best if centered. Be sure to allow extra yardage if you will need to do this.

Bear in mind that all patterns except very small prints should match across seams, and in pairs of curtains also across the leading (center) edges. When estimating yardage, allow one extra pattern repeat (the lengthwise distance from one point in a motif to the same point in the next, identical motif) for each length of fabric that you are joining, after the first. Matching large patterns on slipcovers can be quite difficult, so if you are not experienced at making slipcovers, it might be better to choose a very small pattern or a solid color instead. For the best method of matching patterns across seams, see page 184.

fabrics with a pile or nap

If a fabric has a pile (such as velvet or chenille) or a nap (such as flannel), bear in mind that all the pieces must run in the same direction. This is because the surface looks much richer one way up.

estimating yardage

To estimate the yardage for curtains and shades (blinds), see pages 204 and 208.

cutting out

You will need a large, flat, clean surface and a sharp pair of dressmakers' shears. Check for any fabric defects, and double-check all your calculations. Iron out any wrinkles in the fabric.

1 First "square" the fabric—ie, form a straight line across one end of the fabric at right angles to the selvage. With loosely woven fabrics, you can do this by pulling a crosswise thread from the weave of the fabric. For other fabric types, you will need to use a carpenter's square (set square), dressmakers' chalk, and a long ruler, to mark and cut the fabric at right angles to the selvage. If the pattern does not quite follow the straight grain, cut according to the pattern rather than the grain (though there should not be much difference between them).

2 Many fabrics have a "direction," created by a pattern, pile or nap, finishing process, or shine. The direction is not always noticeable, so to be safe try to have all the pattern pieces running in the same direction. Similarly, even if the fabric looks as though it doesn't have a right side and a wrong side, treat the same side as the right side throughout to be safe.

3 Selvages, the finished edges running the length of the fabric, can make seams pucker, so it is better to trim them off. However, if this would affect the pattern repeat, you could just trim them to ⅝in (1.5cm) or clip into the selvages at intervals of 2–4in (5–10cm). On a pale fabric, trim off information about the care of the fabric printed down the selvages, as this could show through.

4 When cutting lengths of fabric, such as for curtains or a shade, measure each fabric length and mark the cutting point with pins on both edges, then double-check that they are correct. With a long ruler and dressmakers' chalk, draw a line between the pins, then use the carpenter's square to check that the line is square to the long edges.

5 When cutting out rectangles to specified dimensions, measure and mark out the pieces following the grain of the fabric, using a long ruler, a carpenter's square, and dressmakers' chalk. Check the measurements are correct before cutting out.

6 When using a paper pattern to cut out pieces, pin the pattern to the fabric all around the edges with the pins quite close together (checking first whether the seam allowance is included or whether you have to add it). If the pattern says "place on fold," fold the fabric first exactly on the grain line, and then place the pattern's fold line exactly on the fabric fold; the cut-out fabric piece when opened up will be twice the size of the pattern. If the pattern has any markings, such as darts, transfer them to the fabric using tailor's tacks (see page 187), or dressmakers' carbon paper and a tracing wheel.

7 Mark the top of each cut length or rectangle of fabric with dressmakers' chalk, to make sure that you stitch them together all facing in the same direction. Try not to fold cut lengths of fabric—but if you must, fold them lengthwise, so that any creases that form will be hidden in the finished folds of the curtains.

staystitching

This line of machine-stitching is done through a single thickness of fabric just inside the seam line, to prevent the fabric from stretching while being handled and to help prevent any clips made into the seam allowance from going beyond the seam line. It should be done immediately after cutting out the pieces. The project instructions tell you when and where to staystitch.

matching pattern repeats using ladder stitch

Here is the best way to make sure that the pattern lines up correctly across seams.

1 Lay one piece of fabric right side up on a flat surface. Press the seam allowance to the wrong side along the seam line of the other piece of fabric. With this piece also right side up, position the pressed seam line on the seam allowance of the first piece of fabric so the pattern matches. Pin together.

2 The two layers are now sewn together temporarily using ladder stitch, which is worked much like hemstitch (see opposite). Secure the thread inside the folded edge. Bring the needle out through the fold, take it horizontally across the join, and, holding the needle vertically, insert it into the flat fabric close to the seam line and thread. Bring the needle up again immediately below this but ¾in (2cm) farther down.

3 Make a horizontal stitch across the join into the folded edge, and, still holding the needle vertically, run it through the fold and bring it out again ¾in (2cm) farther down. Pull the thread through. Continue in this way along the whole seam.

4 Machine-stitch the seam with right sides together in the usual way, and then remove the ladder stitching.

hand stitches

This is a selection of the stitches most often used in sewing and in this book. It is important to make the stitches an even size and to keep an even tension. Work stitches with a thread that matches the fabric. However, you can use a contrasting color to make temporary stitches easier to see when it's time to remove them. The following instructions are for a right-handed person; simply reverse them if you are left-handed.

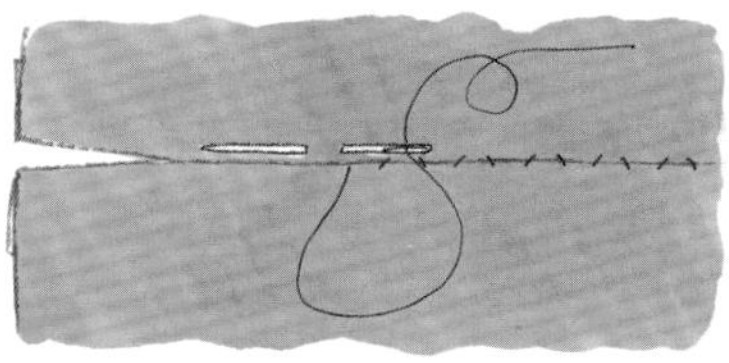

slipstitch

Also occasionally known as even slipstitch, this is an almost invisible stitch that is used to join two folded edges together, for example when attaching curtain lining to the main fabric or when closing the edges of a mitered corner or of an opening.

1 Working from right to left, secure thread on the wrong side. Bring the needle out through one of the folded edges, then insert it into the opposite folded edge, no more than 1/16in (1–2mm) farther along. Run the needle through the fold and bring it out 1/4in (5mm) farther along.

2 Repeat on the opposite edge, and continue working in this way, closing the two edges together.

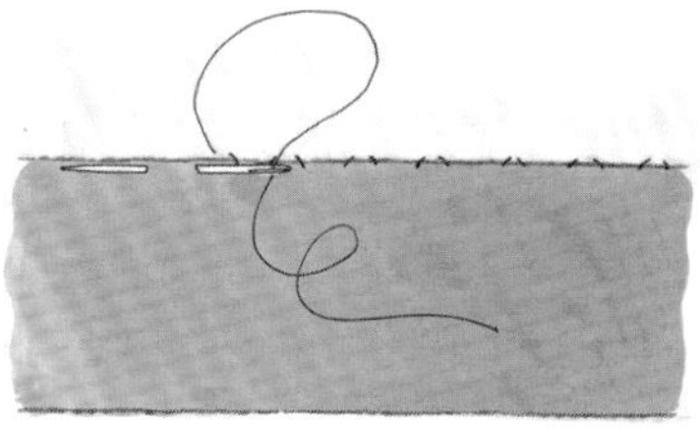

hemstitch

Also known as uneven slipstitch or slip hemming, this stitch is used to hold a folded edge to a flat piece, for example a hem. It is almost invisible on the right side of the fabric.

1 Working from right to left, secure the thread on the inside of the fold. Bring the needle out through the fold and insert it in the flat piece, either directly below or up to 1/16in (1–2mm) farther along. Pick up only two or three threads.

2 Insert the needle back down into the folded edge, no more than 1/16in (1–2mm) farther along. Run the needle through the fold and bring it out 1/4in–3/8in (5mm–1cm) farther along. Continue along the hem in the same way, making sure the stitches are not pulled too tightly or the fabric will look puckered on the right side.

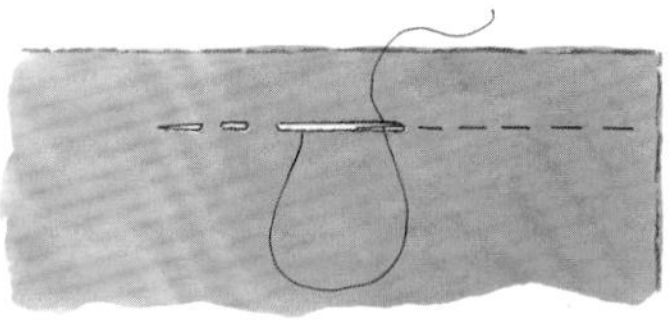

running stitch

This straight stitch is used for gathering.

1 Working from right to left, secure the thread. With the needle pointed left, weave it in and out of the fabric, keeping the stitches small and even, and the spaces between them the same size as the stitches.

2 Pull the thread through and then repeat, continuing in this way along the stitching line.

hand stitches

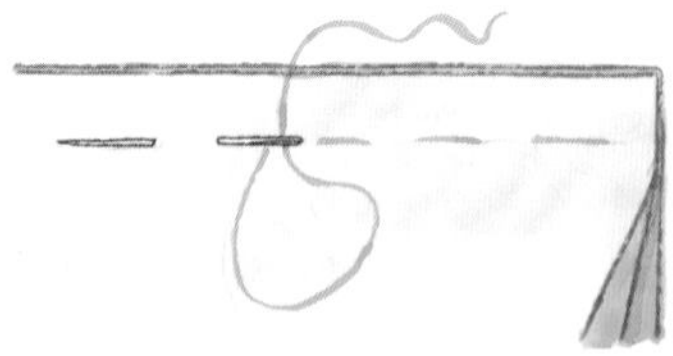

basting (tacking)

This is a temporary stitch used to hold two pieces of fabric together while the permanent stitching is being done. It is worked in much the same way as running stitch but the stitches are longer and the spaces between them can be longer still. Use a contrasting-color thread so it will be easy to see when removing it.

1 Working from right to left with the needle pointing left, work long, straight stitches just inside the seam line by moving the needle in and out of the fabric.

2 The spaces between the stitches can be the same length as the stitches or the stitches can be farther apart.

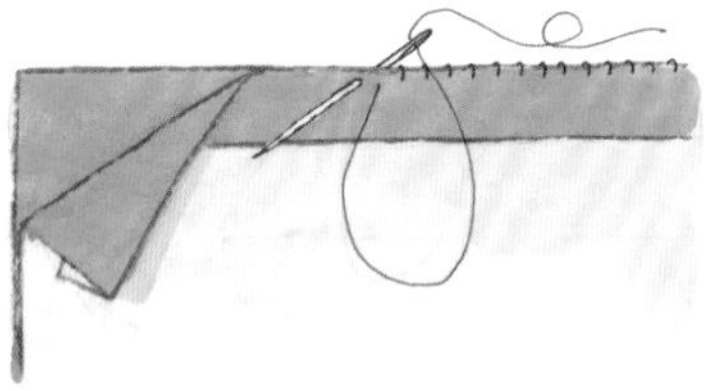

overhand stitch

This tiny, even stitch is used to top-sew two finished or folded edges together securely, for example when attaching ties or tapes. It is similar to whipstitch (see right) but has smaller, vertical stitches.

1 Working from right to left, secure the thread on the wrong side of the fabric. Bring the needle through to the front, close to the working edge. Holding the needle diagonally, insert it in the back edge immediately behind the thread, picking up only two threads, and bring it out through the front edge again.

2 Pick up only two threads in the front edge and then insert the needle into the back edge immediately behind the thread. Continue in this way, keeping the stitches uniform in size and evenly spaced.

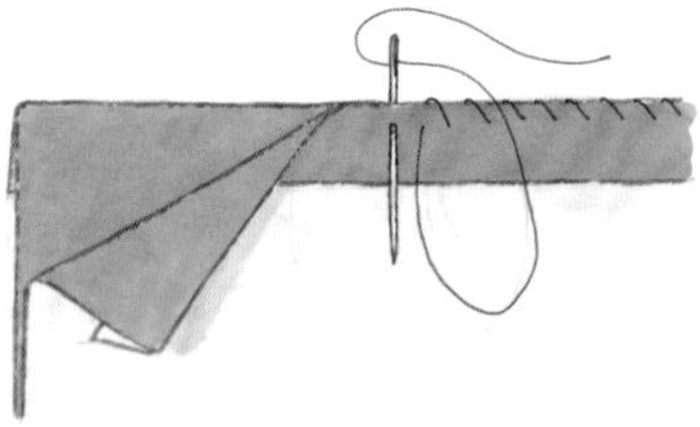

whipstitch

This is similar to overhand stitch (see left) but the stitches are larger and slanting.

1 Working from right to left, secure the thread on the wrong side of the fabric. Bring the needle through to the front, close to the working edge. Holding the needle at a right angle to the edge, insert it in the back edge to the left of the thread, picking up only two or three threads, and bring it out through the front edge again.

2 Pick up only two or three threads in the front edge and then insert the needle into the back edge to the left of the thread. Continue in this way, keeping the stitches uniform in size and evenly spaced.

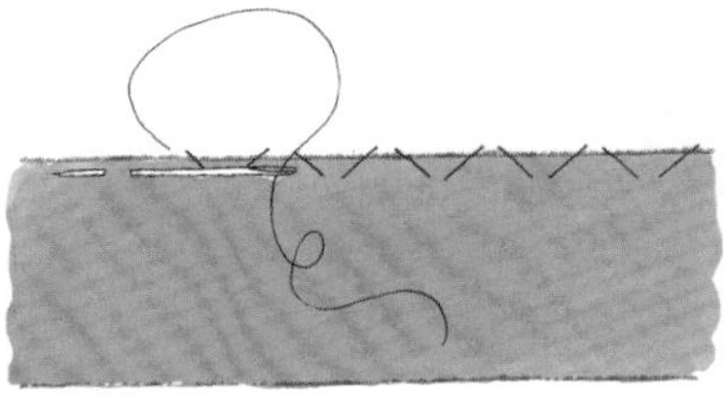

catchstitch

This stitch is used to hold a raw edge against a flat piece, for example in single-fold side hems that will be covered by a lining. Note: the term catchstitch is often used to mean herringbone stitch (see right).

1 Working from right to left, secure the thread on the wrong side of the hem. Bring the needle to the right side about ⅛in (3mm) from the raw edge. Pass the needle up and to the left, picking up two threads from the single layer of fabric.

2 Pull the needle and thread through and pass it down to the left, taking a small stitch in the hem fabric. Continue along the hem in this way.

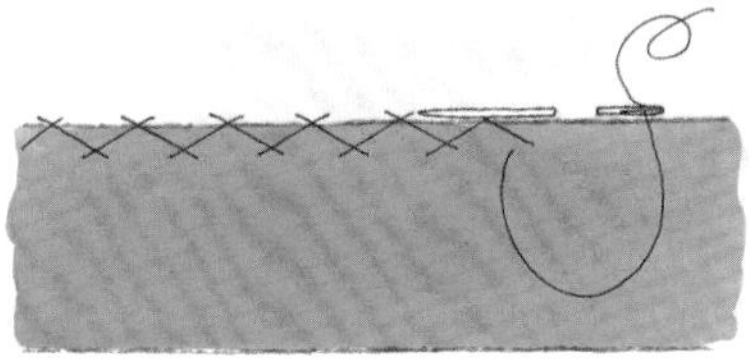

herringbone stitch

This looks similar to catchstitch (see left), and is often called catchstitch, but it is stronger (and is sewn in the opposite direction).

1 Working from left to right, bring the needle up through the hem edge. With the needle pointing left, take a very small backward stitch in the flat piece just above the hem edge, ¼–⅜in (5mm–1cm) to the right of where the thread emerged.

2 Now take a small backward stitch ¼–⅜in (5mm–1cm) to the right in the hem. Continue along the hem in this way.

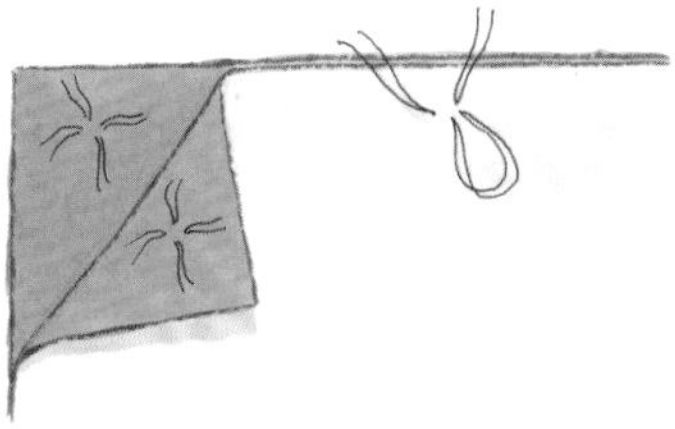

tailor's tacks

Tailor's tacks are used to mark construction details and matching points, as an alternative to using fadeaway pencil, dressmakers' carbon paper or pins, or making a small snip into the seam allowance.

1 Using a long length of doubled thread, make a small stitch through the two layers of fabric at the position you wish to mark. Pull the needle through, leaving a long thread loop. Make a second stitch over the first one, again leaving a long loop.

2 Carefully fold back the top layer of fabric as far as the tailor's tack and pull the loops through to the inside. Using sharp scissors, cut the loops to separate the two layers of fabric.

seams

There are several different types of seams used in this book. The right choice takes into account the weight and thickness of the fabric, and the position of the seam. Allow enough fabric for your seam allowances, especially if the fabric is likely to ravel. In that case, finish the edges with machine-zigzagging, or a serger (overlock machine) if you have one.

plain seam

This is the most commonly used seam for joining fabric, and no stitching is visible from the right side. The seam allowances are specified for each project in this book, but ⅝in (1.5cm) is standard.

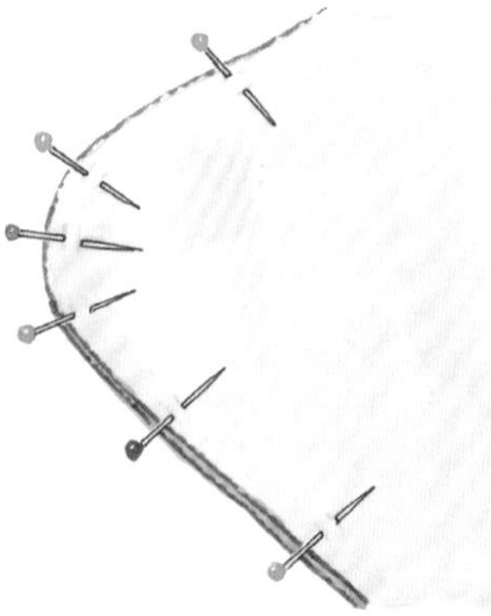

1 Place the two fabric pieces with right sides together and raw edges even. Pin along the seam line or at right angles to it. On a curved seam or on bulky fabric, the pins will need to be closer together than on a straight seam or thin fabric. If the seam is tricky or you are a beginner, hand-baste (see page 186) close to the seam line and remove the pins.

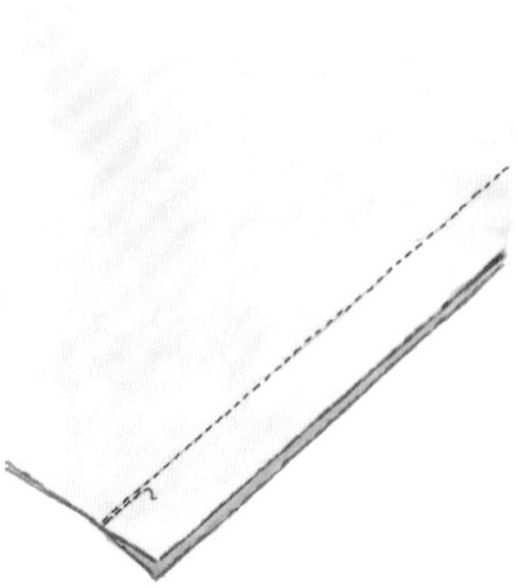

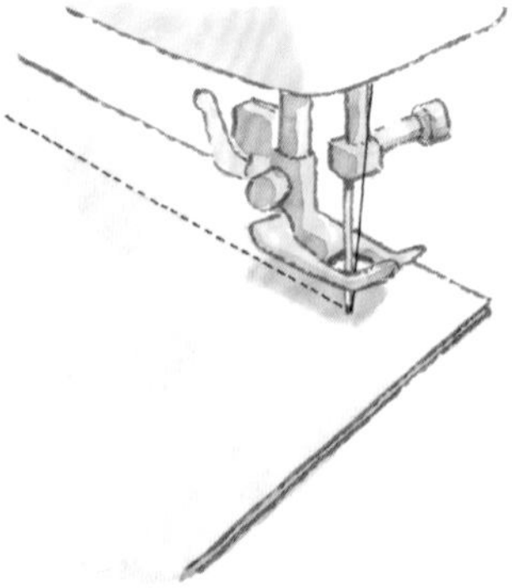

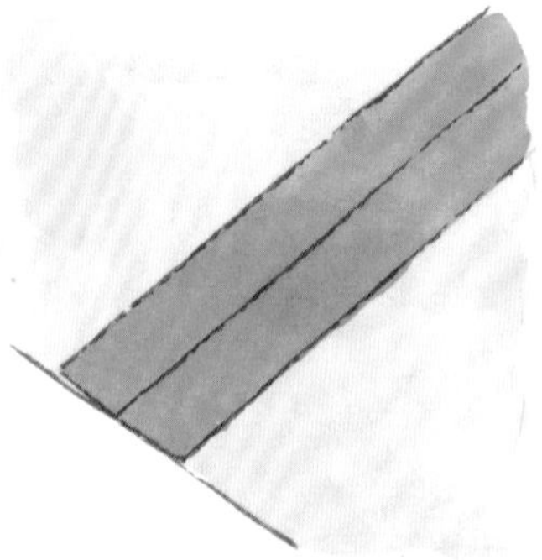

2 Machine-stitch along the seam line, using the stitching guide on the machine to make sure the seam is exactly the right width and doesn't wobble. If you haven't basted the seam, remove the pins as you come to them unless your machine can stitch over pins. Stitch a few reverse stitches at the start and finish of the seam to secure the threads.

3 To stitch around a corner, stop stitching when you reach the seam line of the adjacent edge (ie, the width of the seam allowance from the end). With the needle in the fabric, lift the presser foot and turn the fabric until the new edge is in line with the machine stitching guide. Lower the presser foot and continue stitching.

4 Remove any remaining pins or basting if used. Using a steam iron, press open the seam allowances (or press them to one side, if directed in the project).

french seam

This narrow, self-enclosed seam neatly contains all the raw edges, with no stitching visible from the right side. It is used mainly on unlined items, sheer and lightweight fabrics, and those that ravel easily. For this you need to allow a ¾in (2cm) seam allowance.

Note: To use a French seam when you have only a ⅝in (1.5cm) seam allowance, trim the seam allowance in step 1 to ⅛in (3mm), and stitch a ¼in (5mm) seam in step 2.

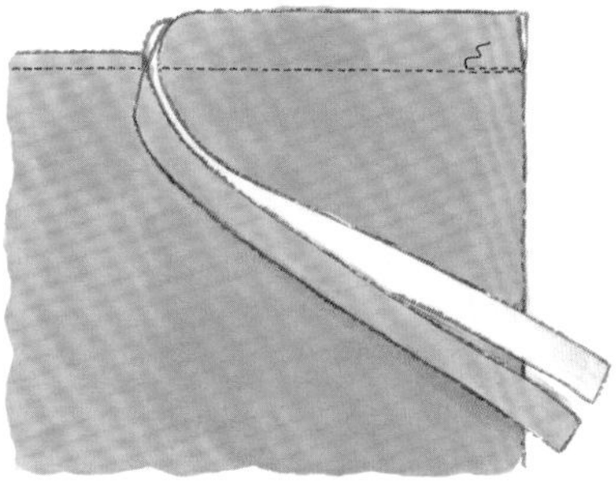

1 Place the two fabric pieces with wrong sides together and raw edges even. Pin along the seam line. Machine-stitch a ⅜in (1cm) seam. Trim the seam allowances to ¼in (5mm) and press them open.

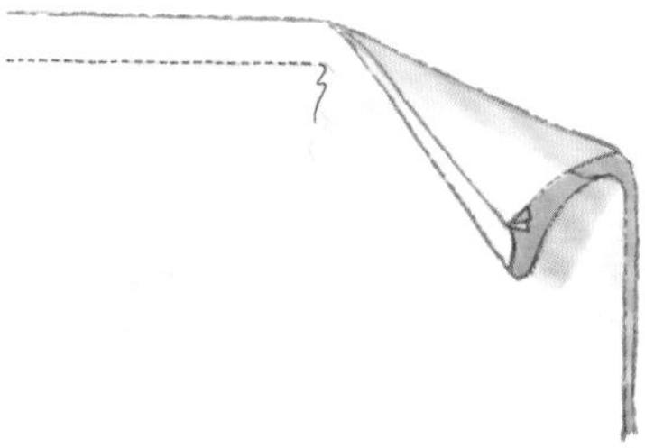

2 Turn the fabric so that right sides are together, pressing the seam back onto itself, with the seam line running along the edge. Pin and machine-stitch a ⅜in (1cm) seam, enclosing the raw edges. Press the finished seam to one side.

flat fell seam

Also known as a run and fell seam, this is another type of self-enclosed seam, used mainly for heavier weight fabrics. As with the French seam, the raw edges are enclosed, but it is stronger and flatter than a French seam, and there is some visible stitching on the right side.

Note: With this method, there will be one line of stitching visible on the right side.

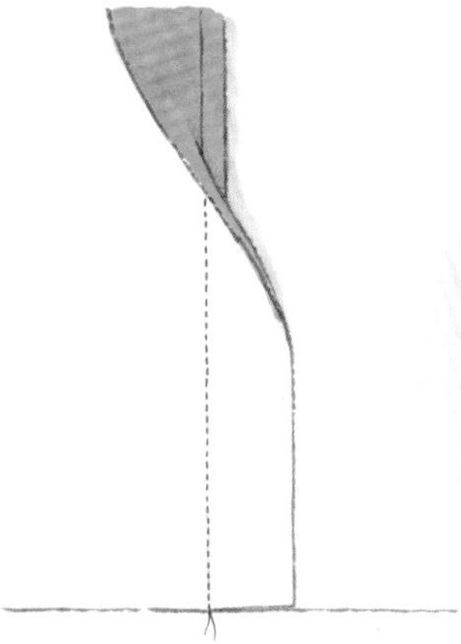

1 Place the two fabric pieces with right sides together and raw edges even. Pin along the seam line. Machine-stitch a ⅝in (1.5cm) seam, making a few reverse stitches at the start and finish of the seam to secure the threads. Press both seam allowances to one side and then trim the underneath seam allowance to ¼in (5mm).

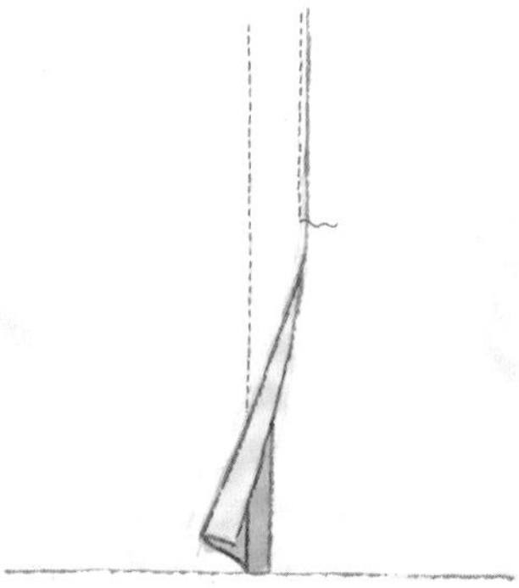

2 Wrap the upper seam allowance over the trimmed seam allowance, enclosing it. Pin in place. Machine-stitch close to the turned-under edge from the wrong side.

reducing bulk on a corner or point

For a corner, before turning it right side out the seam allowances are trimmed, so that they are less bulky and sit flat when pressed.

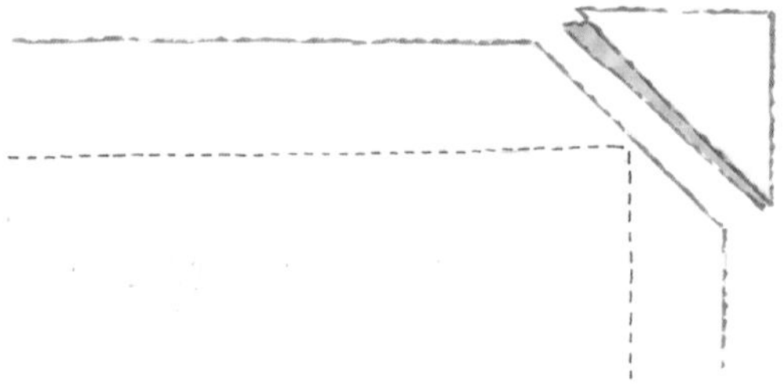

1 Snip the seam allowances at the corner close to the stitched line, as shown. Be careful not to cut too close, otherwise frayed edges will pop out on the right side.

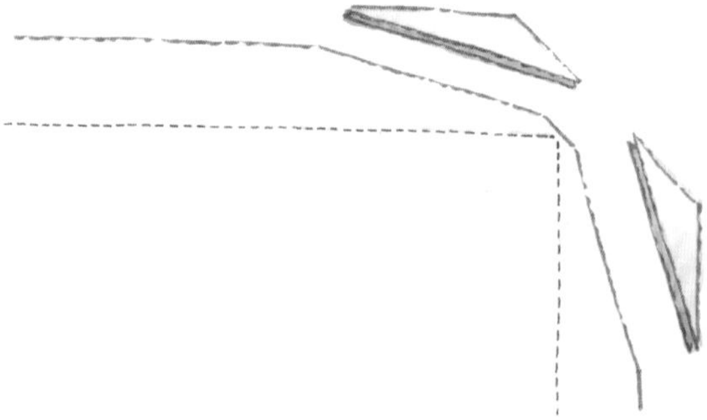

2 If the seam is still bulky because the fabric is thick, snip away more from the seam allowance on each side of the corner in a diagonal line, as shown.

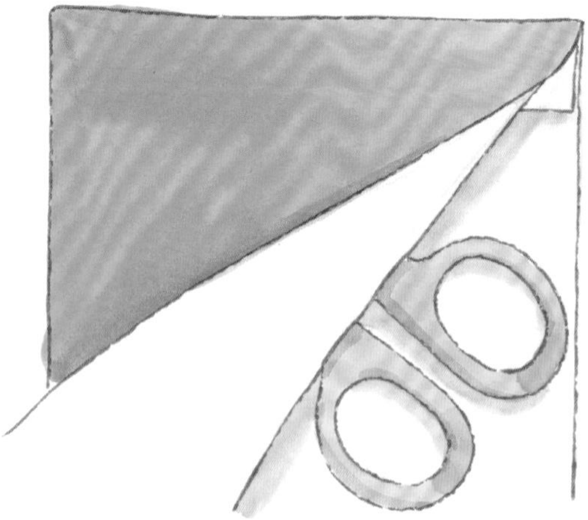

3 Use a pointed object, such as a pair of scissors, to carefully push out the corner on the right side. Be very careful not to push through the seam.

clipping curved seams

For a plain seam stitched on a curve, before turning it right side out the seam allowances are clipped so that the seam lies flat and smooth. Sometimes this is also done to a curve on a single layer of fabric that has been staystitched (see page 183). For an outward (convex) curve, cut slits into the seam allowances. For an inward (concave) curve, snip away wedge-shaped notches.

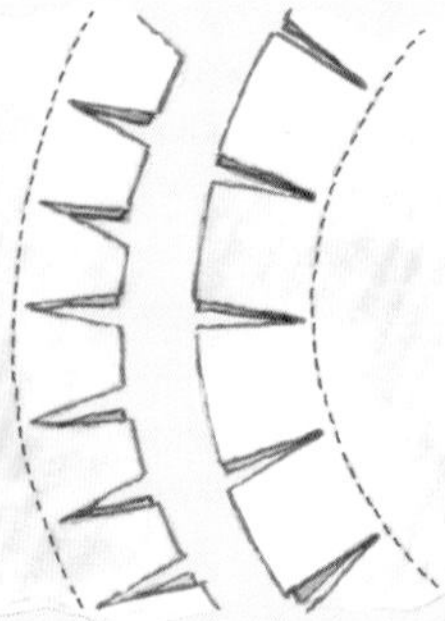

hems

For a flat hem, fabric lengths must be cut straight—it is then simple to fold over the required amount and press it in place with a steam iron. Most base hems are made with a double fold, although a lot of side hems may be just a single fold, especially if they are enclosed within the lining. If you want hems to be invisible from the right side, hem them in place by hand with hemstitch (see page 185). Alternatively, if you don't mind having the stitching visible on the right side, you can machine-stitch hems in place.

simple miters

A miter is used to form a neat, flat finish at a corner where two hems meet. Here is how to do a simple miter where two single hems of the same width meet.

1 Finish both raw edges with machine zigzagging, or use a serger if you have one. Press the single hems to the wrong side along both edges, and then open them out flat again.

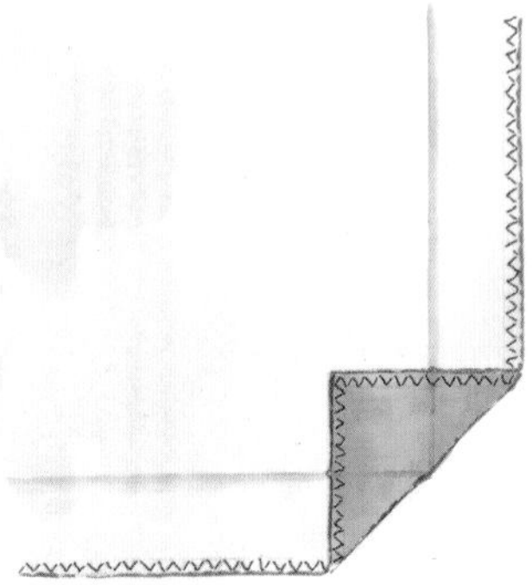

2 Matching up the press lines, turn over the corner of the fabric so that the diagonal fold passes through the point where the two press lines cross.

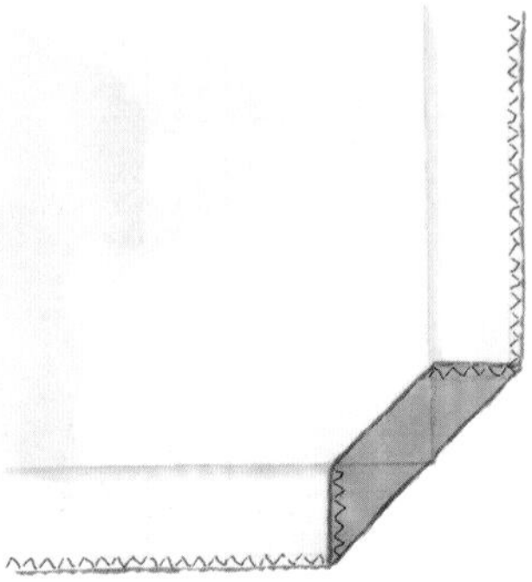

3 Press the diagonal fold in place, and trim away the triangle, leaving a ⅝in (1.5cm) seam allowance.

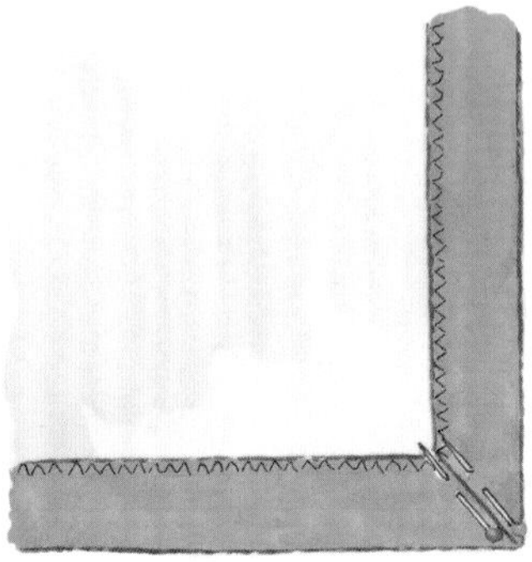

4 Fold the hems back in place and pin the diagonal mitered edges. The hems are now ready to be sewn in place.

uneven miters

Here is how to do a miter at a 45° angle on a corner where two hems of different widths meet. Illustrated below is a curtain with a single side hem (which will later be covered by the curtain lining) and a double bottom hem. An unlined curtain would have a double side hem but the procedure is much the same. The hems on a shade are also mitered in this way.

1 Press the single or double hems along the adjoining edges, such as the side and bottom edges of a curtain.

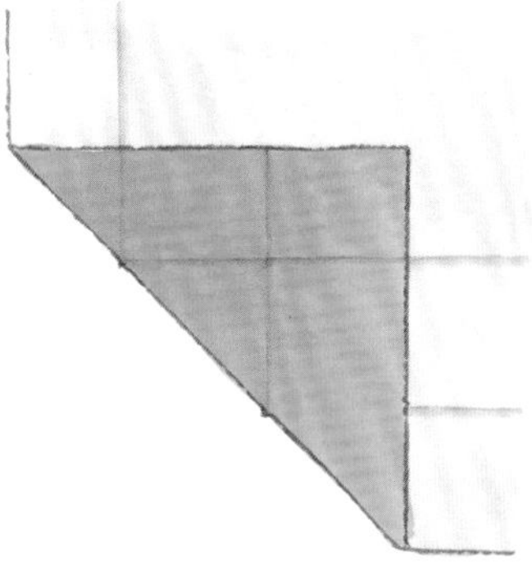

2 Open the hems flat again. Matching up the press lines, turn over the corner of the fabric so that the diagonal fold passes through the point where the two inner press lines cross. Press the diagonal fold flat.

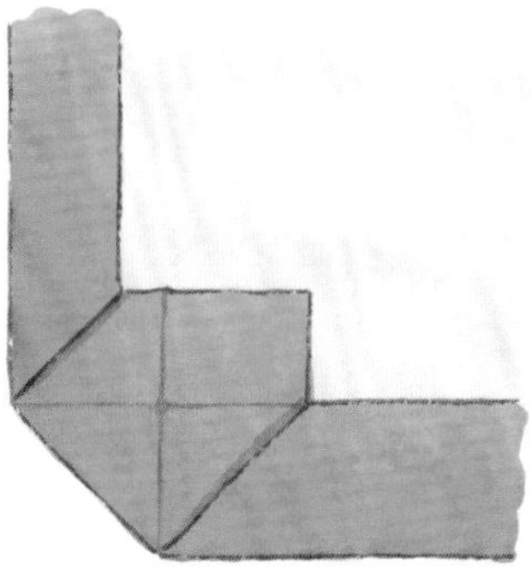

3 Refold the side hem. (If using a curtain weight—see right—slip it under the edge of the side hem, and pin and hand-sew it in place.) Turn the first fold of the double bottom hem back over to the wrong side.

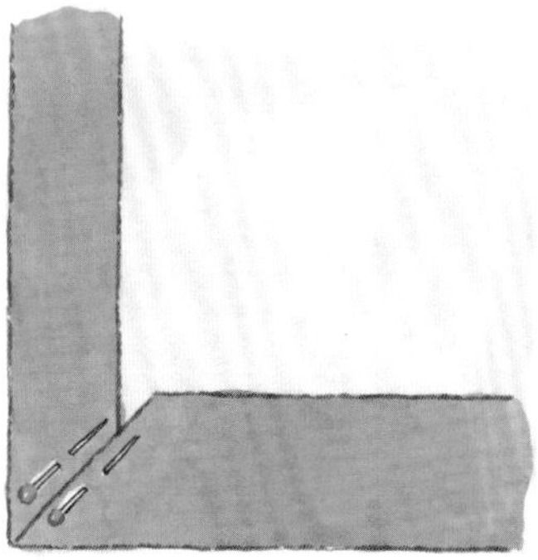

4 Turn the second fold of the double base hem back over to the wrong side, enclosing the covered weight if used. Pin the diagonal mitered edges in place. The hems are now ready to be hand-sewn in place.

weights

It is advisable to insert weights into the hems of curtains, especially if they are full-length panels. Weights help the fabric to hang better by holding it down and keeping the hems straight and even. They are sewn into the mitered corners of each hem and at each fabric width or half-width across the hem. You can buy round or rectangular lead weights. The round ones often have two holes drilled into the center, rather like a button, so you can sew them directly to the fabric. For a neater finish, make small lining pockets to encase the weights, then slipstitch the pockets into the base hem.

1 Cut two square pieces of unbleached muslin about ¾in (2cm) larger than the diameter of the weight. Pin the pieces together along three sides.

2 Machine-stitch the pockets around the three-pinned sides. Insert a weight and machine-stitch across the fourth side to close the bag.

Note: You can also buy lead-weight tape, which is a length of chain that is sold by the yard (meter). Particularly good for lightweight and sheer fabrics, it is threaded into the entire hem and secured at regular intervals with a hand stitch.

bias binding

Bias binding is a strip of fabric cut on the bias (cut at a diagonal angle to the lengthwise and crosswise grain). It can be used in various ways as a decorative edging, including to make piping (see page 196). You can buy bias binding ready-made or make it yourself as shown here.

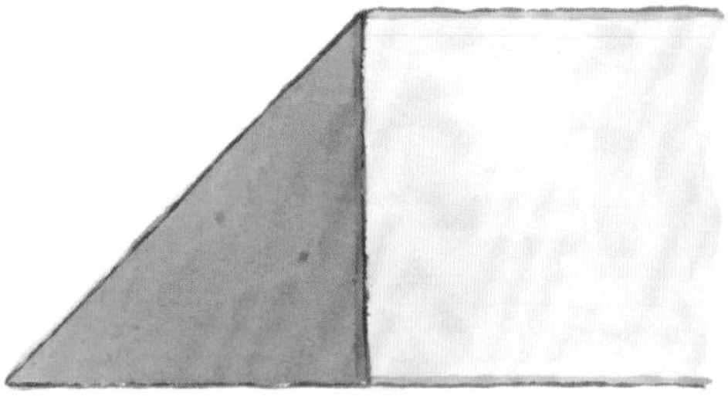

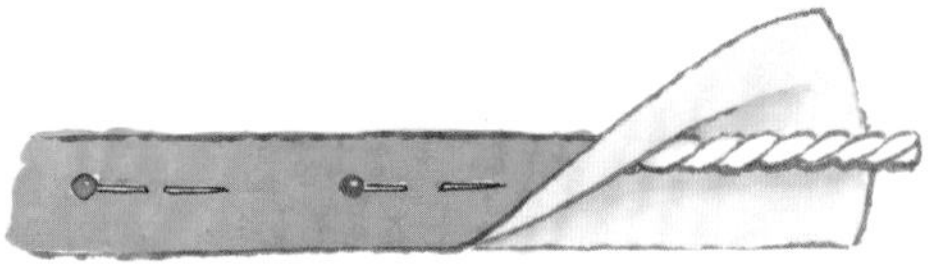

1 To find the bias of the fabric, fold down the raw edge running across the width of the fabric from selvage to selvage to form a triangle. The crosswise and lengthwise grain of the fabric should now be matching. Press and cut along the fold line.

2 If you will be using the bias binding flat, the width of the cut strips should be equal to twice the finished width, plus 1¼in (3cm) for seams. If you will be using it for piping, pin some fabric around the cord—you will need this width plus 1¼in (3cm) for seams.

3 With dressmakers' chalk and a long ruler, draw lines parallel to the bias cut line, with the distance apart equal to the calculated width. You will need enough strips to form the length necessary to go around the edge of your project. Cut along the lines using scissors, or a rotary cutter with a ruler and cutting mat.

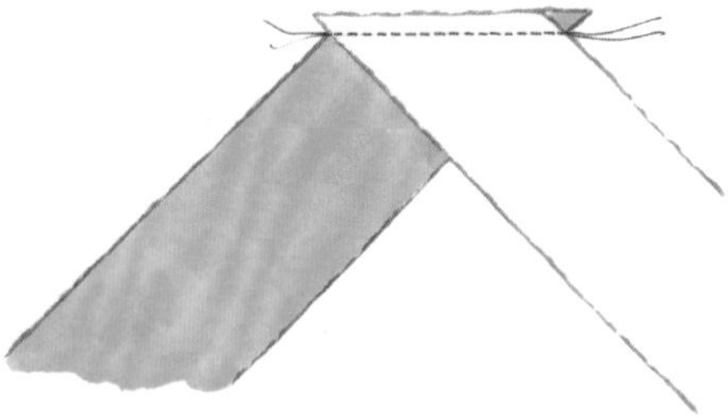

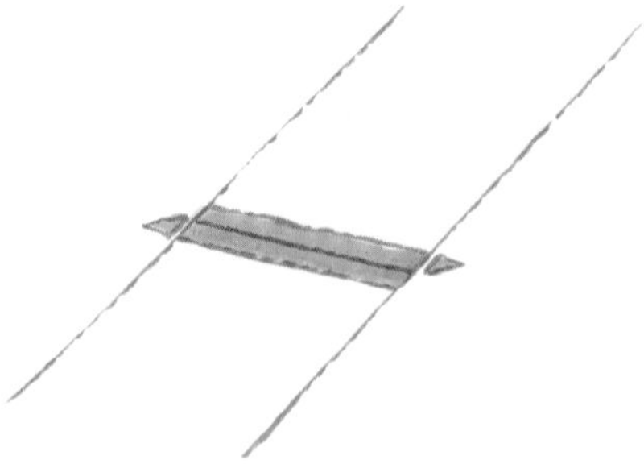

4 To join the bias strips into one length, pin two ends together as shown, and stitch a ¼in (5mm) seam. Repeat until all the strips are joined together with seams slanting in the same direction.

5 Press open the seam and trim the pointed ends of the seam allowances even with the edges of the strip.

piping

A cord covered with a narrow strip of fabric, piping (also known as cording or welting) is sewn into a seam as a decorative edging, which also makes the seam stronger. Ready-made piping is available, but making your own enables you to use fabric to match your project.

Piping cord, which is soft, is available in various diameters, ranging from ⅛in (3mm) to jumbo, although the medium sizes are most commonly used. Cable cord, which is a firmer, twisted cord, can also be used and is available in sizes from 1/16in (2mm) to ⅜in (1cm). If your cord is not preshrunk, wash and dry it at a high temperature.

The cord is normally covered with bias binding (see page 194). However, if the piping is to be used on a straight seam and if you want the lines of the fabric pattern—such as checks or stripes—to run along the piping, you can cut the fabric strips along the straight grain. But if the piping will curve around corners, the strips must be cut on the bias to help them bend.

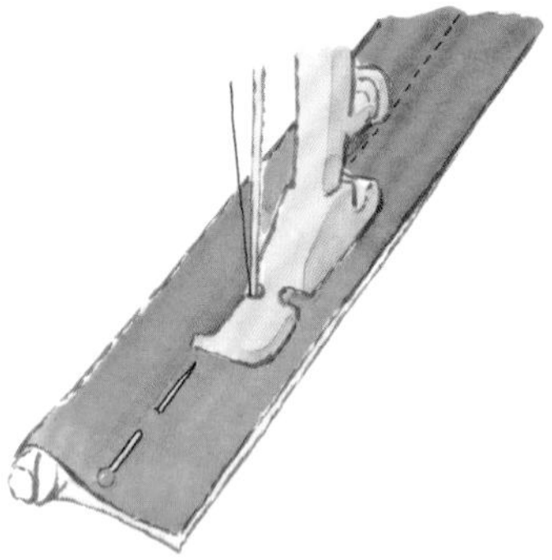

1 Place the cord on the wrong side of the fabric strip and bring the long edges of the strip together, enclosing the cord. Pin the edges together. Using a zipper foot on your sewing machine, machine-stitch down the length of the cord, close to it but without crowding the stitching against it or stretching the fabric.

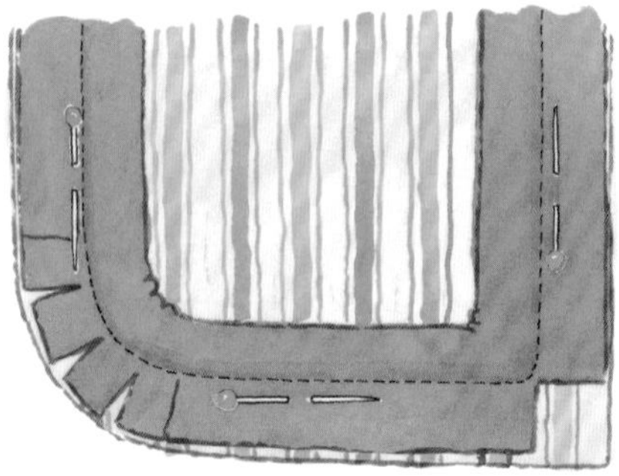

2 Decide where on the project the piping will start and finish. It should ideally be an inconspicuous straight portion of the edge you are piping, rather than on a zipper edge, at a corner, or on a deep curve. Pin the piping to the right side of one fabric piece, with the cord facing inward and the stitching line of the piping along the seam line of the fabric piece. To make the piping turn the corner, clip into the piping seam allowances close to the stitching line and bend the piping around the corner. If the piping is to bend gradually around a curve, snip into the piping seam allowances at several regular intervals so that the cord curves around smoothly.

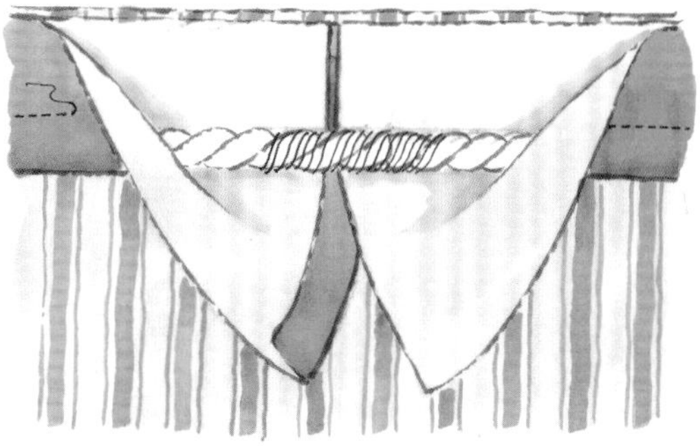

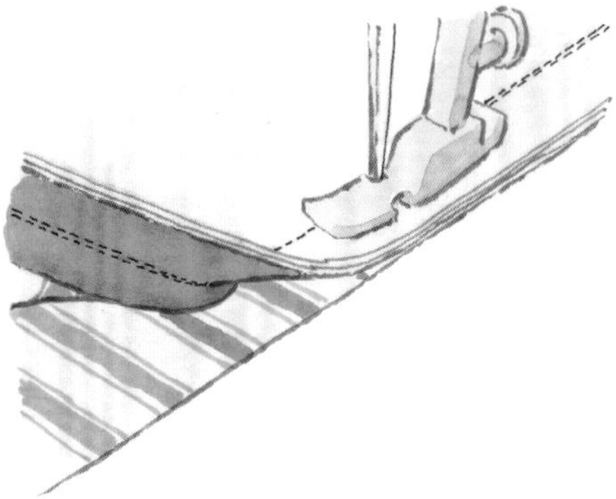

3 With the zipper foot on the sewing machine, machine-baste the piping in place, stitching on top of the piping stitching, and leaving 2in (5cm) unstitched at each end, which should overlap by ¾in (2cm). Unpick about 2in (5cm) of the piping machine-stitching at each end, and fold back the ends of the fabric strip. Trim the two ends of the cord so that they butt together, then bind the cord ends with thread. Turn under ⅜in (1cm) at one end of the fabric strip, and wrap it around the exposed cord, overlapping the raw end of the fabric strip. Machine-baste this portion of the piping in place.

4 With right sides together and raw edges even, pin this piped fabric piece to the other fabric piece. With the zipper foot on the machine, machine-stitch along the seam line very close to the cord, through all four layers. When the project is turned right side out, the seam will be neatly piped.

darts

Darts provide a means of shaping fabric over a curve, as on a chair slipcover. Most darts are shaped like long triangles.

1 Mark the dart on the wrong side of the fabric. With right sides together, bring the two stitching lines together and pin along the line. Baste, removing the pins.

2 Starting at the wide end, stitch along the stitching line in a completely straight line. At the pointed end, where the dart tapers to nothing, you will be stitching very close to the fold. Tie the thread ends and press the dart to one side.

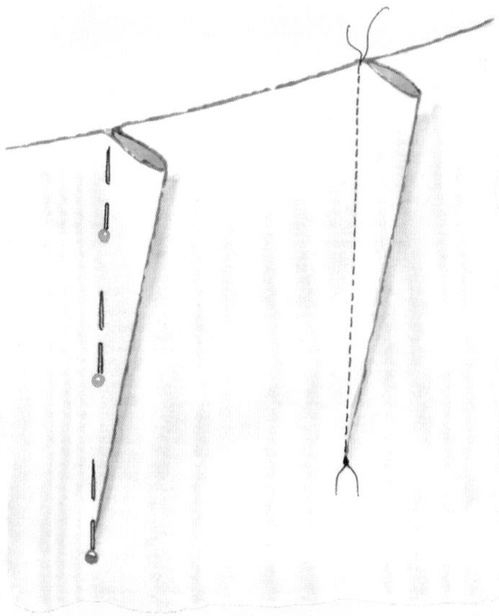

gathers

Gathering involves drawing up parallel lines of stitching to form tiny, soft folds in the fabric. Usually fabric is gathered to about one half to one third its original width.

gathering using machine-stitching

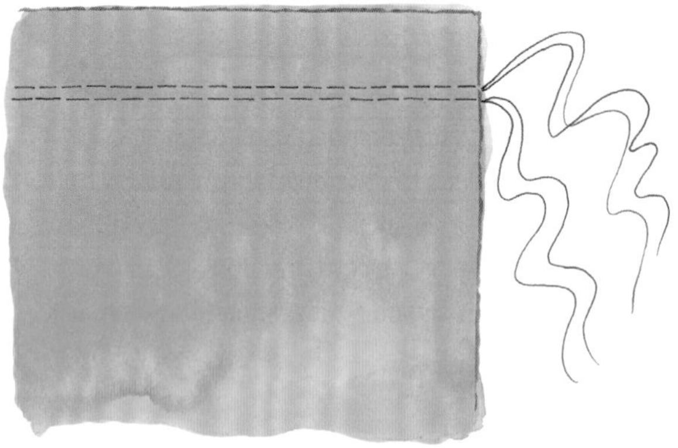

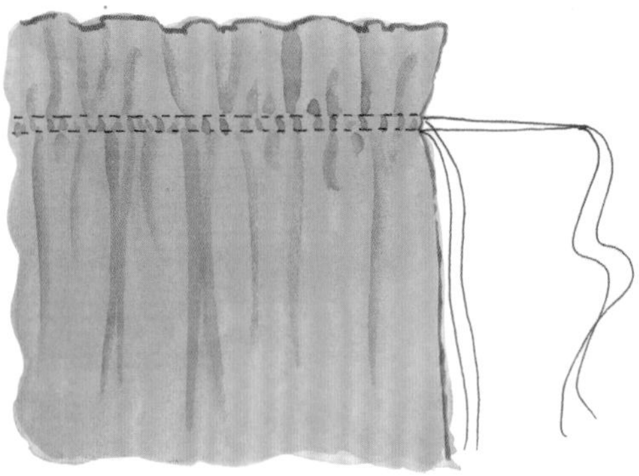

1 Machine-stitch two parallel lines of your longest straight stitch within the seam allowance, with the first just inside the seam line and the other ¼in (5mm) away from the first, leaving long ends of thread at both ends.

2 If you are gathering a small area, knot the thread ends at one end, and at the other end gently pull the two bobbin threads at the same time, pushing the gathers along the threads as you pull. When the piece is gathered to the required size, knot the long thread ends and distribute the gathers evenly.

3 OR, if you are gathering a large area, temporarily secure the bobbin threads at one end by wrapping them around a pin in a figure-eight. Begin gathering as in step 2, but stop when you have gathered up half the length of fabric, then repeat the procedure from the other end. When it is the required size, knot the long thread ends and distribute the gathers evenly.

Note: For very long lengths, it's advisable to stop and then resume stitching (leaving long ends) at each seam or at least every 2–3ft (60–90cm), to reduce the chances of the threads breaking when being pulled up.

gathering using hand-sewing

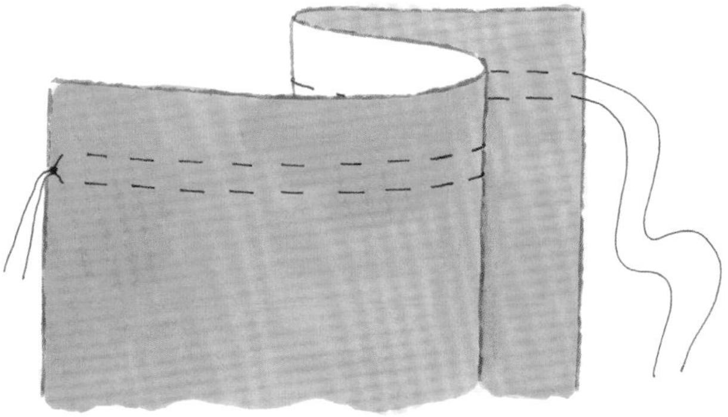

1 To gather small areas, you can, if you prefer, hand-sew two parallel lines of running stitch (see page 185) within the seam allowance, with the first just inside the seam line and the other ¼in (5mm) away from the first, and preferably with the stitches lined up. Knot the threads at one end and leave long thread ends at the other.

2 Carefully pull the long thread ends, pushing the gathers along the threads as you pull. When the piece is gathered to the required size, knot the long thread ends and distribute the gathers evenly.

inverted pleats

Pleats are folds in fabric held in place at the top. Basically, they are folded along a specific fold line, and the fold is then brought over to align with another line, the placement line. Inverted pleats are actually two pleats that face each other—they have two fold lines and a common placement line. Most are made with a continuous length of fabric folded onto itself, but the exception is an inverted pleat with a separate underlay, or backing piece, stitched to the back.

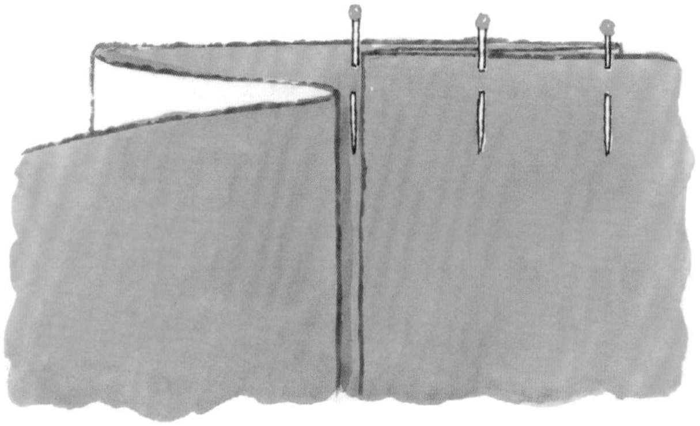

1 A pleat will hang best if the fold lines and placement line run along the straight grain of the fabric. Mark the placement line along the top and lower edges of your fabric piece with pins or tailor's tacks (see page 187). On each side of the placement line, measure the width of each pleat along the top and lower edges of the fabric piece, and mark with pins or tailor's tacks. With wrong sides together, fold the fabric along each fold line and press the folds in place.

2 Working from the right side of the fabric, fold along one of the pressed fold lines and, matching the tailor's tacks, bring the pressed edge over to align with the center placement line. Pin in place. Repeat with the second side of the pleat. Baste the pleats in place along the top and lower edges. The top will be held in place by the seam, while the bottom will be hemmed and will hang free after the basting is removed.

zippers

Zippers are used in many of the projects to form a neat, unobtrusive opening. Insert the zipper before you begin to assemble the cover, as it is much easier to work on one flat piece. The zipper is usually 3–4in (7.5–10cm) shorter than the finished seam it is inserted into.

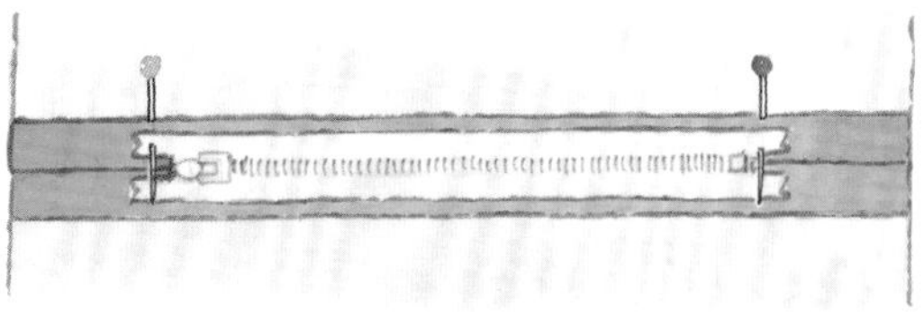

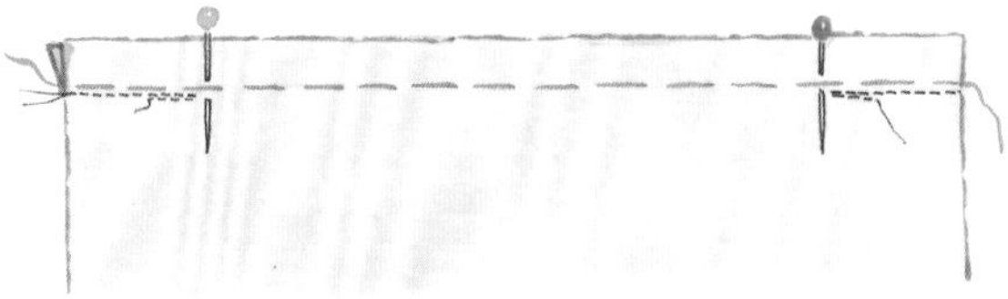

1 With right sides together and raw edges even, pin and baste the two edges of the seam in which the zipper is to be inserted. Lightly press open the seam. Lay the zipper over the seam allowances, centered between the ends of the seams, and mark the ends of the zipper with pins.

2 Remove the zipper and, with right sides together, machine-stitch the seam from the edge to the pin marker at each end. Reverse-stitch at each end of the stitching to secure. Leave the basting intact between the machine-stitched ends. Press open the seam.

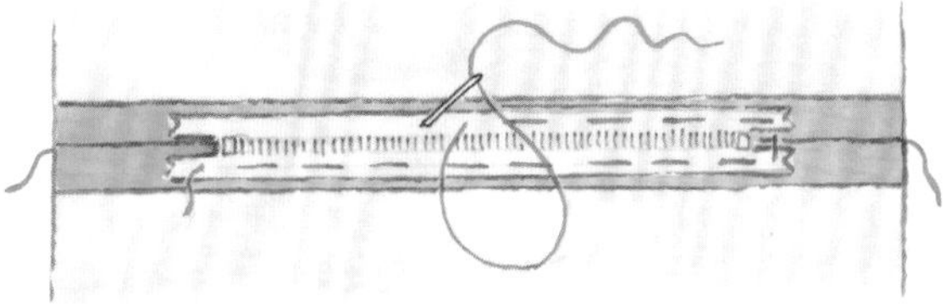

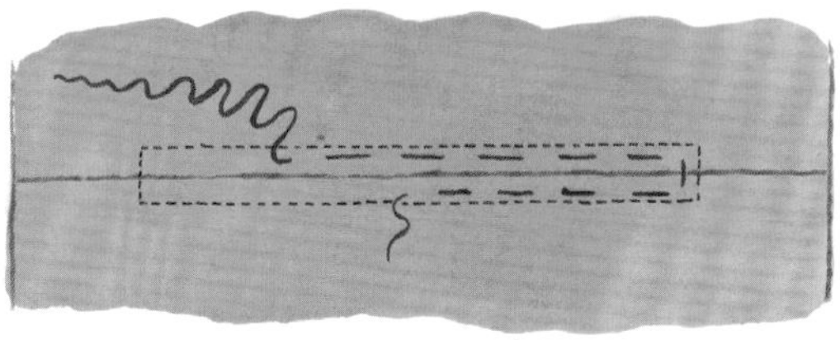

3 Lay the closed zipper face down on the seam allowances, along the basted section of the seam. Make sure the zipper teeth are exactly over the seam line, then hand-baste the zipper in place through all layers.

4 Working from the right side, and using a zipper foot on your machine, carefully sew the zipper in place. Stitch ¼in (5mm) from the seam line along each side and across the top and bottom of the zipper, being careful to avoid the zipper stops. Do this all in one go (unless the fabric has a tendency to creep, in which case stitch the long sides in the same direction). Instead of reverse-stitching at the ends, tie the threads on the wrong side. Remove the basting.

ties

Narrow fabric ties provide a useful way to attach seat cushions to chairs, fasten tablecloths, or attach simple curtains to a pole for an informal look. Wider ties, made from lightweight fabric, will form an elegant bow at the back of a dining chair slipcover.

making ties: method 1

This method has the advantage of not having to be turned right side out after stitching (which can be difficult with narrow ties), but the stitching shows from the right side.

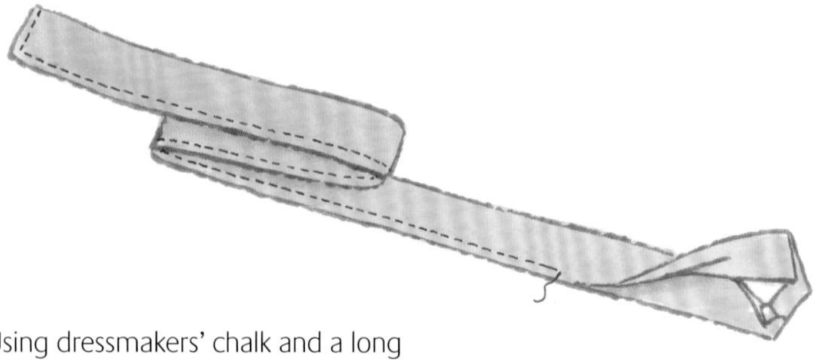

1 Using dressmakers' chalk and a long ruler, draw parallel lines along the straight grain of your fabric, with the distance between them equal to four times the finished width of the ties, and the length equal to the finished length of the ties plus two hem or seam allowances (see step 2)—or to the dimensions specified in the project. Cut along the lines using scissors, or a rotary cutter with a ruler and cutting mat.

2 If an end of a tie will be stitched into a seam on your project, there is no need to finish it, but if it will be exposed, press ¼in (5mm) to the wrong side at that end.

3 Press each strip in half along the length, wrong sides together. Open the strip and press the long raw edges to the wrong side to meet at the center.

4 Fold each strip in half again along the length, bringing the pressed long edges together and enclosing the raw edges completely. Pin and machine-stitch close to the turned-under edges along the full length of the strip, and across the end(s) if the hems have been pushed inside in step 2.

Note: If you need to make a lot of ties, it can be easier to make one long strip and then cut it into the required lengths and appropriate number of ties. Finish any raw ends that will be exposed by pushing them up inside the tie tubes and slipstitching in place (see page 185).

making ties: method 2

These ties are made from strips of fabric that are stitched with right sides together and turned right side out, so no stitching is visible.

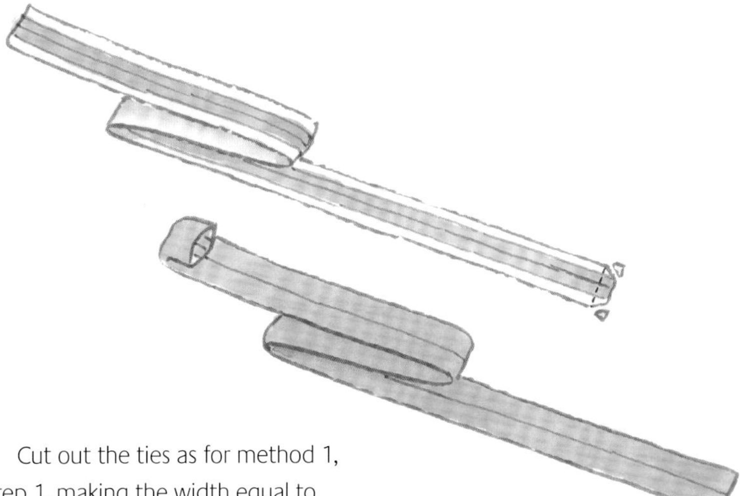

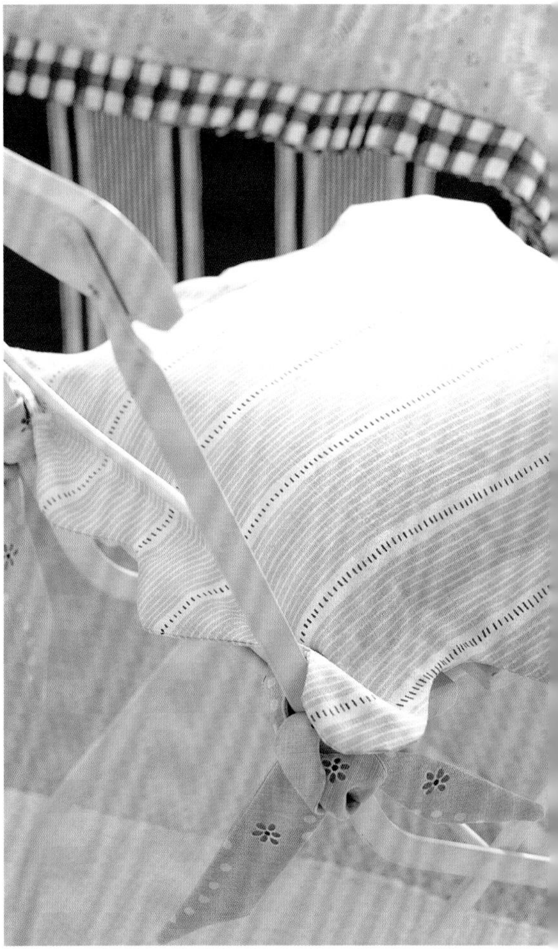

1 Cut out the ties as for method 1, step 1, making the width equal to twice the finished width, plus 1$\frac{1}{4}$in (3cm), and the length equal to the finished length plus two seam allowances—or to the dimensions specified in the project.

2 Fold each strip in half lengthwise, right sides together. Pin and machine-stitch a $\frac{5}{8}$in (1.5cm) seam down the long edges.

3 Trim the seam allowances to $\frac{1}{4}$in (5mm). Refold the tie so that the seam runs down the middle of one side, and press open the seam allowances. If one end will be exposed, stitch across the end with a $\frac{5}{8}$in (1.5cm) seam, and trim this to $\frac{1}{4}$in (5mm), then snip off the corners of the seam allowance.

4 Turn right side out and press flat, making sure the seam is still running down the center of one side.

Note: Placing the stitched end on the blunt end of a knitting needle or skewer and pulling the tie down over it makes it easier to turn the tube right side out.

calculating quantities of ties

To work out the number of ties needed for a curtain, take the finished width of your curtain panel and divide the finished curtain panel width by the spacing measurement recommended in the project instructions. You will need one more tie than the number of spaces calculated. For example, a curtain that is 60in (152cm) wide with a tie spacing of 8in (20cm) will have seven and a half spaces. If you round down the figure to seven spaces, you will need eight ties. If you round up the figure to eight spaces, you will need nine ties. Whether you round the figure up or down will depend on how close together you want the ties to be.

measuring for curtains

When measuring for curtains, it is helpful if the hardware (poles or rods) is in place before you begin, and also carpets or any other flooring if the curtains are to be full-length.

Always use a long, retractable, steel measuring tape, and ask someone to help you when measuring large windows. Decide on the type of heading you will be making, because it can affect the location of the pole in relation to the top of the window or the trim.

If you are making curtains or a shade in a fabric with a pattern repeat, place an entire pattern repeat at the lower edge, rather than the top.

curtain width or fullness

The fabric fullness required will depend on the curtain heading (see the individual projects). As a general rule, for each curtain in a pair, allow one-and-a-half to two-and-a-half times the width of the rod, divided by two.

curtain length or drop

For the finished length (drop) of the curtains, measure as follows:

- For curtains hung from an exposed rod, work out where the heading will finish in relation to the rod. If you are unsure, use curtain hooks to attach a piece of heading tape to the rod, and measure down from the top of the tape.
- For curtains hung from a pole, measure the length from the bottom of the curtain ring or the eyelet.
- For curtains hung from a pole that is attached to a valance shelf (mounting board) or cornice box (pelmet box), measure the finished length from the underside of the board, then deduct the hook drop. This will depend on the type of heading and hardware you are using. If you are unsure, hook a piece of the chosen heading tape to the pole with curtain hooks. Measure the clearance between the top edge of the tape and the bottom edge of the board.
- For full-length curtains, deduct ⅜in (1cm) from measurement B (see diagram) for clearance. If you prefer curtains to puddle, or pool, on the floor, add another 6–8in (15–20cm) to measurement B.
- For sill-length curtains, add 2–4in (5–10cm) to measurement C so that they hang just below the windowsill. If the sill protrudes, deduct ⅜in (1cm) from measurement C (see diagram), to allow the curtains to hang clear.

estimating yardage

When making curtains, don't skimp on the fabric yardage. Full curtains made from inexpensive fabrics look much better than ones that have been made from half the amount of a high-price fabric.

Start by calculating how many fabric widths are needed. Take your finished curtain-width (fullness) measurement and divide it by the width of your fabric. For example, for a finished curtain width of 90in (230cm) and a fabric width of 55in (139cm), you will need two widths per curtain.

- If the number of fabric widths works out to be just under or over a number of full widths, round up or down to the nearest full width.
- If it is nearer a half width, round it up or down to the nearest half width, and place the half widths on the outer edges of the curtains when stitching them together.

Next, calculate the total yardage. Add the top and lower hem allowances (see the individual projects) to the length measurements and multiply this number by the quantity of fabric widths calculated. If your fabric has a pattern repeat, add one full pattern repeat per width of fabric, after the first width.

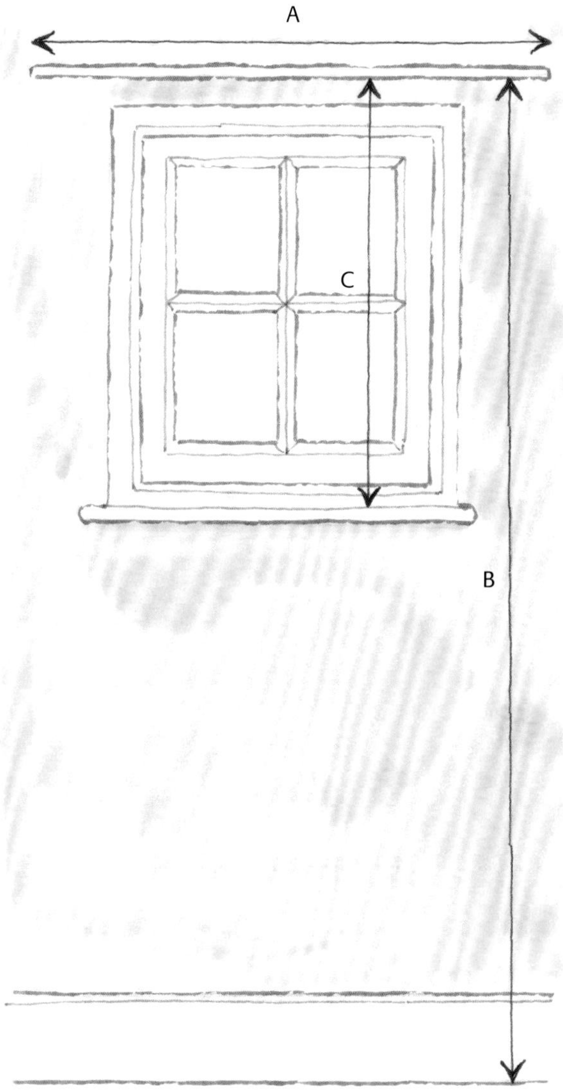

where to measure

There are two main measurements needed for working out the fabric yardage:

- The length of the pole, rod (including any overlap arms at the center, if your rod has them), valance shelf or cornice box (measurement A on the diagram)
- The length (drop) from the curtain hardware to the floor (measurement B on the diagram) or windowsill (measurement C on the diagram), depending on the style of your curtains.

Measure the finished length (drop) a few times at different points across the window, as floors can be uneven. Check whether the window is plumb (an even square or rectangle), by measuring the width at both the top and bottom. Check every measurement twice.

measuring for pinch pleats

These are pleats that create a deep formal heading in which the flat curtain is punctuated at regular intervals by double or triple pleats, as in the projects on pages 48 and 44 respectively. Here is how to calculate the sizes of the pleats and spaces for a pinch-pleat heading:

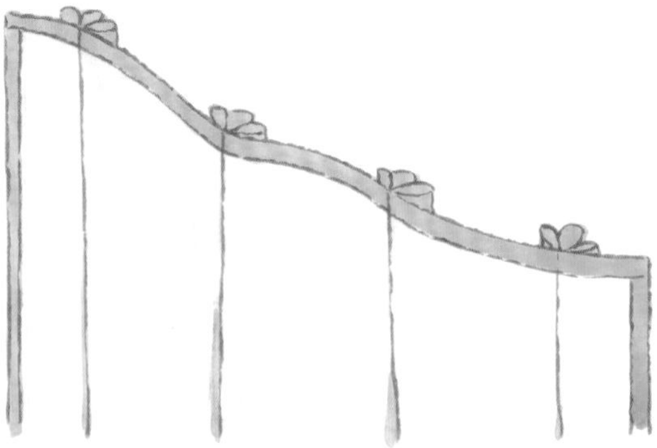

1 Lay the made-up curtain panel out flat and measure the width. Subtract from this the width of the finished (pleated) curtain. The difference between the two is the amount left over for the pleats. At each edge, there should be a flat allowance of 3¼in (8.5cm) for rod overlap arms and returns.

2 As a rough guide, allow four double or triple pleats for every width of fabric. Divide the amount left over for the pleats (see step 1) by the total number of pleats calculated, to work out the size of the pleats.

3 On the finished heading, excluding the overlap and return allowances at each side, you will have one less space than pleats. For example, if a panel is two fabric widths wide, it will have eight pleats and seven spaces—plus the space at each side for the overlap and return allowances, which are each 3¼in (8.5cm) wide.

4 To calculate the size of the spaces, subtract the overlap and return allowances—6½in (17cm) in total—from the finished width of the curtain panel, and divide the remaining width by the number of spaces (seven in this example).

curtain-hanging methods

Curtain panels are traditionally hung from rods (tracks) or poles. Unless you plan to use a cornice (pelmet) or valance, which will cover the system or utilitarian rod, choose a wooden or metal pole that can stand on its own decoratively speaking. The finials can be sculptural or ornate, such as acanthus leaf and pineapple finials, or much simpler round knobs. Cast-iron poles can have decorative scrolled or curled ends. The poles are supported by brackets on either side of the window. A very long pole will need a center bracket for additional support.

The usual method of hanging curtains is to attach hooks to the back of the curtain heading and insert these into the slides on the rod or into the eyelets on the pole's rings. Look again at all the photos in the curtains chapter to see the variety of headings used. Alternatives include:

- Ties attached to the top of the curtain and tied around a pole.
- Large grommets (eyelets) installed in the curtain heading, through which the pole is slotted.
- Casings at the top of curtain panels, through which a narrow pole is slotted.
- Fine, high-tension wires that are slotted through a casing at the top of the curtain and have eyelets at the ends to attach to hooks in the wall.
- Clip-on rings that hold lightweight fabric in place without sewing.
- Small metal clips with teeth that suspend a swathe of fabric from a pole. Be sure that they won't rip a delicate sheer fabric.

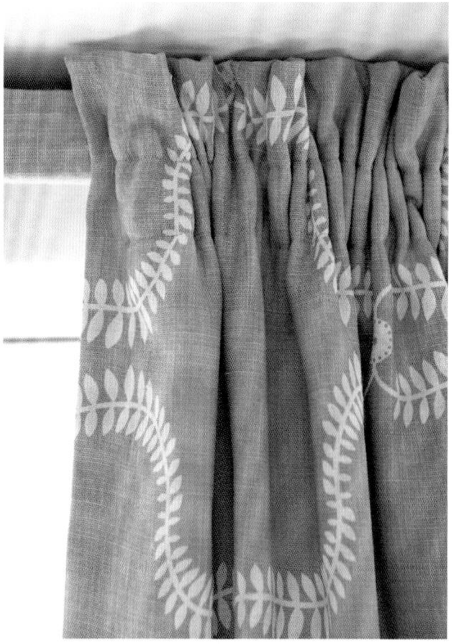

measuring for shades

A shade (blind) requires a wooden lath for installation. As with curtains, it is helpful to have the lath in place before you measure (see Wooden Laths for Shades, page 210). Shades can be installed either inside the window recess or frame, or outside it, on or above the top trim. Inside mounts look neater with Swedish and Roman shades, but they may block out some daylight or obstruct some windows from opening. Outside mounts allow more flexibility if you need to disguise the shape of a window, and they also admit more light.

where to measure for shades

- Width of inside-mounted shade: The wooden lath is screwed directly to the top of the window recess or into the top of the frame. The lath should therefore be the width of the window recess or the width inside the window casing from left to right (measurement D on the diagram), minus ⅜in (1cm) on each side, so the shade will not touch the sides of the window, which could restrict it from moving up and down correctly.
- Width of outside-mounted shade: The wooden lath is screwed either directly into the wall above the window (measurement E on the diagram) or onto the top trim. The lath should therefore be the width of the window plus 4–6 in (10–15cm) on each side.
- Length of inside-mounted shade: For the finished length (drop), measure from the top of the wooden lath to the sill, minus ⅜in (1cm) (measurement F on the diagram).
- Length of outside-mounted shade: For the finished length (drop), measure from the top of the wooden lath to a point that is 2in (5cm) below the sill (measurement G on the diagram). If you will be applying the hook-and-loop tape to the top of the lath, as shown for Wooden Laths for Shades, step 3 (see page 210), allow extra for the shade to extend over the top of the lath.

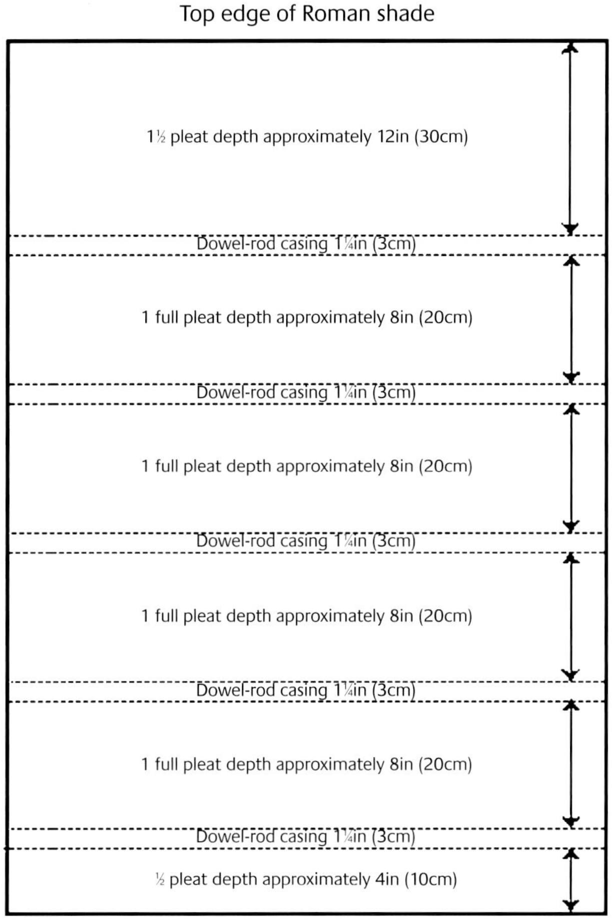

dowel-rod spacing for roman shades

Measure your window, as illustrated opposite, to find the finished width and length of your shade.

For an average shade, allow 4in (10cm) between the position of the lowest dowel-rod casing and the hem edge (half a pleat depth), unless otherwise specified, as in the diagram above. Place the top dowel-rod casing 12in (30cm) from the top edge of the shade (one and a half times the pleat depth). Space the remaining dowel-rod casings evenly, approximately 8in (20cm) apart (a full pleat depth), depending on the size of your window.

For a lined Roman shade, add 1¼in (3cm) per dowel-rod casing to the finished length of the shade (plus the hem allowances).

estimating yardage for shades

To calculate yardage, use the length of the wooden lath for the width measurement and multiply by the length (drop) of the shade. Remember, these are your finished shade measurements only—turn to the individual projects to find out the hem and seam allowances required.

wooden laths for shades

The wooden lath for a shade is used to attach the shade to the window frame or the surrounding wall. It is made from a piece of wood measuring 1 x 2in (2.5 x 5cm), which is usually covered in fabric to match your shade. The instructions here are for a lath that is screwed to the wall, but you could mount it using angle brackets instead if you prefer, as for Valance Shelves, step 4 (opposite).

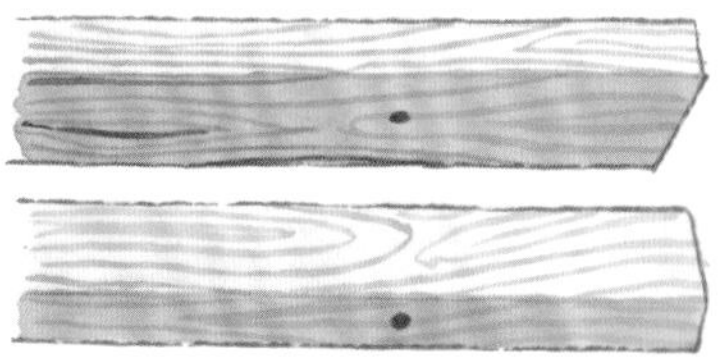

1 Cut a wooden lath to the finished width of the shade (see Where to Measure for Shades, page 208). For an inside-mounted shade, drill holes on the underside of the lath, 6in (15cm) from the ends. For an outside-mounted shade, drill holes into the face of the lath, 6in (15cm) from the ends.

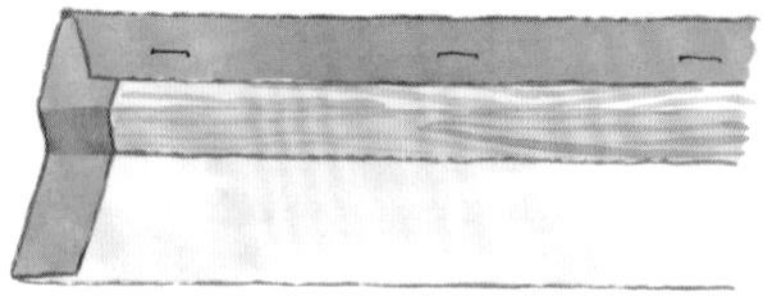

2 Cut a strip of fabric wide enough to wrap around the lath and hang about 4in (10cm) longer than it. Place the lath in the center on the wrong side of the fabric strip, and fold the fabric ends up and onto the top. Staple in place. Fold the ends of the fabric into envelope corners, wrap the sides of the fabric around the lath, and staple in place along the entire length.

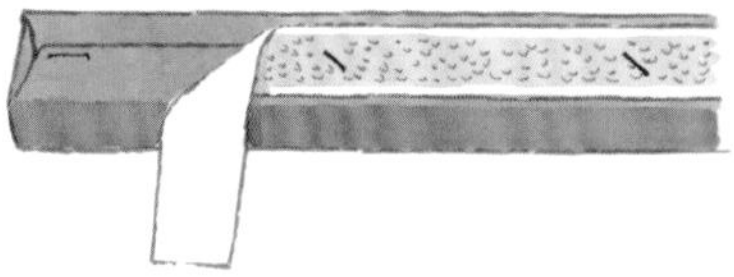

3 Staple the hook side of hook-and-loop tape to the front of the lath (for inside- or outside-mounted shades) or to the top of the lath (for outside-mounted shades only). Stapling it to the top, as shown, will hide the stitching at the top of the shade, but remember to allow for the extra length (the depth of the board) when calculating the finished length of the shade.

4 Using an awl (bradawl), mark the positions of the screw eyes on the underside of the lath. Line them up with the rows of cording rings on the shade and screw them in place. Attach an extra eye 1in (2.5cm) from one end of the lath, on the cord-operating side.

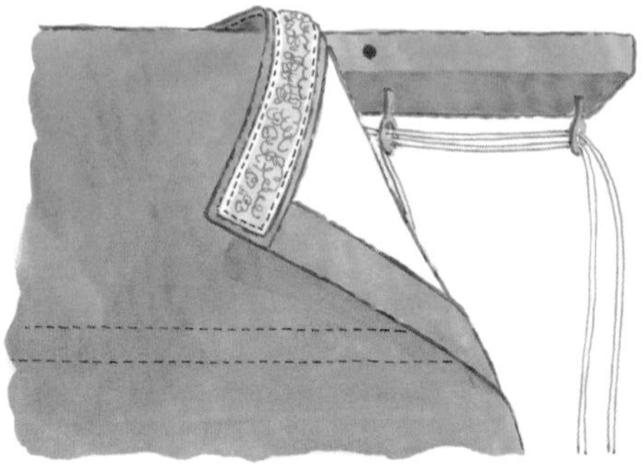

5 For an outside-mounted shade, it is easiest to attach it to the lath with the hook-and-loop tape before mounting the lath, stringing the cord through all the rings, tape, and screw eyes (see individual projects). Then, to mount the lath, open the hook-and-loop tape to beyond the drilled holes, and pierce the fabric covering the drilled holes. Screw it directly into the wall or the trim above the window and rejoin the hook-and-loop tape. For an inside-mounted shade, screw the lath to the top of the window recess.

valance shelves

A valance shelf, also sometimes called a mounting board, is a shelf attached to the wall above a window, to hold a valance. The valance is attached to the front and sides of the shelf, and the curtain rod is mounted on the underside of the shelf so the curtains can hang behind the valance.

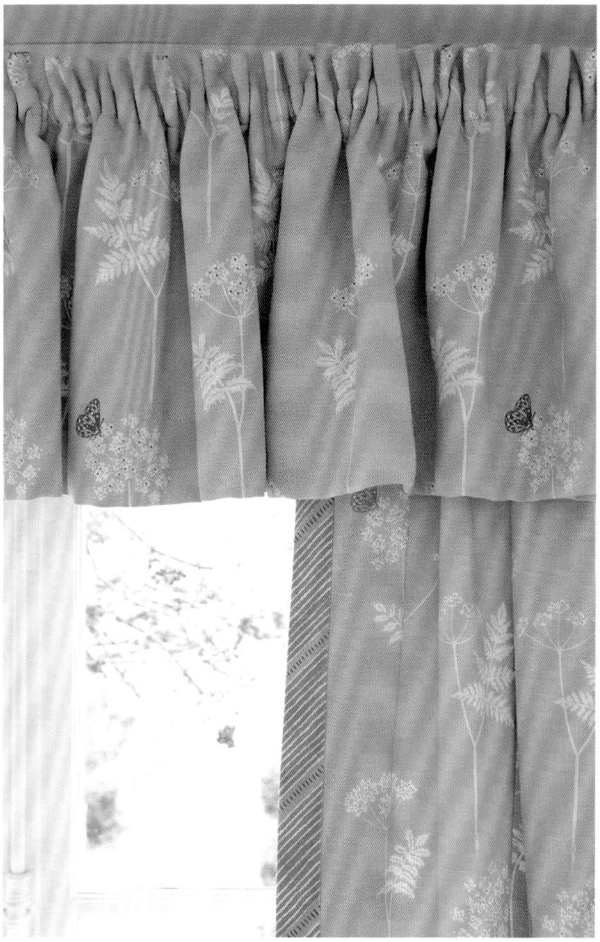

1 Choose sturdy wood that does not bend, such as pine or plywood, about 1in (2.5cm) thick. Make the shelf 5–8in (12.5–20cm) deep, depending on your project, by the length of the rod plus 2in (5cm).

2 Cover the shelf with fabric as for Wooden Laths for Shades, step 1 (opposite), or paint it to match your room decor.

3 Staple the hook side of a length of hook-and-loop tape to the narrow front and side edges of the shelf, for attaching the valance later.

4 Using angle irons, attach the valance shelf to the wall above the window, just above the trim. Mount the rod on the underside of the board halfway in from the edge, so that the curtains can be drawn easily when the valance is in place.

care advice

Regular care and attention will prevent your soft furnishings from becoming too dirty and will help them to last longer.

vacuuming

Regular vacuuming and spot-cleaning will prevent household dirt, grease, and stains from settling deep down into the fibers of your slipcovers, bed covers, pillows, and window treatments. Once grime has penetrated, it is often difficult to remove. Vacuum with a soft brush attachment, paying particular attention to the inside of pleats and ruffles.

airing

One of the simplest ways to freshen up curtains is to throw the windows wide open on a fine, dry, breezy day, then draw the curtains closed and let them blow freely for a few hours (making sure there's nothing they could knock over as they flap in the breeze!). This will help to remove any stale household smells or dust mites. If possible, hang them on an outdoor clothesline for the afternoon on a fine day.

laundering

Unlined curtains may be washed if you wish, but the fabric may lose any special finishes, which could affect the curtains' body. If there is a care label attached to the roll of fabric when you buy it, save it for your reference. Also, do a test: Cut an 8in (20cm) square of the fabric (use an offcut or remnant) and wash it. After it is dry and you've ironed it, measure the sample to see if it has shrunk. If it has, either hand-wash the curtains in cold water or have them professionally cleaned.

Iron the curtain while it is still damp, taking particular care when pressing over seams, so that the ridges do not make marks to show through. Set the iron on a cool temperature and use a pressing cloth to prevent shine and scorching. If you have a steamer, use it to take out any other wrinkles once the curtain is hung.

dry-cleaning

This is really the only option for lined draperies and shades. However, with regular airing and vacuuming, you can minimize the amount of dry-cleaning that is necessary.

hardware maintenance

To keep your curtain hardware in good working order, treat the inside of rods (tracks) and the top of poles with an anti-static spray from time to time. Use a soft brush to keep finials and curtain rings dust-free, too.

using color

Working with color is the most enjoyable way to decorate, but it's an individual choice and one that is completely personal to you. Using color way is a powerful way to affect the mood of a room—different colors can make you feel relaxed or invigorated, depending on the purpose of the room.

Despite working closely with color for the last 18 years, I am still on a journey with my fabrics, and choosing colors today feels no different from the time I mixed the palette for my first collection. Color can help set a mood, creating a sense of warmth and energy, or create an atmosphere imbued with tranquility and calm. I find I internalize good color combinations all the time and store them in my memory, both consciously and subconsciously, to reappear later when I am designing. The colors of nature are always with me, and the interior of our house keeps these memories vibrant. So use what you love to inspire you to create a home that expresses your personality and individuality.

Try using three colors together; color 1 for the walls, color 2 for the curtains, and color 3 for accessories like cushions and other small accessories.

how color works

When I began decorating our converted cow byre 20 years ago, I started by looking through magazines and keeping a folder of pages I really liked. This was such a helpful way to focus on the overall style I liked, and certainly helped me to make my first color choices. Since then I find that understanding color is not difficult, and there are a few simple guidelines that will help you get started.

When we look at a rainbow, the arrangement of colors demonstrates how they work together. Blue fades into green, green into yellow, yellow into orange, orange into red, and red into purple, which fades in turn back to blue. If you imagine these colors arranged in a circle, on one side we find the cool colors of purple, blue, and green, and on the other side, the warmer hues of red, yellow, and orange. This starting point is a great help when you are choosing colors to go together. Harmonious schemes, using a few colors next to each other on the circle, with perhaps a contrasting accent, are restful and relaxing. Contrasting schemes, using colors roughly opposite each other, preferably with cooler colors predominating, are dynamic and stimulating.

Choosing the same color for the walls, floor, and upholstery allows you to give the room an instant update simply by changing the cushions and rug.

Using cool colors for the walls and woodwork, and warm colors in your choice of fabrics for the soft furnishings is a useful way to combine colors.

There are so many glorious tints of white paint available, so use them as the basis of a room on the walls, paintwork, and flooring, with a selection of mix-and-match fabrics that will add a homely, informal feel.

Choose a main color, and liven it up by adding small amounts of a contrasting shade. This is often called an accent color, which can be brought in with accessories, such as pillows and cushions.

TIP

Paint large pieces of cardstock using sample pots before you buy paint (or paint patches directly on the walls) and use removable sticky pads to attach them to the wall in different positions, near the window and in darker corners. Live with the colors to see how they look in the evening as well as in the daylight.

working with light

When you are choosing colors for your home, it's always a good idea to take into account where you live, looking carefully at how the light falls in each room. If you live in the northern hemisphere, for example, where the light is blue and cool, you need to choose a very different palette from one useful for the warm light of the sunny south. A dark, north-facing room needs warm shades to balance the lack of light, and greens and blues can be too cool—choose warm hues, like yellow, red, and orange, to bring a sunny feel to the darkest corner. On the other hand, if your room is full of warm, natural sunlight, using colors from the blue and green side of the spectrum will tone down the heat of the sun, and balance it with the deliciously cool feeling of walking in a green woodland on a hot day.

color effects

There is no doubt that color has a strong effect on us, both emotionally and physically. For instance, strong red has been shown to raise blood pressure, being vivid and energetic, green is used to calm and pacify heightened emotions, and orange stimulates appetite. Yellow is cheerful and makes us happy, and purple provides a sense of spiritual well-being. Colors can be used to trick the eye and change the apparent shape of a room too. Warm shades, like red, orange, or terra-cotta, appear to come forward, so they can have the effect of making a large room feel smaller. Painting a high ceiling in a warm color will help it appear lower, while painting one or both short walls in a wide room will give the effect of making it look more square. On the other hand, cool colors, like pale blue, green, and lavender—colors of the landscape and atmosphere—are receding hues, so use them to make small spaces seem more spacious.

Use warm colors like yellows and reds to bring a sunny aspect to a dark room.

Cool, pale blues are most suitable in a room that is full of light.

Mix and match fabrics and find combinations I haven't thought of. Combine stripes with spots, patterns with solid colors, and make a house you can call home.

Opposite: A classic wood-framed sofa with charcoal gray upholstery is given a pop of color with this assortment of scatter pillows in shades of charcoal, tangerine, and indigo. Pillow covers provide an easy way to add cohesion to your colorscheme.

starting points

Before you start planning a new decorating project, think about what you want to keep. This could be a length of beautiful fabric, a set of Victorian tiles around a fireplace, a sofa you don't want to change, or a favorite colorful painting. Any of these can become the starting points for designing a color scheme. Even if a feature is not to your taste, it can be transformed with color. A coat of an off-white paint will quickly make a dark wooden fireplace feel more contemporary, for example. If you have nothing else to set off your imagination, follow your instincts, choose a fabric you love, and work the color scheme around it. Many of my fabrics are available in one main color, with small dashes of one or two other shades as accents, so use them as the basis of a whole room.

enjoy yourself

Have fun and enjoy using color, fabric, and pattern to express your mood and personality and your home will always be welcoming and individual. The fabrics in my collections are wonderfully interchangeable, and so it's up to you to play with different combinations to find out which will give you the effect you feel most happy with.

Pick up on a wall color with an accent color in the fabric used for accessories.

TIP

To help you visualize your room scheme, hang fabric samples near windows and place them on the backs of chairs and sofas, then leave them for a few days. Ask for larger, returnable samples if you need more help. Try to use at least three colors in each room.

templates

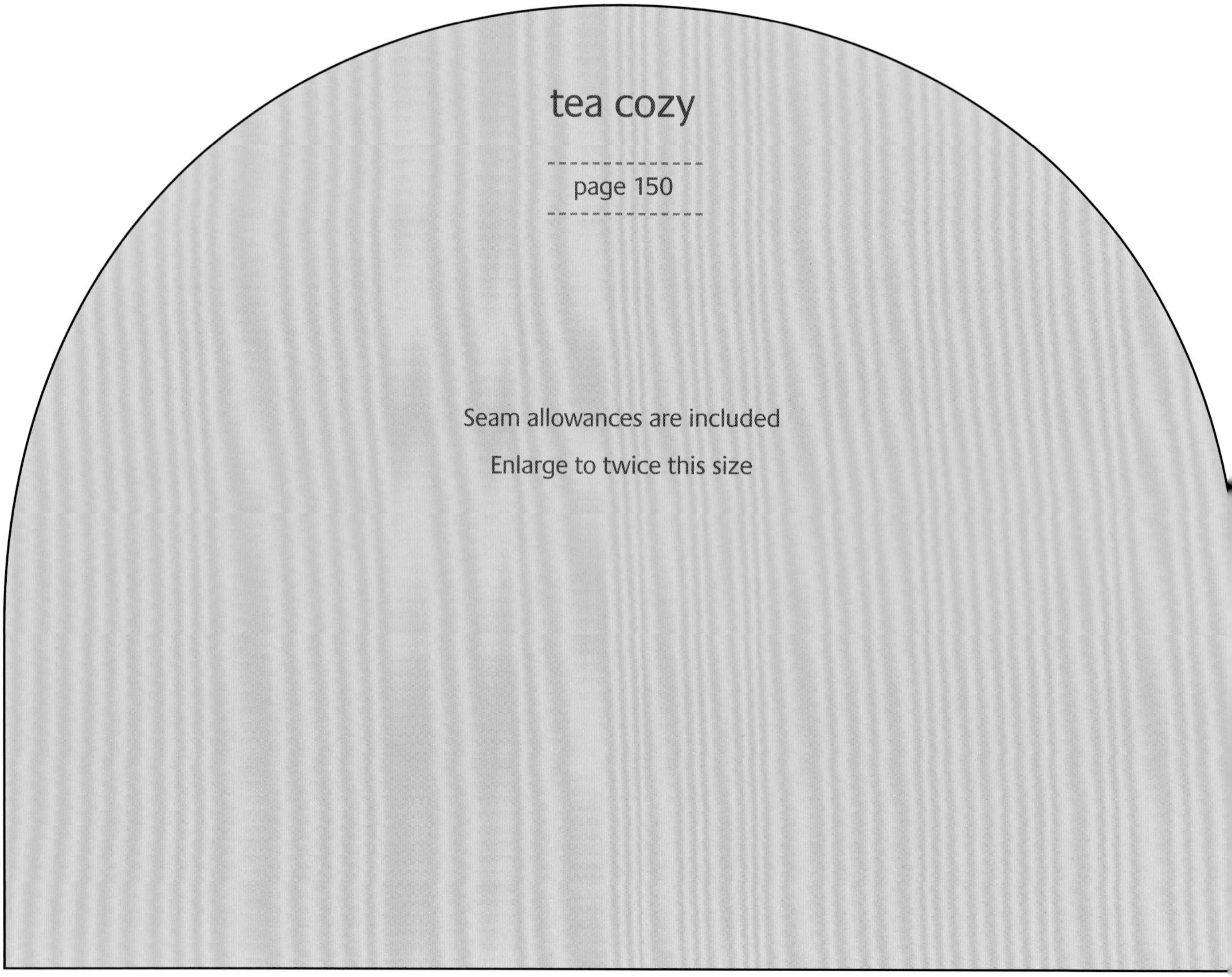
tea cozy
page 150
Seam allowances are included
Enlarge to twice this size

clothespin bag

page 162

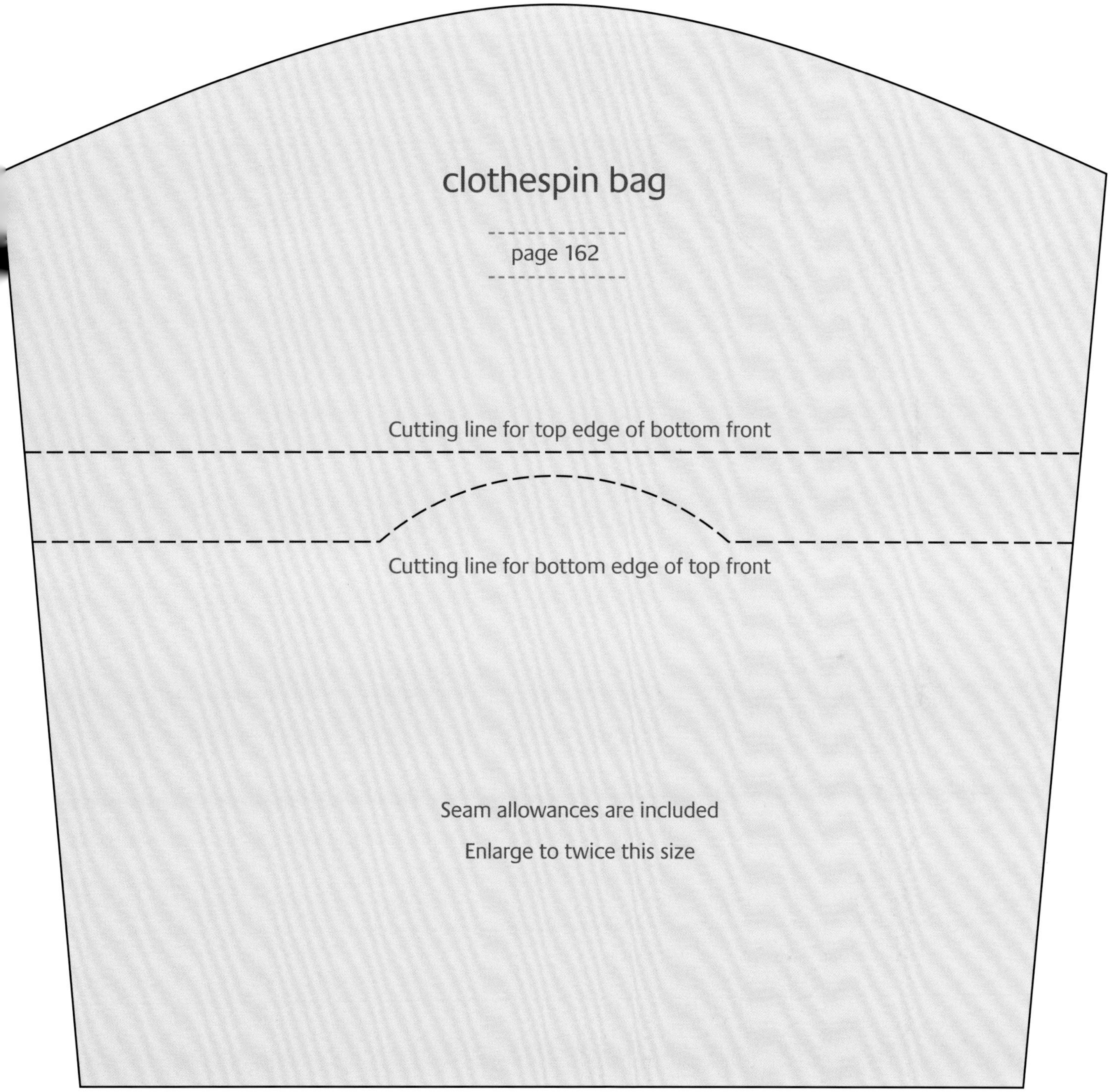

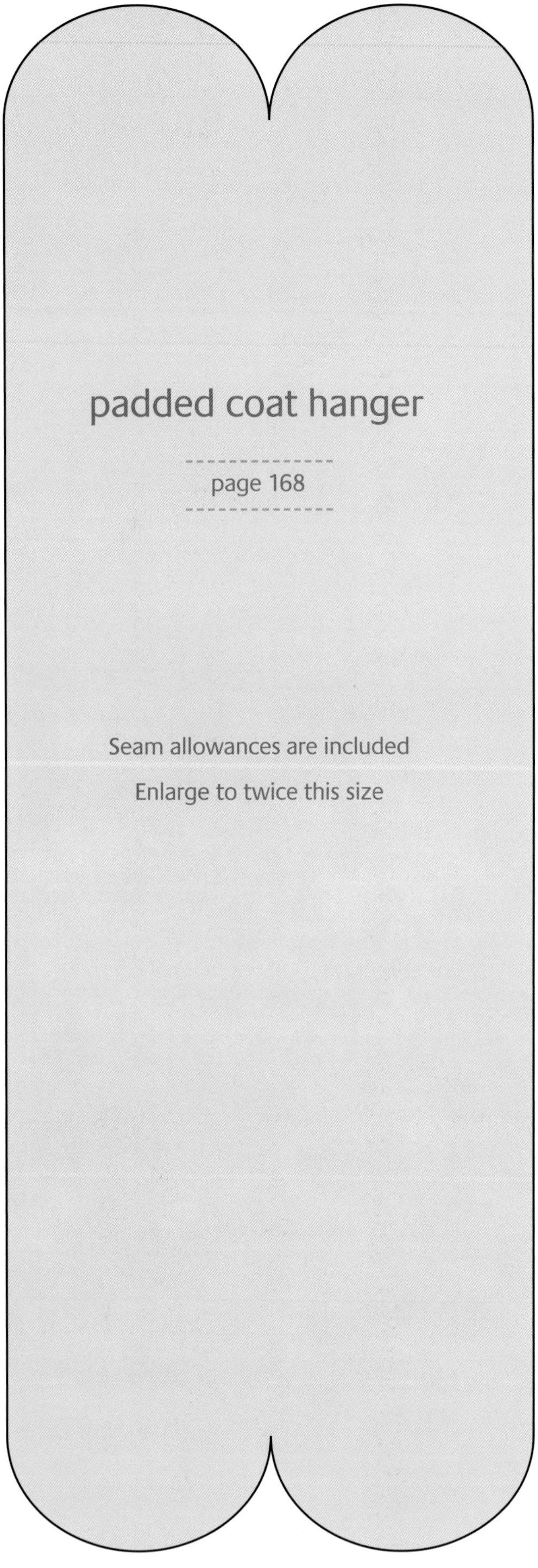

acknowledgments

I would like to thank my Mother for giving me a creative childhood which must be one of the best gift of all. Huge thanks to my wonderful family for putting up with the ever-changing decoration in our home, and also to Rose whose passion for color has been an inspiration.

Thank you to Laura Spencer for her huge help with the technical side of designing.

Thanks also to my wonderful sewing team: Sarah Mackay, Lena Kamber, Terri Davies, and Lucy Lane-Fox. To all my staff for their endless tolerance and loyal assistance. To all my resident artists for their hard work creating the sets for our shoots.

Also, thanks to Sally Denning for her ability to take my fabrics on a wonderful journey with her skilled styling (www.sallydenning.co.uk), and to Mark Scott for his incredible photography (www.markscottphotography.co.uk). And, of course, thanks go to Gail Abbott (www.gailabbott.co.uk) for her gentle encouragement, styling, and support with this book.

Vanessa Arbuthnott
www.vanessaarbuthnott.co.uk

With many thanks to Nord Design (nordesign.co.uk) for letting us use their stylish Scandinavian-designed ceramics and accessories, and to Sandra Jane (sandrajane.co.uk) for lending us a selection of beautiful homewares, all of which made a difference to our lovely photographs.

Gail Abbott

index